Great Thinkers

This is a collection of some of the most important ideas of Eastern and Western culture – drawn from the works of those philosophers, political theorists, sociologists, artists and novelists whom we believe have the most to offer to us today. We've worked hard to make the thinkers in this book clear, relevant and charming, mining the history of knowledge to bring you the ideas we think have the greatest importance to our times. This book contains the canon of **The School of Life**, the gallery of individuals across the millennia who help to frame our intellectual project – and we will have succeeded if, in the days and years ahead, you find yourself turning to our thinkers to illuminate the multiple dilemmas, joys and griefs of daily life.

Published in 2016 by The School of Life
70 Marchmont Street, London WC1N 1AB
Copyright © The School of Life 2016
Designed and typeset by FLOK, Berlin
Illustrated by Stuart Patience
Printed in Latvia by Livonia Print

A proportion of this book has appeared online at thebookoflife.org.

Every effort has been made to contact the copyright holders of the material
reproduced in this book. If any have been inadvertently overlooked, the
publisher will be pleased to make restitution at the earliest opportunity.

The School of Life offers programmes, publications and services to assist
modern individuals in their quest to live more engaged and meaningful lives.
We've also developed a collection of content-rich, design-led retail products
to promote useful insights and ideas from culture.

www.theschooloflife.com

ISBN 978-0-9935387-0-4

Great Thinkers

Contents

Sociology

Psychotherapy

Art & Architecture

Literature

Credits

Introduction

This is a book that gathers together the canon of The School of Life: it is our selection of the greatest thinkers from the fields of philosophy, political theory, sociology, psychotherapy, art, architecture and literature whom we believe have the most to offer to us today.

The idea of assembling a 'canon' can feel a bit awkward – maybe even oppressive. It can feel unfair to leave out so many people. And anyway, who decides? Surely the people making the canon are bringing some bias to their task?

We happily admit to bias. We're sometimes taught to think ill of bias, as if the only good kind of information was that which carried absolutely no intention or design, and left everything up to the audience instead. This emphasis on neutrality is understandable; there has historically – especially in the 20th century – been a lot of bad bias around. But we ultimately believe that the goal isn't to have no bias at all but to put forward 'good' bias; by which we mean bias in favour of a selection of thinkers who point us to valuable and important ideas. At The School of Life, we are heavily biased towards emotional intelligence and the use of culture as a tool for consolation and enlightenment.

We have some quite specific views about what makes a thinker 'great'. Typically, great thinkers are included in encyclopedic works on the basis of reputation: a list is drawn up asking what names have been most influential, and what ideas have most memorably shaped the intellectual world. However, we've got our sights on a different aim: we want to work out what ideas offer help with some of the leading problems of our own times. For us, a 'great' thinker is someone whose ideas stand the very highest chance of being helpful in our lives now.

Because a canon is necessarily so selective, it is always vulnerable to attack. We have a sanguine view of selection;

selection is simply an inescapable feature of living in an information-rich world. The ideal isn't to avoid being selective; the challenge is to try to select as well as possible. In our eyes, this means picking out thinkers who can untangle some of the greatest difficulties in our political, professional and personal lives. We aren't historians recovering ideas for their own sakes; we are applied philosophers seeking intellectual concepts that can be put to work in the here and now.

We've worked hard to make the thinkers in this book sound simple, easy and (hopefully) quite charming. In the past, many of these thinkers have been caught in a fiendish trap. What they have had to say has been hugely relevant and important. But *how* they have said it has guaranteed that they went unheard: because their books were a little too dense, some of their ideas sounded odd and many of their most crucial concepts were prone to get lost amidst a welter of subsidiary information. We've recovered what we see as the important ideas in our chosen thinkers by following a number of principles:

· Only a few things that any mind, however great, has ever said are likely to be of central lasting importance.

· These key points are detachable from the full body of a thinker's work.

· We are forgetful, time-pressured creatures. We are liable to forget every intricacy of a complex sustained argument. So we need central messages spelt out memorably and simply.

· Whatever academic culture tells us, context is not decisive. Important truths get lodged in odd places and can be extricated from them; they may lie in 3rd-century China, in an aristocratic salon in 18th-century Paris or in a small house in an alpine village in the 19th century. Yet what always matters in the end is what they can do for us now.

· It's a tragic paradox that there are ways of showing reverence for the great thinkers that end up preventing them from having an impact in the world – the exact opposite of what reverence was hoping to achieve. Being a little casual with a great thinker is the biggest homage one could pay to him or her.

· Our guiding concern is that great ideas should be widely known and that they should be active in our lives.

That said, we recognise that there are proper worries around 'simplification'. There is a concern – fed by the academic world – that if you simplify, you inevitably betray: you omit the stuff that really matters. We understand the anxiety but don't want to let it triumph, for we are equally aware of the dangers of listening to it too closely: needless complexity can lead to good ideas being ignored altogether. We think that the important truths about how we might live are capable of popular formulation. We're against the tragic view that what is important is condemned always to be unpopular or incomprehensible to most citizens.

Popularising is, from our perspective, a great and noble task, especially in a democratic consumer-led world where elite culture has (more or less) lost its sway. It's what makes ideas real in the life of a society. In any case, our lives are never entirely bookish or intellectual. We're always driven by, and to an extent reliant on, straightforward thoughts that guide our conduct. Those ideas are the ones that matter to the day-to-day flourishing of a community. Preciousness can be the downfall of the best concepts.

The modern world has to date left the study and transmission of cultural ideas largely to university departments in the humanities. Their main focus has been on trying to understand what great thinkers were about in and of themselves. Here, somewhat heretically, we're doing something very different: we want to know what they can do for *us*.

We've mined history to bring you the ideas we believe to be of the greatest relevance to our own times. We will have succeeded if, in the days and years ahead, you find yourself turning to them to illuminate the multiple dilemmas and griefs of daily life.

Philosophy

Plato

c.428–c.348 BC

A thens, 2,400 years ago. It's a compact place: around 250,000 people live here. There are fine baths, theatres, temples, shopping arcades and gymnasiums. Art is flourishing, and science too. You can pick up excellent fish down at the harbour in Piraeus. It's warm for more than half the year.

This is also home to the world's first true – and probably greatest – philosopher: Plato.

Born into a prominent and wealthy family in the city, Plato devoted his life to one goal: helping people to reach a state of what he termed εὐδαιμονία, or *eudaimonia*.

This peculiar but fascinating Greek word is a little hard to translate. It almost means 'happiness' but is really closer to 'fulfilment', because 'happiness' suggests continuous chirpiness – whereas 'fulfilment' is more compatible with periods of great pain and suffering – which seem to be an unavoidable part even of a good life.

How did Plato propose to make people more fulfilled? Four central ideas stand out in his work.

1. Think harder

Plato proposed that our lives go wrong in large part because we almost never give ourselves time to think carefully and logically enough about our plans. And so we end up with the wrong values, careers and relationships. Plato wanted to bring order and clarity to our minds.

He observed how many of our ideas are derived from what the crowd thinks, from what the Greeks called '*doxa*', and we'd call 'common sense'. And yet, repeatedly, across the thirty-six books he wrote, Plato showed this common sense to be riddled with errors, prejudice and superstition. Popular ideas about love, fame, money or goodness simply don't stand up to reason.

Plato also noticed how proud people were about being led by their instincts or passions (jumping into decisions on the basis of nothing more than 'how they felt'), and he

LEO VON KLENZE, *The Acropolis*, 1846

compared this to being dragged dangerously along by a group of blindfolded wild horses.

As Freud was happy to acknowledge, Plato was the inventor of therapy, insisting that we learn to submit all our thoughts and feelings to reason. As Plato repeatedly wrote, the essence of philosophy came down to the command to γνῶθι σεαυτόν – 'know yourself'.

2. Love more wisely

Plato is one of the great theorists of relationships. His book, *The Symposium*, is an attempt to explain what love really is. It tells the story of a dinner party given by Agathon, a handsome poet, who invites a group of his friends around to eat, drink and talk about love.

The guests all have different views about what love is. Plato gives his old friend Socrates – one of the main characters in this and all his books – the most useful and interesting theory. It goes like this: when you fall in love, what's really going on is that you have seen in another person some good quality that you haven't got. Perhaps they are calm, when you get agitated; or they are self-disciplined, while you're all over the place; or they are eloquent when you are tongue-tied.

The underlying fantasy of love is that by getting close to this person, you can become a little like they are. They can help you to grow to your full potential.

In Plato's eyes, love is in essence a kind of education: you couldn't really love someone if you didn't want to be improved by them. Love should be two people trying to grow together – and helping each other to do so. Which means you need to get together with the person who contains a key missing bit of your evolution: the virtues you don't have.

This sounds entirely odd nowadays when we tend to interpret love as finding someone perfect just as they are. In the heat of arguments, lovers sometimes say to one another: 'If you loved me, you wouldn't try to change me.'

Plato thinks the diametric opposite. He wants us to enter relationships in a far less combative and proud way. We should accept that we are not complete and allow our lovers to teach us things. A good relationship has to mean we won't love the other person exactly as they are. It means committing to helping them become a better version of themselves – and to endure the stormy passages this inevitably involves – while also not resisting their attempts to improve us.

3. The importance of beauty

Everyone – pretty much – likes beautiful things. But we tend to think of them as a bit mysterious in their power over us and, in the greater scheme, not terribly important.

But Plato proposed that it really matters what sorts of houses or temples, pots or sculptures you have around you.

No one before Plato had asked the key question: why do we like beautiful things? He found a fascinating reason: we recognise in them a part of 'the good'.

There are lots of good things we aspire to be: kind, gentle, harmonious, balanced, peaceful, strong, dignified. These are qualities in people. But they are also qualities in objects. We get moved and excited when we find in objects the qualities we need but are missing in our lives.

Beautiful objects therefore have a really important function. They invite us to evolve in their direction, to become as they are. Beauty can educate our souls.

It follows that ugliness is a serious matter too, for it parades dangerous and damaged characteristics in front of us. It encourages us to be like it: harsh, chaotic, brash. It makes it that much harder to be wise, kind and calm.

Plato sees art as therapeutic: it is the duty of poets and painters (and, nowadays, novelists, television producers and designers) to help us lead good lives.

Plato believed in the censorship of the arts. It's not the paradox it seems. If artists can help us live well, they can, unfortunately, equally give prestige and glamour to unhelpful attitudes and ideas. Just being an artist doesn't guarantee the power of art will be wisely used.

That's why Plato believed that artists should work under the command of philosophers, who would give them the right ideas and ask them to make these convincing and popular. Art was to be a sort of propaganda – or advertising – for the good.

4. Changing society

Plato spent a lot of time thinking how the government and society should ideally be. He was the world's first utopian thinker.

In this, he was inspired by Athens's great rival: Sparta. This was a city-sized machine for turning out great soldiers. Everything the Spartans did – how they raised their children, how their economy was organised, whom they admired, how they had sex, what they ate – was tailored to that one goal. And Sparta was hugely successful, from a military point of view.

But that wasn't Plato's concern. He wanted to know: how could a society get better at producing not military power but *eudaimonia*? How could it reliably help people towards fulfilment?

In his book, *The Republic*, Plato identifies a number of changes that should be made:

a. We need new heroes

Athenian society was very focused on the rich, like the louche aristocrat Alcibiades, and sports celebrities, like the boxer Milo of Croton. Plato wasn't impressed: it really matters whom we admire, for celebrities influence our outlook, ideas and conduct. And bad heroes give glamour to flaws of character.

Plato therefore wanted to give Athens new celebrities, replacing the current crop with ideally wise and good people he called 'guardians': models for everyone's good development. These people would be distinguished by their record of public service, their modesty and simple habits, their dislike of the limelight and their wide and deep experience. They would be the most honoured and admired people in society.

b. We need censorship

Today, censorship makes us anxious. But Plato was worried about the wrong sort of freedom: Athens was a free-for-all for the worst opinion-sellers. Crazy religious notions and sweet-sounding, but dangerous, ideas sucked up mass enthusiasm and led Athens to disastrous governments and misguided wars (like a fateful attack on Sparta).

Continuous exposure to a storm of confused voices was – Plato thought – seriously bad for us, so he wanted to limit the activities of public orators and dangerous preachers. He would – nowadays – have been very sceptical about the power of mass media.

Roman mosaic showing Plato seated (second from left) among students and
other philosophers in his school, The Academy.

c. We need better education

Plato believed passionately in education but wanted to re-
focus the curriculum. The primary thing we need to learn
is not just maths or spelling, but how to be good: we need
to learn about courage, self-control, reasonableness, independence and calm.

To put this into practice, Plato founded a school called
The Academy in Athens, which flourished for over 400
years. You went there to learn nothing less than how to live
and die well.

It's fascinating and not a little sad how modern academic institutions have outlawed this ambition. If a student

showed up at Oxford or Harvard universities today seeking to be taught how to live, the professors would call the police – or the insane asylum.

d. We need better childhoods

Families try their best. And sometimes children strike lucky. Their parents are well balanced, good teachers, reliably mature and wise. But pretty often parents transmit their confusions and failings to their children.

Plato thought that bringing up children well was one of the most difficult (and most needed) skills. He was acutely sympathetic to the child who is held back by the wrong home environment.

So he proposed that many children would in fact be better off if they could take their vision of life not from their parents but from wise guardians, paid for by the state. He proposed that a sizeable share of the next generation should be brought up by people more qualified than their own parents.

Conclusion

Plato's ideas remain deeply provocative and fascinating. What unites them is their ambition and their idealism. He wanted philosophy to be a tool to help us change the world. We should continue to be inspired by his example.

Aristotle

384–322 BC

Aristotle was born around 384 BC in the ancient Greek kingdom of Macedonia, where his father was the royal doctor. He grew up to be arguably the most influential philosopher ever, with modest nicknames like 'the master', and simply 'the philosopher'. One of his big jobs was tutoring Alexander the Great, who soon after went out and conquered the known world.

Aristotle studied in Athens, worked with Plato for several years, and then branched out on his own. He founded a research and teaching centre called The Lyceum: French secondary schools, *lycées,* are named in honour of this venture. He liked to walk about while teaching and discussing ideas. His followers were named Peripatetics, the wanderers. His many books are actually lecture notes.

Aristotle was fascinated by how things really work. How does an embryo chick develop in an egg? How do squid reproduce? Why does a plant grow well in one place and hardly at all in another? And, most importantly, what makes a human life and a whole society go well? For Aristotle, philosophy was about practical wisdom. Here are four big philosophical questions he answered:

1. What makes people happy?

In the *Nicomachean Ethics* – the book got its name because it was edited by his son, Nicomachus – Aristotle set himself the task of identifying the factors that lead people to have a good life, or not. He suggested that good and successful people all possess distinct virtues, and proposed that we should get better at identifying what these are, so that we can nurture them in ourselves and honour them in others.

Aristotle also observed that every virtue seems to be bang in the middle of two vices. It occupies what he termed 'the golden mean' between two extremes of character. For example, in book four of his *Ethics*, under the charming title of 'conversational virtues and vices', Aristotle looks at ways in which people are better or worse at talking to one another – buffoonery, wit, boorishness.

Knowing how to have a good conversation is one of the key ingredients of the good life, Aristotle recognised. Some people go wrong because they lack a subtle sense of humour: that's the bore, 'someone useless for any kind of social intercourse, because he contributes nothing and takes offence at everything'. But others carry humour to excess: 'the buffoon cannot resist a joke, sparing neither himself nor anybody else, provided that he can raise a laugh and saying things that a man of taste would never dream of saying'. So the virtuous person is in the golden mean in this area: witty but tactful.

In a fascinating survey of personality and behaviour, Aristotle analyses 'too little', 'too much' and 'just right' around a whole host of virtues. We can't change our behaviour in any of these areas just at the drop of a hat. But change is possible, eventually. Moral goodness, says Aristotle, is the result of habit. It takes time, practice, encouragement. So Aristotle thinks people who lack virtue should be understood as unfortunate, rather than wicked. What they need isn't scolding or being thrown into prison, but better teachers and more guidance.

2. What is art for?

The blockbuster art at the time was tragedy. Athenians watched gory plays at community festivals held at huge open-air theatres. Aeschylus, Euripides and Sophocles were household names. Aristotle wrote a how-to-write-great-plays manual, *The Poetics*. It's packed with great tips: for example, make sure to use *peripeteia*, a change in fortune, when, for the hero, things go from great to awful. And *anagnorisis*, the moment of dramatic revelation, when suddenly the hero realises their life is going very wrong – and is, in fact, a *catastrophe*.

But what is tragedy actually for? What is the point of a whole community coming together to watch horrible things

TABLE OF VIRTUES AND VICES

SPHERE OF ACTION OR FEELING	EXCESS	MEAN	DEFICIENCY
Fear and Confidence	Rashness *thrasutēs*	Courage *andreia*	Cowardice *deilia*
Pleasure and Pain	Licentiousness *akolasia*	Temperance *sōphrosunē*	Insensibility *anaisthēsia*
Getting and Spending (minor)	Prodigality *asōtia*	Liberality *eleutheriotēs*	Illiberality *aneleutheria*
Getting and Spending (major)	Vulgarity *apeirokalia, banausia*	Magnificence *megaloprepeia*	Pettiness *mikroprepeia*
Honour and Dishonour (major)	Vanity *chaunotēs*	Magnanimity *megalopsūchia*	Pusillanimity *mikropsūchia*
Honour and Dishonour (minor)	Ambition *philotimia*	Proper ambition	Unambitiousness *aphilotimia*
Anger	Irascibility *orgilotēs*	Patience *prāotēs*	Lack of spirit *aorgēsia*
Self-expression	Boastfulness *alazoneia*	Truthfulness *alētheia*	Understatement *eirōneia*
Conversation	Buffoonery *bōmolochia*	Wittiness *eutrapelia*	Boorishness *agroikia*
Social Conduct	Obsequiousness *areskeia* Flattery *kolakeia*	Friendliness *philia(?)*	Cantankerousness *duskolia (duseris)*
Shame	Shyness *kataplēxis*	Modesty *aidōs*	Shamelessness *anaischuntia*
Indignation	Envy *phthonos*	Righteous indignation *nemisis*	Malicious enjoyment *epichairekakia*

Table of Aristotle's Virtues and Vices

happening to lead characters? Like Oedipus, in the play by Sophocles, who by accident kills his father, gets married to his mother, finds out he's done these things and gouges out his eyes in remorse and despair. Aristotle's answer is *catharsis*. *Catharsis* is a kind of cleaning: you get rid of bad stuff. In this case, cleaning up our emotions – specifically, our confusions around the feelings of fear and pity.

We've got natural problems here: we're hard-hearted, we don't give pity where it's deserved, and we're prone to either exaggerated fears or not getting frightened enough. Tragedy reminds us that terrible things can befall decent people, including ourselves. A small flaw can lead to a whole life unravelling. So we should have more compassion or pity for those whose actions go disastrously wrong. We need to be collectively retaught these crucial truths on a regular basis. The task of art, as Aristotle saw it, is to make profound truths about life stick in our minds.

3. What are friends for?

In books eight and nine of the *Nicomachean Ethics*, Aristotle identifies three different kinds of friendship: there's friendship that comes about when each person is seeking fun, their chief interest is in their own pleasure and the opportunity of the moment, which the other person provides. Then there are friendships that are really strategic acquaintances, where people take pleasure in each other's company only in so far as they have hopes of taking advantage of it.

Then, there's the true friend. Not someone who's just like you, but someone who isn't you, and about whom you care as much as you care about yourself. The sorrows of a true friend are your sorrows. Their joys are yours. It makes you more vulnerable, should anything befall this person. But it's hugely strengthening too. You're relieved from the too-small orbit of your own thoughts and worries. You expand into the life of another, and together you become larger, cleverer, more resilient, more fair-minded. You share virtues and cancel out each other's defects. Friendship teaches us what we ought to be: it is, quite literally, the best part of life.

4. How can ideas cut through in a busy world?

Like a lot of people, Aristotle was struck by the fact that the best argument doesn't always win the debate or gain popular traction. He wanted to know why this happens and what we can do about it. He had lots of opportunity for observations. In Athens, many decisions were made in public meetings, often in the *agora*, the town square. Orators would vie with one another to sway popular opinion.

Aristotle plotted the ways audiences and individuals are influenced by many factors but don't strictly engage with logic or the facts of the case. It's maddening, and many serious people can't stand it. They avoid the marketplace and popular debate. Aristotle was more ambitious. He invented what we still call rhetoric – the art of getting people to agree with you. He wanted thoughtful, serious and well-intentioned people to learn how to be persuasive, to reach those who don't agree already.

He makes some timeless points: you have to soothe people's fears, you have to see the emotional side of the issue – is someone's pride on the line? Are they feeling embarrassed? – and edge around it accordingly. You have to make it funny because attention spans are short, and you might have to use illustrations and examples to make your point come alive.

We're keen students of Aristotle. Today, philosophy doesn't sound like the most practical activity; maybe that's because we've not paid enough attention recently to Aristotle.

The Stoics

Stoicism was a philosophy that flourished for some 400 years in ancient Greece and Rome, gaining widespread support among all classes of society. It had one very large and highly practical ambition: to teach people how to be calm and brave in the face of overwhelming anxiety and pain.

We still honour this school whenever we call someone 'stoic' or plain 'philosophical' when fate turns against them: when they lose their keys, are humiliated at work, rejected in love or disgraced in society. Of all philosophies, Stoicism remains perhaps the most immediately relevant and useful for our uncertain and panicky times.

Many hundreds of philosophers practised Stoicism, but two figures stand out as our best guides to it: the Roman politician, writer and tutor to Nero, Seneca (4 BC–AD 65); and the kind and magnanimous Roman emperor (who philosophised in his spare time while fighting the Germanic hordes on the edges of the empire) Marcus Aurelius (AD 121–180). Their works remain highly readable and deeply consoling, ideal for sleepless nights, those breeding grounds for runaway terrors and paranoia.

Stoicism can help us with four problems in particular:

1. Anxiety
At all times, so many terrible things might happen. The standard way for people to cheer us up when we're mired in anxiety is to tell us that we will, after all, be OK: the embarrassing email might not be discovered, sales could yet take off, there might be no scandal …

But the Stoics bitterly opposed such a strategy, because they believed that anxiety flourishes in the gap between what we fear *might*, and what we hope *could*, happen. The larger the gap, the greater will be the oscillations and disturbances of mood.

To regain calm, what we need to do is systematically and intelligently crush every last vestige of hope. Rather than appease ourselves with sunny tales, it is far better – the Stoics proposed – to courageously come to terms with the very worst possibilities – and then make ourselves entirely at home with them. When we look our fears in the face and imagine what life might be like if they came true, we stand to come to a crucial realisation: *we will cope*. We will cope even if we had to go to prison, even if we lost all our money, even if we were publicly shamed, even if our loved ones left us, and even if the growth turned out to be malignant (the Stoics were firm believers in suicide).

We generally don't dare do more than glimpse the horrible eventualities through clenched eyelids, and therefore they maintain a constant sadistic grip on us. Instead, as Seneca put it: 'To reduce your worry, you must assume that what you fear may happen is certainly *going* to happen.' To a friend wracked with terror he might be sent to prison, Seneca replied bluntly: 'Prison can always be endured by someone who has correctly understood existence.'

The Stoics suggested we take time off to practise worst-case scenarios. We should, for example, mark out a week a year where we eat only stale bread and sleep on the kitchen floor with only one blanket, so we stop being so squeamish about being sacked or imprisoned.

We will then realise, as Marcus Aurelius says, 'that very little is needed to make a happy life.'

Each morning, a good Stoic will undertake a *praemeditatio*: a premeditation on all the appalling things that might occur in the hours ahead. In Seneca's stiffening words: 'Mortal have you been born, to mortals have you given birth. So you must reckon on everything, expect everything.'

Stoicism is nothing less than an elegant, intelligent dress rehearsal for catastrophe.

2. Fury

We get angry – especially with our partners, our children, and politicians. We smash things up and hurt others. The

Stoics thought anger a dangerous indulgence, but most of all, a piece of stupidity, for in their analysis, angry outbursts are only ever caused by one thing: an incorrect picture of existence. They are the bitter fruits of naivety.

Anger is, in the Stoic analysis, caused by the violent collision of hope and reality. We don't shout every time something sad happens to us, only when it is sad *and* unexpected. To be calmer, we must, therefore, learn to expect far less from life. *Of course* our loved ones will disappoint us, *naturally* our colleagues will fail us, *invariably* our friends will lie to us ... None of this should be a surprise. It may make us sad. It must never – if we are Stoics – make us angry.

The wise person should aim to reach a state where simply nothing could suddenly disturb their peace of mind. Every tragedy should already be priced in. 'What need is there to weep over parts of life?' asked Seneca. 'The whole of it calls for tears.'

3. Paranoia

It is easy to think we've been singled out for terrible things. We wonder why it has happened to us. We tear ourselves apart with blame or direct bitter venom at the world.

The Stoics want us to do neither: it may neither be our, nor anyone else's, fault. Though not religious, the Stoics were fascinated by the Roman goddess of fortune, known as Fortuna, whom they took to be the perfect metaphor for destiny. Fortuna, who had shrines to her all over the empire, was popularly held to control the fate of humans, and was judged to be a terrifying mixture of the generous and the randomly wilful and spiteful. She was no meritocrat. She was represented holding a cornucopia filled with goodies (money, love, etc.) in one hand, and a tiller, for changing the course of life, in the other. Depending on her mood, she might throw you down a perfect job or a beautiful relationship, and then the next minute, simply because she felt like it, watch you choke to death on a fishbone.

It is an urgent priority for a Stoic to respect just how much of life will always be in the hands of this demented character. 'There is nothing which Fortune does not dare,' warned Seneca.

Understanding this ahead of time should make us both suspicious of success and gentle on ourselves around failure. In every sense, much of what we get, we don't deserve.

The task of the wise person is therefore never to believe in the gifts of fortune: fame, money, power, love, health – these are never our own. Our grip on them must at all times be light and deeply wary.

4. Loss of perspective

We naturally exaggerate our own importance. The incidents of our own lives loom very large in our view of the world. And so we get stressed and panicked, we curse and throw things across the room.

View of Star-Forming Region S106 from NASA's Hubble Telescope

To regain composure, we must regularly be reduced in our own eyes. We must give up on the very normal but very disturbing illusion that it really matters what we do and who we are.

The Stoics were keen astronomers and recommended the contemplation of the heavens to all students of philosophy. On an evening walk, look up and see the planets: you'll see Venus and Jupiter shining in the darkening sky. If the dusk deepens, you might see some other stars – Aldebaran, Andromeda and Aries, along with many more. It's a hint of the unimaginable extensions of space across the solar system, the galaxy and the cosmos. The sight has a calming effect that the Stoics revered, for against such a backdrop, we realise that none of our troubles, disappointments or hopes have any relevance.

Nothing that happens to us, or that we do, is – blessedly – of any consequence whatsoever from the cosmic perspective.

Conclusion

We need the Stoics more than ever. Every day confronts us with situations that they understood and wanted to prepare us for.

Their teachings are dark and sobering, yet, at the same time, profoundly consoling and, at points, even rather funny.

They invite us to feel heroic and defiant in the face of our many troubles.

As Seneca reminded us, 'Look at your wrists. There – at any time – lies freedom.'

To counterbalance the enragingly cheerful and naive optimism of our times, there is nothing better than the bittersweet calming wisdom of these ancient sages.

Epicurus

341–270 BC

The ancient Greek philosopher Epicurus was born in 341 BC, on the island of Samos, a few miles off the coast of modern Turkey. He had an unusually long beard, wrote over 300 books, and was one of the most famous philosophers of his age.

What made him famous was his skilful and relentless focus on one particular subject: *happiness*. Previously, philosophers had wanted to know how to be good; Epicurus insisted he wanted to focus on how to be *happy*.

Few philosophers had ever made such a frank, down-to-earth admission of their interests before. It shocked many, especially when they heard that Epicurus had started a school for happiness called The Garden. The idea of what was going on inside was both entirely shocking and deeply titillating. A few disgruntled Epicureans made some damaging leaks about what was going on in the school. Timocrates said that Epicurus had to vomit twice a day because he spent all his time on a sofa being fed luxurious meats and fish by a team of slaves. And Diotimus the Stoic published fifty lewd letters that he said had been written by Epicurus to some young students when he'd been drunk and sexually obsessed. It's because of such gossip that we still sometimes now use the adjective 'Epicurean' to describe luxury and decadence.

But such associations are unfounded. The truth about Epicurus is far less sensational – but far more interesting. The Greek philosopher really was focused on happiness and pleasure, but he had no interest in expensive meals or orgies. He owned only two cloaks and lived on bread, olives and – as a treat – the occasional slice of cheese. Instead, having patiently studied happiness for many years, Epicurus came to a set of remarkable and revolutionary conclusions about what we actually need to be happy, conclusions wholly at odds with the assumptions of his age – and of our own.

Epicurus proposed that we typically make three mistakes when thinking about happiness:

1. We think we need romantic relationships

Then, as now, people were obsessed with love. But Epicurus observed that happiness and love (let alone marriage) almost never go together. There is too much jealousy, misunderstanding and bitterness. Sex is always complicated and rarely in harmony with affection. It would be best, Epicurus concluded, never to put too much faith in relationships. By contrast, he noted how rewarding most friendships are: here we are polite, we look for agreement, we don't scold or berate and we aren't possessive. But the problem is we don't see our friends enough. We let work and family take precedence. We can't find the time. They live too far away.

2. We think we need lots of money

Then, as now, people were obsessed by their careers, motivated by a desire for money and applause. But Epicurus emphasised the difficulties of employment: the jealousy, the backbiting and frustrated ambitions.

What makes work really satisfying, Epicurus believed, is when we're able to work either alone or in very small groups, and when it feels meaningful, when we sense that we're helping others in some way or making things that improve the world. It isn't really cash or prestige we want; it's a sense of fulfilment through our labour.

3. We put too much faith in luxury

We dream of luxury: a beautiful home, elegant rooms and pleasant views. We imagine trips to idyllic locations, where we can rest and let others look after us …

But Epicurus disagreed with our longings. Behind the fantasy of luxury, what he believed we really want is calm. Yet calm won't possibly arise simply through changing the view or owning a delightful building.

Calm is an internal quality that is the result of analysis: it comes when we sift through our worries and correctly understand them. We therefore need ample time to read, to write, and, most of all, to benefit from the regular support of a good listener: a sympathetic, kind, clever person who in Epicurus's time would have been a philosopher, and whom we would now call a therapist.

With his analysis of happiness in hand, Epicurus made three important innovations:

· Firstly, he decided that he would live together with friends. Enough of seeing them only now and then. He bought a modestly priced plot of land outside of Athens and built a place where he and his friends could live side by side on a permanent basis. Everyone had their rooms, and there were common areas downstairs and in the grounds. That way, the residents would always be surrounded by people who shared their outlooks, were entertaining and kind. Children were looked after in a rota. Everyone ate together. One could chat in the corridors late at night. It was the world's first proper commune.

· Secondly, everyone in the commune stopped working for other people. They accepted cuts in their income in return for being able to focus on fulfilling work. Some of Epicurus's friends devoted themselves to farming, others to cooking, a few to making furniture and art. They had far less money, but ample intrinsic satisfaction.

· Thirdly, Epicurus and his friends devoted themselves to finding calm through rational analysis and insight. They spent periods of every day reflecting on their anxieties, improving their understanding of their psyches, and mastering the great questions of philosophy.

Epicurus's experiment in living caught on. Epicurean communities opened up all around the Mediterranean and drew in thousands of followers. The centres thrived for generations – until they were brutally suppressed by a jealous and aggressive Christian Church in the 5th century. But even then, their essence survived when many of them were turned into monasteries.

Epicurus's influence continues into the modern age. Karl Marx did his PhD thesis on him and thought of him as his favourite philosopher. What we call communism is at heart just a bigger – and rather more authoritarian and joyless – version of Epicureanism.

Even today, Epicurus remains an indispensable guide to life in advanced consumer capitalist societies because advertising – on which this system is based – functions on cleverly muddling people up about what they think they need to be happy.

An extraordinary number of adverts focus on the three very things that Epicurus identified as false lures of happiness: romantic love, professional status and luxury.

Adverts wouldn't work as well as they do if they didn't operate with an accurate sense of what our real needs are. Yet while they excite us by evoking them, they refuse to quench them properly. Beer ads will show us groups of friends hugging – but only sell us alcohol (that we might end up drinking alone). Fancy watch ads will show us high-status professionals walking purposefully to the office, but won't know how to answer the desire for intrinsically satisfying work. And adverts for tropical beaches may titillate us with their serenity, but can't – on their own – deliver the true calm we crave.

Epicurus invites us to change our understanding of ourselves and to alter society accordingly. We mustn't exhaust ourselves and the planet in a race for things that wouldn't possibly satisfy us even if we got them. We need a return to philosophy and a lot more seriousness about the business of being happy.

Augustine

AD 354-430

Augustine was a Christian philosopher who lived in the early 5th century AD on the fringes of the rapidly declining Roman Empire, in the North African town of Hippo (present-day Annaba, in Algeria). He served as bishop for over thirty years, proving popular and giving inspirational guidance to his largely uneducated and poor congregation. In his last days, a Germanic tribe known as the Vandals burned Hippo to the ground, destroyed the legions, made off with the town's young women, but left Augustine's cathedral and library entirely untouched out of respect for the elderly philosopher's achievements.

He matters to us non-Christians today because of what he criticised about Rome, its values and its outlook – and because Rome has so many things in common with the modern West, especially the United States, which so revered the empire that it wanted its capital city on the Potomac to look as if it might have been magically transported from the banks of the Tiber.

The Romans believed in two things in particular:

1. Earthly happiness

They were, on the whole, an optimistic lot. The builders of the Pont du Gard and the Coliseum had faith in technology, in the power of humans to master themselves, and in their ability to control nature and plot for their own happiness and satisfaction. In writers like Cicero and Plutarch, one finds a degree of pride, ambition and confidence in the future that, with some revisions, would not be out of place in Palo Alto or the pages of *Wired*. The Romans were keen practitioners of what we would nowadays call self-help, training their audiences to greater success and effectiveness. In their eyes, the human animal was something eminently open to being perfected.

2. A just social order

For long periods, the Romans trusted that their society was marked by justice: *justitia*. Although inheritance was a major factor, they also believed that people of ambition and intelligence could succeed. The army was trusted to be meritocratic. The capacity to make money was held to reflect both practical ability and also a degree of inner virtue. Therefore, showing off one's wealth was deemed honourable and a point of pride. Consumption was conspicuous and fame a wholly respectable ideal.

With these two attitudes in particular, Augustine disagreed furiously. In his masterpiece, *The City of God*, he dissected each one in turn in ways that continue to prove relevant to anyone who might harbour doubts of their own about them – even if his proposed solutions, drawn from Christian theology, will only ever appeal to believers. Augustine's rebuttals ran like this:

1. We're all lustful, mad, erratic, deluded deviants with no earthly chance of happiness

It was Augustine who came up with the idea of 'Original Sin'. He proposed that all humans, not merely this or that unfortunate example, were crooked, because all of us are unwitting heirs to the sins of Adam. Our sinful nature gives rise to what Augustine called a *'libido dominandi'* – a desire to dominate – which is evident in the brutal, blinkered, merciless way we treat others and the world around us. We cannot properly love, for we are constantly undermined by our egoism and our pride. Our powers of reasoning and understanding are fragile in the extreme. Lust – a particular concern of Augustine's, who had spent much of his youth fantasising about women in church – haunts our days and nights. We fail to understand ourselves, we chase phantoms, we are beset by anxieties … Augustine concluded his assault by chiding all those philosophers who 'have wished, with amazing folly, to be happy here on earth and to achieve bliss by their own efforts.'

It might sound depressing, but it may turn out to be a curious relief to be told that our lives are awry not by coincidence but by definition, because we are human, and because nothing human can ever be made entirely straight (perfection being an exclusive prerogative of the divine). We are creatures fated to intuit virtue and love, while never quite being able to secure them for ourselves. Our relationships, careers, countries are necessarily not as we'd want them to be. It isn't anything we have done – the odds have been stacked against us from the start.

Augustinian pessimism takes off some of the pressure we might feel (especially late at night, on Sunday evenings, and at any time after 40) when we slowly come to terms with the imperfect nature of pretty much everything we do and are. We should not rage or feel that we have been persecuted or singled out for undue punishment. It is simply the human condition, the legacy of what we might as well, even if we don't believe in Augustine's theology, call 'Original Sin'.

2. All hierarchies are unfair; there is no social justice; those at the top naturally won't all be good or those at the bottom bad – and vice versa

Romans had – in their most ambitious moments – thought themselves to be running a society with some strongly meritocratic features. Family tended to influence opportunity, but you couldn't get near the top just on that; you had to rely on your genuine virtues and abilities. Above all, they saw the grandeur of the Roman state as a sign of the collective merits of the Roman population. Romans ruled large parts of the earth because they deserved to. Empire was the reward for their virtue. It's a hugely tempting view today for those on the inside of successful corporations or states – to see their great prosperity and power as the just rewards for merit.

What arrogant, boastful and cruel claims, responded Augustine. There never was nor could ever be *justitia* in Rome or anywhere else on earth. God didn't give good people wealth and power – nor did he necessarily condemn

Fig. 49.—Miniature of the "City of God," by St. Augustine, translated by Raoul de Presles.—Manuscript of the Fifteenth Century. St. Geneviève Library. The upper enclosure represents the saints who have been already received into heaven; the seven lower enclosures represent those who are preparing themselves, by the exercise of Christian virtues, for the heavenly kingdom, or who are excluding themselves from it by committing one or other of the seven capital sins.

The *City of God* from a 15th-century manuscript

those who lacked them to poverty. The social order was a complete muddle of the deserving and the undeserving – and moreover, any attempt by human beings to judge who was a good person and who a bad one was a gross sin, an attempt to appropriate a task that only God could carry out, and then only at the end of time, on the Day of Judgement, to the sound of trumpets and phalanxes of angels.

Augustine distinguished between what he called two cities: the City of Men and the City of God. The latter was an ideal, a heavenly paradise, where the good would finally dominate, where power would be properly allied to justice and where virtue would reign. But men could never build such a city, and should never believe themselves capable of doing so. They were condemned to dwell only in the City of Men or Earthly City, which was a pervasively flawed society, where money could never accurately track virtue. In Augustine's formulation: 'True justice has no existence save in that republic whose founder and ruler is Christ.' That is, the fully fair distribution of reward is not something we can or should expect on earth.

Again, it may sound bleak, but it makes Augustine's philosophy extremely generous towards failure, poverty and defeat – our own and that of others. Unlike what the Romans might claim, earthly failure is no indication of being an inherently bad person – just as triumph can't mean anything too profound either. It is not for humans to judge each other by outward markers of success. From this analysis flows a lack of moralism and snobbery. It is our duty to be sceptical about power and generous towards weakness.

We don't need to be Christians to be comforted by both these points. They are the religion's universal gifts to political philosophy and human psychology. They stand as permanent reminders of some of the dangers and cruelties of believing that life can be made perfect or that poverty and obscurity are reliable indicators of vice.

Thomas Aquinas

1225–1274

t seems, at first, weird that we might learn from him. Thomas Aquinas was a medieval saint, said in moments of high excitement to levitate and have visions of the Virgin Mary. He was much concerned with explaining how angels speak and move. And yet ...

He continues to matter because he helps us with a problem that continues to bedevil us: how we can reconcile religion with science and faith with reason. Aquinas was both a philosopher and a holy saint. Refusing either to lose his faith or mindlessly believe, he developed a new understanding of the place of reason in human life. Aquinas's monumental contribution was to teach Western European civilisation that any human being – not just a Christian – could have access to great truths whenever they made use of God's greatest gift to human beings: reason. He broke a logjam in Christian thinking: the question of how non-Christians could have both wisdom and at the same time no interest in, or even knowledge of, Jesus. He universalised intelligence and opened the Christian mind to the insights of all of humanity from across the ages and continents. The modern world, in so far as it insists that good ideas can come from any quarter regardless of creed or background, remains hugely in his debt.

Thomas Aquinas was born to a noble family in Italy in 1225. As a young man, he went to study at the University of Naples and there came into contact with a source of knowledge that was just then being rediscovered: that of the ancient Greek and Roman authors, who had previously been shunned by Christian academics. At university, Aquinas also came under the influence of the Dominicans, a new order of monks who, unlike other groups, believed that they should live in the outside world, rather than a cloister.

Against the will of his family, Aquinas decided to join the order. His family's questionably pious response was to kidnap him and lock him in a tower they owned. Aquinas wrote desperate letters to the Pope, arguing his cause and

DIEGO VELAZQUEZ, *Temptation of St. Thomas Aquinas*, 1630

pleading to be set free. However, the Pope was busy with political matters, and so Aquinas stayed locked up and passed the time writing letters to Dominican monks and tutoring his sisters. According to one legend, during this period Aquinas's family even furnished him with a prostitute in a low-cut top in the hopes of seducing him away from his idea of being a monk, but Aquinas drove the young lady away with an iron bar.

Seeing they were getting nowhere, finally, his family un-locked the door and the (in their eyes) wayward Aquinas joined the Dominican order for good. Resuming his inter-rupted education, Aquinas went to study at the University of Paris, where he was a remarkably quiet student, but an ex-ceptionally prolific author, writing nearly 200 pieces about Christian theology in less than three decades. His books bear beautiful and strange titles, like the *Summa Theologica* and *Summa contra Gentiles*. He also became a hugely popu-lar and influential teacher and was eventually allowed by the Dominican leadership to found his own school in Naples. Such was his devotion to knowledge, even at the moment of his death (at the age of 49), he is reputed to have been in the middle of delivering an extended commentary on the Song of Songs. After he died, he was canonised in the Catholic Church and is now the patron saint of teachers.

One of Aquinas's central intellectual ambitions was to understand how people could know what was right and wrong – a far from academic concern, because, as a Chris-tian, he wanted to know how a person could be sure that their actions would allow them to go to heaven. Aquinas was aware that many ideas that seemed extremely right were not the work of Christians. For example, he especially ad-mired Aristotle: a man utterly unacquainted with the truths of the Gospels. It was in response to this dilemma that Aqui-nas made a highly important argument for the compatibility of religious belief and rational thought.

Many great philosophers were pagans, Aquinas knew, but this did not bar them from insight because, as he now pro-posed, the world could usefully be explored through reason alone. To explain how this could work, Aquinas proposed that the universe and all its dynamics operated according to two kinds of law: 'natural law' and divine 'eternal law'.

For Aquinas, many 'laws' could be worked out from our own experience of the world. We could find out for our-selves how to smelt iron, build an aqueduct or organise a just economy. These were the natural laws. But there were other revealed 'eternal' laws: that is, things that reason could not arrive at on its own. To know (as he thought) that after our deaths we would be judged by a merciful God or that Jesus was simultaneously human and divine, we would have to depend upon revelation in sacred books: we'd have to take them on trust from a higher authority.

In a commentary he wrote on the Roman philosopher Boethius, Aquinas defined a then prevailing assumption: 'the human mind cannot know any truth unless it is illuminated by light from God.' This was the view that everything that it is important for us to understand has to come from the single approved source: God. But it was in opposition to this idea that Aquinas argued that 'it is not necessary that the human mind should be endowed with any new light from God in order to understand those things which are within its natural field of knowledge.'

The radical move Aquinas was making was to allow important space for 'natural law' too. He was standing up for the importance of personal observation and experience. His worry was that the Bible was such a prestigious source that it could swamp observation: people would be so impressed by revelation from authority that they would discount the power of observation and what we can discover on our own.

The point Aquinas made was that both natural and revealed eternal law are important. They are not – he argued – essentially opposed. The problems come when we insist exclusively on either one. Which we need to develop depends upon the bias we currently have.

Today, the tension between higher authority and personal experience remains, though of course today the 'revelation' by a higher authority doesn't mean consulting the Bible. It means organised science. The modern version is the refusal of any kind of knowledge that doesn't come with the backing of experiments, data, mathematical modelling and peer-reviewed journal references.

The arts, literature and philosophy are today in the position Aquinas defined for natural law. They attempt to understand the world on the basis of personal experience, observation and individual thinking. They don't come with the stamp of higher authority (meaning, now, science rather than the Bible).

Aquinas's contemporaries were broadly aware of the ancient Greeks and Romans, but they took the view that 'pagans' simply could not have anything important to say on any topics that they felt really mattered to them. It wasn't the fault of the ancients – they lived before Jesus. But they were held to be in error on the single most important issue of life: religious belief. This seemed so terrible a flaw that nothing else the pagan philosophers thought could be in any way useful or important. Aquinas argued that people who are misguided on some fundamental things can still have a lot to teach you. He was diagnosing a form of intellectual snobbery. We have a tendency to dismiss a given idea because of its background: we feel we won't listen unless it comes from the right place. We might define 'the right place' in terms of the labs at MIT rather than the Bible, but the impulse is the same.

So, today, an atheistic modernist sitting in London might find it incredible that they could have anything at all to learn from reading the Gospel According to John. The Bible, they think, is so obviously in error on fundamental points. It contains primitive mistakes about the origins of the world; it is filled with supposed miracles. Which is similar to the way medieval Christians felt about ancient pagan writers.

The key point for Aquinas is that natural law is a subsection of eternal law, and it can be discovered through the faculty of independent reason. Aquinas gave as an example Jesus's injunction to 'Do unto others as you would have them do unto you'. Jesus may have given this idea a particularly memorable formulation, but it has in fact been a cornerstone of moral principles in most societies at all times. How is this

Portrait of Averroës (Ibn Rushd) (1126–1198), who was an
Andalusian-Arab philosopher and physician, by 14th-century
Florentine artist Andrea Bonaiuto.

possible? The reason, Aquinas argued, is that natural law doesn't need God's direct intervention in order to make itself known to man. Just by reasoning carefully, one is intuitively following God's intentions. Aquinas allowed that in a few situations God works simply through divine law, outside of the limits of human reason; and he gave the example of prophetic revelations and the visits of angels. However, most useful knowledge could be found within the realm of natural law.

Aquinas's ideas unfolded at a time when Islamic culture was going through very similar dilemmas as Christianity, in terms of how to reconcile reason and faith. For a long time, the Islamic caliphates in Spain, Morocco and Egypt had flourished, generating a wealth of new scientific knowledge and philosophy. However, due to the increasing influence of rigid religious leaders, they had become more dogmatic and oppressive by the time Aquinas was born. They had, for example, reacted violently against the Islamic philosopher Averroës (Arabic name Ibn Rushd). Like Aquinas, Averroës had been deeply influenced by Aristotle and had argued that reason and religion were compatible. However, the caliphates – anxious never to depart from the literal words of God – had made sure Averroës' ideas were banned and his books burned.

Aquinas read Averroës and saw that he and the Muslim scholar were engaged on similar projects. He knew that the Muslim world's increasingly radical rejection of reason was harming what had once been its thriving intellectual culture. It was partly thanks to Aquinas's ideas that Christianity did not suffer the same process of stultification as Islam.

Though Aquinas was a man of deep faith, he therefore provided a philosophical framework for the process of doubt and open scientific inquiry. He reminds us that wisdom (that is, the ideas we need) can come from multiple sources. From intuition but also from rationality, from science but also from revelation, from pagans but also from monks: he's sympathetic to all of these, and he takes and uses whatever works, without caring where the ideas come from. That sounds obvious, until we notice just how often we don't do this in our own lives: how often we get dismissive if an idea comes from an (apparently) 'wrong' source, someone with the wrong accent, a newspaper with a different political creed to ours, a prose style that seems too complicated, or too simple – or an old lady with a woolly hat.

Michel de Montaigne

1533–1592

We generally think that philosophers should be proud of their big brains, and be fans of thinking, self-reflection and rational analysis.

But there's one philosopher, born in France in 1533, with a refreshingly different take. Michel de Montaigne was an intellectual who spent his writing life knocking the arrogance of intellectuals. In his great masterpiece, the *Essays*, he comes across as relentlessly wise and intelligent – but also as constantly modest and keen to debunk the pretensions of learning. Not least, he is extremely funny: 'to learn that we have said or done a stupid thing is nothing; we must learn a more ample and important lesson; that we are but blockheads ... On the highest throne in the world, we are seated, still, upon our arses.' And, lest we forget: 'Kings and philosophers shit, and so do ladies.'

Montaigne was a child of the Renaissance, and the ancient philosophers popular in Montaigne's day had explained that our powers of reason could afford us a happiness and greatness denied to other creatures. Reason allowed us to control our passions and temper the wild demands of our bodies, wrote philosophers like Cicero. Reason was a sophisticated, almost divine, tool offering us mastery over the world and ourselves. But this character-isation of human reason enraged Montaigne. After hanging out with academics and philosophers, he wrote: 'In practice, thousands of little women in their villages have lived more gentle, more equable and more constant lives than [Cicero].'

His point wasn't that human beings can't reason at all, simply that they tend to be far too arrogant about their brains. 'Our life consists partly in madness, partly in wisdom,' he wrote. 'Whoever writes about it merely respectfully and by rule leaves more than half of it behind.'

Perhaps the most obvious example of our madness is the struggle of living with a human body. Our bodies smell, ache, sag, pulse, throb and age. Montaigne was the world's first and possibly only philosopher to talk at length about impotence, which seemed to him a prime example of how crazy and fragile our minds are.

Montaigne had a friend who had grown impotent with a woman he particularly liked. Montaigne did not blame his penis: 'Except for genuine impotence, never again are you incapable if you are capable of doing it once.' The problem was the mind, the oppressive notion that we had complete control over our bodies, and the horror of departing from an unfair portrait of normality. The solution was to redraw the portrait; it was by accepting a loss of command over the penis as a harmless possibility in love-making that one could pre-empt its occurrence – as the stricken man eventually discovered. In bed with a woman, he learned to: 'Admit beforehand that he was subject to this infirmity and spoke openly about it, so relieving the tensions within his soul. By bearing the malady as something to be expected, his sense of constriction grew less and weighed less heavily on him.'

Montaigne's frankness allowed the tensions in the reader's own soul to be relieved. A man who failed with his girlfriend, and was unable to do any more than mumble an apology, could regain his forces and soothe the anxieties of his beloved by accepting that his impotence belonged to a broad realm of sexual mishaps, neither very rare nor very peculiar. Montaigne knew a nobleman who, after failing to maintain an erection with a woman, fled home, cut off his penis and sent it to the lady 'to atone for his offence.' Montaigne proposed instead that:

> If [couples] are not ready, they should not try to rush things. Rather than fall into perpetual wretchedness by being struck with despair at a first rejection, it is better ... to wait for an opportune moment ... a man who suffers a rejection should make gentle assays and overtures with various little sallies; he should not stubbornly persist in proving himself inadequate once and for all.

Throughout his work, Montaigne took farts, penises, and shitting as serious topics for contemplation. He told his readers, for example, that he liked quiet when sitting on the toilet: 'Of all the natural operations, that is the one during which I least willingly tolerate being disrupted.'

Ancient philosophers had recommended that one try to model oneself on the lives of certain esteemed people, normally philosophers. In the Christian tradition, one should model one's life on that of Christ. The idea of modelling is attractive; it suggests we need to find someone to guide and illuminate our path. But it matters a lot what kind of portraits are around. What we see evidence for in others, we will attend to within; what others are silent about, we may stay blind to or experience only in shame. Montaigne is refreshing because he provides us with a life that is recognisably like our own and yet inspiring still – a very human ideal.

Academia was deeply prestigious in Montaigne's day, as in our own. Montaigne was an excellent scholar but he hated pedantry. He only wanted to learn things that were useful and relentlessly attacked academia for being out of touch: 'If man were wise, he would gauge the true worth of anything by its usefulness and appropriateness to his life,' he said. Only that which makes us feel better may be worth understanding.

Montaigne noted snobbery and pretension in many areas – and constantly tried to bring us back to earth.

> Storming a breach, conducting an embassy, ruling a nation are glittering deeds. Rebuking, laughing, buying, selling, loving, hating and living together gently and justly with your household – and with yourself – not getting slack nor being false to yourself, is something more remarkable, more rare and more difficult. Whatever people may say, such secluded lives sustain in that way duties which are at least as hard and as tense as those of other lives.

In this vein, Montaigne mocked books that were difficult to read. He admitted to his readers that he found Plato more than a little boring – and that he just wanted to have fun with books:

> I am not prepared to bash my brains for anything, not even for learning's sake however precious it may be. From books all I seek is to give myself pleasure by an honourable pastime ... If I come across difficult passages in my reading I never bite my nails over them: after making a charge or two I let them be ... If one book wearies me I take up another.

He could be pretty caustic about incomprehensible philosophers:

'Difficulty is a coin which the learned conjure with so as not to reveal the vanity of their studies and which human stupidity is keen to accept in payment.'

Montaigne observed how an intimidating scholarly culture had made all of us study other people's books before we study our own minds. And yet, as he put it: 'We are richer than we think, each one of us.'

We may all arrive at wise ideas if we cease to think of ourselves as so unsuited to the task because we aren't 2,000 years old, aren't interested in the topics of Plato's dialogues and have a so-called ordinary life. 'You can attach the whole of moral philosophy to a commonplace private life just as well as to one of richer stuff.'

It was perhaps to bring the point home that Montaigne offered so much information on exactly how ordinary his own life was – why he wanted to tell us:

That he didn't like apples.
'I am not overfond ... of any fruit except melons.'
That he had a complex relationship with radishes.
'I first of all found that radishes agreed with me; then they did not; now they do again.'

That he practised the most advanced dental hygiene
'My teeth ... have always been exceedingly good ...
Since boyhood I learned to rub them on my napkin,
both on waking up and before and after meals.'
That he ate too fast.
'In my haste I often bite my tongue and occasionally
my fingers.'
And liked wiping his mouth.
'I could dine easily enough without a tablecloth, but
I feel very uncomfortable dining without a clean nap-
kin ... I regret that we have not continued along the
lines of the fashion started by our kings, changing
napkins likes plates with each course.'

Trivia, perhaps, but symbolic reminders that there was a
thinking 'I' behind his book, that a moral philosophy had
issued – and so could issue again – from an ordinary, fruit-
eating soul.

There is no need to be discouraged if, from the outside,
we look nothing like those who have ruminated in the past.

In Montaigne's redrawn portrait of the adequate, semi-
rational human being, it is possible to speak no Greek, fart,
change one's mind after a meal, get bored with books, be
impotent, and know none of the ancient philosophers.

A virtuous, ordinary life, striving for wisdom but never
far from folly, is achievement enough.

Montaigne remains the great, readable intellectual with
whom we can laugh at intellectuals and pretensions of many
kinds. He was a breath of fresh air in the cloistered, un-
worldly, snobbish corridors of the academia of the 16th century – and because academia has, sadly, not changed very
much, he continues to be an inspiration and a solace to all
of us who feel routinely oppressed by the pedantry and arrogance of so-called clever people.

La Rochefoucauld

1613–1680

There's a belief that philosophy, when properly done, should sound dense, forbidding, a little confusing, as if it might have been awkwardly translated from the German. But at the dawn of the modern age lived a French philosopher who trusted in a very different way of presenting his thoughts, a man who wrote a very slim book, barely sixty pages long, that can deservedly be counted as one of the true masterpieces of philosophy, a compendium of acerbic, melancholy observations about the human condition, each of them only a sentence or two long, that retains an exceptional number of timely, wise and oddly consoling lessons for our morally confused and distracted age.

The Duc de La Rochefoucauld was born in Paris in 1613, and, despite his many initial advantages (wealth, connections, good looks and a very beautiful and ancient name), he had a thoroughly difficult and often miserable life. He fell in love with a couple of duchesses who didn't treat him well; he ended up in prison after some bungled but honourable political manoeuvring; he was forced into exile from his beloved Paris on four occasions; he never advanced as far as he wanted at court; he got shot in the eye during a rebellion and almost went blind; he lost most of his money; and some enemies published what they falsely purported to be his memoirs, full of insults against people whom he liked and depended upon – who then turned against him and refused to believe in his innocence.

After all this – betrayal, imprisonment, impoverishment, injury, plagiarism and libel – La Rochefoucauld can readily be forgiven when he declared that he'd had enough of the active life and would henceforth retreat to quieter contemplative pursuits instead. So he hung up his sword and spent his time in the living rooms of two leading intellectual figures of his day, the Marquise de Sablé and the Comtesse de Lafayette, who regularly invited writers and artists to sit with them in their Parisian salons in order to discuss the great themes of existence – often over lemonade and light snacks.

The salons rewarded wit and spark. They were not lecture halls or seminar rooms, and there was no tolerance for leadenness or pomposity here, so winning over listeners required particular skills that came to shape La Rochefoucauld's mind and work.

It was in the salons that La Rochefoucauld developed the literary genre for which he has become known: that of the maxim, or aphorism, a pithy statement that deftly captures a dark insight into the human soul, reminding us of a wise and often uncomfortable truth. In good hands, an aphorism should deliver its punch in less than three seconds (one might be competing with the arrival of an asparagus tart).

In the salons, La Rochefoucauld perfected and honed the 504 aphorisms that made his name. He watched how his fellow guests reacted, and tweaked his work accordingly. His aphorisms covered all manner of psychological topics, though issues of envy, vanity, love and ambition were recurring themes. A typical La Rochefoucauld aphorism begins by addressing the reader with a 'we' or 'one', inviting consent with gentle coercion. The aphorism then subverts an accepted piety about human nature in a cynical or sceptical direction. It's in the last third of the sentence that the sting is generally delivered, and it often makes us laugh, as can happen when we are forced to acknowledge the falsity of a previous sentimental or hypocritical position.

Perhaps the most classic and perfect of all La Rochefoucauld's aphorisms is:

> We all have strength enough to bear the misfortunes of others.

It is closely followed by the equally effective:

> There are some people who would never have fallen in love, if they had not heard there was such a thing.

And the no less accomplished:

> He that refuses praise the first time it is offered does
> it because he would like to hear it a second.

Voltaire said that La Rochefoucauld's *Maxims* was the book
that had most powerfully shaped the character of the French
people, giving them their taste for psychological reflection,
precision and cynicism. Behind almost every one of the maxims lies a challenge to an ordinary, flattering view of ourselves. La Rochefoucauld relishes revelations of the debt that
kindness owes to egoism and insists that we are never far
from being vain, arrogant, selfish and petty – and, in fact,
never nearer than when we trust in our own goodness.

Having suffered unduly in its name, he was particularly
suspicious of romantic love:

> The reason lovers never tire of one another's com-
> pany is because they never talk of anything but
> themselves.

> If one were to judge of love according to the greatest
> part of the effects it produces, it might very justly
> pass for hatred rather than kindness.

> To say that one never flirts is in itself a form of
> flirtation.

It only looks easy. Nietzsche, who was deeply inspired by La
Rochefoucauld, wrote aphorisms (collected in his book *Human, All Too Human*), which sorely lack the Frenchman's
mixture of darkness and good sense:

> A few men have sighed because their women were
> abducted; most, because no one wanted to abduct
> them.

La Rochefoucauld wrote as he did because he wanted his ideas to persuade people whom he knew had little time and would not necessarily be on his side. If most philosophers since have (with the odd exception) felt no need to write with his elegance, wit and concision, it is because they have trusted (fatefully) that, so long as one's ideas are important, the style in which one delivers them is of no issue.

La Rochefoucauld knew otherwise. Most of us are so distracted, if someone wants to get a point across to us, they must use all the devices of art to seize our attention and cauterise our boredom for the necessary span. The history of philosophy would have been very different if its practitioners had all imagined themselves to be writing for an impatient non-professional audience with meandering minds in the midst of a chatty Parisian salon.

Baruch Spinoza

1632–1677

Baruch Spinoza was a 17th-century Dutch philosopher who tried to reinvent religion – moving it away from something based on superstition and ideas of direct divine intervention to being a discipline that was far more impersonal, quasi-scientific and yet also, at all times, serenely consoling.

Baruch – the word means 'Blessed' in Hebrew – was born in the Jewish quarter of Amsterdam in 1632, a thriving centre of Jewish commerce and thought.

His ancestors were Sephardic Jews, who had fled Spain following the Catholic-inspired expulsion of 1492. Baruch, a studious, highly intelligent child, received an intensely traditional Jewish education: he went to the local Jewish school – the yeshiva – and followed all the Jewish High Holidays and rituals.

But gradually, he began to distance himself from the faith of his ancestors: 'Although I have been educated from boyhood in the accepted beliefs concerning Scripture,' he later wrote with characteristic caution, 'I have felt bound in the end to embrace [other] views.'

His fully fleshed-out ideas were to be expressed in his great work, the *Ethics*, written entirely in Latin and published in 1677. In the *Ethics*, Spinoza directly challenged the main tenets of Judaism in particular and organised religion in general:

· God is not a person who stands outside of nature.
· There is no one to hear our prayers.
· Or to create miracles.
· Or to punish us for misdeeds.
· There is no afterlife.
· Man is not God's chosen creature.
· The Bible was only written by ordinary people.
· God is not a craftsman or an architect. Nor is he a king or a military strategist who calls for believers to take up the Holy Sword. God does not see anything, nor does he

expect anything. He does not judge. He does not even reward the virtuous person with a life after death. Every representation of God as a person is a projection of the imagination.
· Everything in the traditional liturgical calendar is pure superstition and mumbo-jumbo.

However, despite all this, remarkably, Spinoza did not declare himself an atheist. He insisted that he remained a staunch defender of God.

God plays an absolutely central role in Spinoza's *Ethics*, but it isn't anything like the God who haunts the pages of the Old Testament.

Spinoza's God is wholly impersonal and indistinguishable from what we might variously call nature, or existence, or a world soul: God is the universe, and its laws; God is reason and truth; God is the animating force in everything that is and can be. God is the cause of everything, but he is the *eternal* cause. He doesn't participate in change. He is not in time. He cannot be individuated.

Spinoza writes: 'Whatever is, is in God, and nothing can exist or be conceived without God.'

Throughout his text, Spinoza was keen to undermine the idea of prayer. In prayer, an individual appeals to God to change the way the universe works. But Spinoza argues that this is entirely the wrong way around. The task of human beings is to try to understand how and why things are the way they are – and then accept it, rather than protest at the workings of existence by sending little messages up into the sky.

As Spinoza put it, beautifully but rather caustically: 'Whosoever loves God cannot strive that God should love him in return.'

In other words, only naive (but perhaps rather touching) narcissism would lead someone at once to believe in a God who made the eternal laws of physics and then to imagine that this same God would take an interest in bending the

Baruch Spinoza – walking with book in hand in Amsterdam, ostracised
by the local Jewish community.

rules of existence to improve his or her life in some way.

Spinoza was deeply influenced by the philosophy of the Stoics of ancient Greece and Rome. They had argued that wisdom lies not in protest against how things are, but in continuous attempts to understand the ways of the world – and then bow down peacefully to necessity.

Seneca, Spinoza's favourite philosopher, had compared human beings to dogs on a leash being led by the necessities of life in a range of directions. The more one pulls against what is necessary, the more one is strangled; and therefore the wise must always endeavour to understand ahead of time how things are – for example, what love is like, or how politics works – and then change their direction accordingly so as not to be strangled unnecessarily. It is this kind of Stoic attitude that constantly pervades Spinoza's philosophy.

To understand God traditionally meant studying the Bible and other holy texts. But Spinoza now introduces another idea.

The best way to know God is to understand how life and the universe work: it is through a knowledge of psychology, philosophy and the natural sciences that one comes to understand God.

In traditional religion, believers will ask special favours of God. Spinoza proposes instead that we should understand what God wants, and we can do so in one way above all: by studying everything that is. By reasoning, we can accede to a divine eternal perspective.

Spinoza makes a famous distinction between two ways of looking at life. We can either see it egoistically, from our limited point of view, as he put it: *Sub specie durationis* – under the aspect of time. Or we can look at things globally and eternally: *Sub specie aeternitatis* – under the aspect of eternity.

Our nature means that we'll always be divided between the two. Sensual life pulls us towards a time-bound, partial view. But our reasoned intelligence can give us unique access to another perspective. It can quite literally allow us – here Spinoza becomes beautifully lyrical – to participate in eternal totality.

Normally, we call 'bad' whatever is bad for us, and 'good' whatever increases our power and advantage, but to be truly ethical means rising above these local concerns. It might all sound forbidding, but Spinoza envisaged his philosophy as a route to a life based on freedom from guilt, from sorrow, from pity or from shame.

Happiness involves aligning our will with that of the universe. The universe – God – has its own projects and it is our task to understand rather than rail against these. The free person is one conscious of the necessities that compel us all.

Spinoza writes that the wise man, the person who understands how and why things are, 'possesses eternally true complacency (*acquiescentia*) of spirit.'

Needless to say, these ideas got Spinoza into very deep trouble. He was excommunicated from the Jewish

REMBRANDT VAN RIJN, *Philosopher in Meditation*, 1632

community of Amsterdam in 1656. The rabbis issued a writ known as a *cherem* against the philosopher: 'By the decree of the angels' – it went – 'and by the command of the holy men, we excommunicate, expel, curse and damn Baruch de Espinoza ... with all the curses which are written in the Book of the Law. Cursed be he by day and cursed be he by night; cursed be he when he lies down, and cursed be he when he rises up.'

Spinoza was forced to flee Amsterdam, and he eventually settled in The Hague, where he lived quietly and peacefully as a lens grinder and private tutor till his death in 1677.

Spinoza's work was largely ignored. In the 19th century, Hegel took an interest, as did Wittgenstein – and some 20th-century scholars.

But on the whole Spinoza offers us a warning about the failures of philosophy.

The *Ethics* is one of the world's most beautiful books. It contains a calming, perspective-restoring take on life. It replaces the God of superstition with a wise and consoling pantheism.

And yet Spinoza's work failed utterly to convince any but a few to abandon traditional religion and to move towards a rationalist, wise system of belief.

The reasons are in a way simple and banal.

Spinoza failed to understand – like so many philosophers before and since – that what leads people to religion isn't just reason, but, far more importantly, emotion, belief, fear and tradition.

People stick with their beliefs because they like the rituals, the communal meals, the yearly traditions, the beautiful architecture, the music and the sonorous language read out in synagogue or church.

Spinoza's *Ethics* arguably contains a whole lot more wisdom than the Bible – but because it comes without any of the Bible's supporting structure, it remains a marginal work, studied here and there at universities in the West – while the traditional religion that he thought outmoded in the 1670s continues to thrive and convince people.

If we're ever to replace traditional beliefs, we must remember just how much religion is helped along by ritual, tradition, art and a desire to belong – all things that Spinoza, despite his great wisdom, ignored at his peril in his bold attempt to replace the Bible.

Arthur Schopenhauer

1788–1860

Arthur Schopenhauer was a German 19th-century philosopher who deserves to be remembered today for the insights contained in his great work: *The World as Will and Representation.*

Schopenhauer was the first serious Western philosopher to get interested in Buddhism – and his thought can best be read as a Western interpretation of, and response to, the enlightened pessimism found in Buddhist thought.

'In my seventeenth year,' he wrote in an autobiographical text, 'I was gripped by the misery of life, as Buddha had been in his youth when he saw sickness, old age, pain and death. The truth was that this world could not have been the work of an all-loving Being, but rather that of a devil, who had brought creatures into existence in order to delight in their sufferings.' And like the Buddha, it was his goal to dissect and then come up with a solution to this suffering.

It is chiefly the fault of universities that Schopenhauer is taught in such an academic way, as it has stopped him from being widely known, read and followed. And yet, in truth, this is a man who – no less than the Buddha – deserves disciples, schools, artworks and monasteries to put his ideas into practice.

Schopenhauer's philosophy starts by giving a name to a primary force within us, which he says is more powerful than anything else – our reason, logic or moral sense, and which he terms the Will-to-Life. The Will-to-Life is a constant force that makes us thrust ourselves forward, cling to existence and look to our own advantage. It's blind, dumb and very insistent. What the Will-to-Life makes us focus on most of all is sex. From adolescence onwards, this Will thrums within us, turns our heads constantly to erotic scenarios and makes us do very odd things – the oddest of which is to fall in love.

Schopenhauer was very respectful of love, as one might be towards a hurricane or a tiger. He deeply resented the disruption caused to intelligent people by infatuations – or what we'd call crushes – but he refused to conceive of these as either disproportionate or accidental. In his eyes, love is connected to the most important (and miserable) underlying project of the Will-to-Life and hence of all our lives: having children.

'Why all this noise and fuss about love? Why all the urgency, uproar, anguish and exertion?' he asked. 'Because the ultimate aim of all love-affairs … is actually more important than all other aims in anyone's life; and therefore it is quite worthy of the profound seriousness with which everyone pursues it.'

The romantic dominates life because '[w]hat is decided by it is nothing less than the *composition of the next generation* … the existence and special constitution of the human race in times to come.'

Of course, we rarely think of future children when we are asking someone out on a date. But in Schopenhauer's view, this is simply because the intellect 'remains so much excluded from the real resolutions and secret decisions of its own will.'

Why should such deception even be necessary? Because, for Schopenhauer, we would never reliably be able to reproduce unless we first had – quite literally – lost our minds. This was a man deeply opposed to the boredom, routine, expense and sheer sacrifice of having children.

Furthermore, he argued that, most of the time, if our intellect were properly in charge of choosing who to fall in love with, we would pick radically different people to the ones we end up with.

But we're ultimately driven to fall in love not with people we'll get on with, but with people whom the Will-to-Life recognises as ideal partners for producing what Schopenhauer bluntly called 'balanced children'. All of us are in any case a bit unbalanced, he thought: we're a bit too masculine, or too feminine, too tall or too short, too rational or too impulsive. If such imbalances were allowed to persist, or were aggravated, in the next generation, the human race would, within a short time, sink into oddity.

The Will-to-Life must therefore push us towards people who can, on account of their compensating imbalances, cancel out our own issues – a large nose combined with a button nose promise a perfect nose. He argued that short people often fall in love with tall people, and more feminine men with more assertive and masculine women.

Unfortunately, this theory of attraction led Schopenhauer to a very bleak conclusion: namely, that a person who is highly suitable for producing a balanced child is almost never (though we cannot realise it at the time because we have been blindfolded by the Will-to-Life) very suitable for us. We should not be surprised by marriages between people who would never have been friends: 'Love ... casts itself on people who, apart from sex, would be hateful, contemptible, and even abhorrent to us. But the will of the species is so much more powerful than that of individuals, that lovers overlook everything, misjudge everything, and bind themselves forever to an object of misery.'

The Will-to-Life's ability to further its own ends rather than our happiness may, Schopenhauer's theory implies, be sensed with particular clarity in that rather scary, lonely moment just after orgasm: 'Directly after copulation the devil's laughter is heard'.

Watching the human spectacle, Schopenhauer felt deeply sorry for us. We are just like animals – except, because of our greater self-awareness, even more unhappy.

There are some poignant passages where he discusses different animals but dwells especially on the mole: a stunted monstrosity that dwells in damp narrow corridors, rarely sees the light of day, and whose offspring look like gelatinous worms – but who still does everything in its power to survive and perpetuate itself.

We're just like them and just as pitiful: we are driven frantically to push ourselves forward, get good jobs to impress prospective partners, wonder endlessly about finding 'The One' (imagining they'll make us happy), and are eventually briefly seduced by someone long enough to produce a child, and then have to spend the next forty years in misery to atone for our error.

Schopenhauer is beautifully and comically gloomy about human nature:

> There is only one inborn error, and that is the notion that we exist in order to be happy ... So long as we persist in this inborn error ... the world seems to us full of contradictions. For at every step, in great things and small, we are bound to experience that the world and life are certainly not arranged for the purpose of being content. That's why the faces of almost all elderly people are etched with such disappointment.

Schopenhauer offers two solutions to deal with the problems of existence. The first is for rather rare individuals that he called 'sages'.

Sages are able, by heroic efforts, to rise above the demands of the Will-to-Life: they see the natural drives within themselves towards selfishness, sex and vanity... and override them. They overcome their desires, live alone (often away from big cities), never marry and quell their appetites for fame and status.

In Buddhism, Schopenhauer points out, this person is known as a monk – but he recognises that only a tiny number of us can go in for such a life.

The second and more easily available and realistic option is to spend as long as we can with art and philosophy, whose task is to hold up a mirror to the frenzied efforts and unhappy turmoil created in all of us by the Will-to-Life. We may not be able to quell the Will-to-Life very often, but in the evenings at the theatre, or on a walk with a book of poetry, we can step back from the day-to-day and look at life without illusion.

The art Schopenhauer loved best is the opposite of sentimental: Greek tragedies, the aphorisms of La Rochefoucauld and the political theories of Machiavelli and Hobbes. Such works speak frankly about egoism, suffering, selfishness and the horrors of married life – and extend a tragic, dignified, melancholy sympathy to the human race.

It's fitting that Schopenhauer's own work fitted his own description of what philosophy and art should do perfectly. It, too, is deeply consoling in its morbid bitter pessimism. For example, he tells us:

'To marry means to do everything possible to become an object of disgust to each other.'

'Every life history is the history of suffering.'

'Life has no intrinsic worth, but is kept in motion merely by want and illusion.'

After spending a lot of time trying, yet failing to be famous, and trying, yet failing to have good relationships, towards the end of his life, Schopenhauer eventually found an audience who adored his writings. He lived quietly in an apartment in Frankfurt with his dog, a white poodle whom he called Atman, after the world soul of the Buddhists – but whom the neighbouring children called Mrs Schopenhauer. Shortly before his death, a sculptor made a famous bust of him. He died in 1860 at the age of 72, having achieved calm and serenity.

He is a sage for our own times, someone whose bust should be no less widespread and no less revered than that of the Buddha he so loved.

Georg Hegel

1770–1831

G eorg Wilhelm Friedrich Hegel was born in Stutt-gart in 1770. He had a very middle-class existence: he was obsessed by his career path and his income. He was a newspaper editor and then a headmaster before becoming an academic professor. He never quite got his hair under control. When he was older, he liked going to the opera. He was very fond of champagne. Intellectually he was adventurous but in externals he was respectable, con-ventional – and proud of it. He ascended the academic tree and reached the topmost branch – head of the University of Berlin – in 1830 (when he was 60 years old). He died the following year.

Hegel has had a terrible influence on philosophy. He writes horribly. He is confusing and complicated when he should be clear and direct. He tapped into a weakness of human nature: to be trustful of grave-sounding, incompre-hensible prose. He made it seem as if the mark of reading deep thought is that one cannot quite understand what is go-ing on. This has made philosophy much weaker in the world than it should be. And the world has paid another heavy price for Hegel's problems with communication. It has made it much harder to hear the valuable things he has to say to us. Among these, a small number of lessons stand out:

1. Important parts of ourselves can be found in history
Hegel was rare among philosophers in taking history serious-ly. In his day, a standard European way of looking at the past was to consider it as 'primitive' – and to feel proud of how much progress had been made to get us to the modern age.

But Hegel preferred to believe that every era can be looked at as a repository of a particular kind of wisdom. It will manifest with rare clarity certain very useful attitudes and ideas, which then become submerged, unavailable or more muddled in later periods. We need to go back in time to rescue things that have gone missing, even in a so-called advanced era.

So, for example, we might need to mine the history of ancient Greece to grasp fully the idea of what community could be; the Middle Ages can teach us – as no other era can – about the role of honour; an inspiring vision of how money can pay for art is to be found in the Florence of the 14th century, even if this period featured appalling attitudes to children and the rights of women.

Hegel held that progress is never linear. The present may be better in some respects, but is likely to be worse than the past in others. There is wisdom at every stage – which points us to the task of the historian: to rescue those ideas most needed to counterbalance the blind spots of the present.

It means that what we might be tempted to call nostalgia may have a tinge of wisdom to it. If people say that life was better in the 1950s or say that they admire Victorian values of thrift, self-reliance and hard work, it's tempting to tell them that the clock can't be turned back and that, anyway, there was so much wrong with those times that it would be appalling to return to them. But there's a more sympathetic attitude that Hegel explored in *The Phenomenology of Spirit*, which he finished in 1807. That's the view that each era contains an important insight that is (unfortunately) mired in a confused set of errors. So, of course, it would be terrible to go back in total, but the nostalgia is latching onto what was good. And that good aspect is something we still need to pay attention to in the present. Hegel imagined an ideal history in which gradually all the good aspects of the past would be liberated from the unfortunate things that accompanied them. And that the best future would gradually amalgamate them all. We need to learn something from the 19th-century industrialist and from the 1968 hippy, from the medieval bishop and from the 18th-century French peasant.

'World history' he says, 'is the record of the mind's efforts to understand itself.' At different points in history, different aspects of the mind are more prominent. The same happens on a micro scale in our own lives. In childhood, wonder or trust may be more to the fore; in late childhood, it might be conformity and the desire to please those thought to be superior; in adolescence, the theme of doubt might get played out conspicuously. Later, there might be episodes of pragmatism, or the experience of authority, or the fear of death. At each of these stages, we are gradually learning about ourselves, and we need to go through them all to fully grasp who we are. The ideal picture of maturity would be the accumulated wisdom of what is learned from all ages.

2. Learn from ideas you dislike

Hegel was a great believer in learning from one's intellectual enemies, from points of view we disagree with or that feel alien. That's because he held that bits of the truth are likely to be scattered even in unappealing or peculiar places – and that we should dig them out by asking always, 'What sliver of sense and reason might be contained in otherwise frightening or foreign phenomena?'

Nationalism, for instance, has had many terrible manifestations (even in Hegel's day). So, the temptation of thoughtful people is to give up entirely on this field. But Hegel's move was to ask what underlying good idea or important need might be hiding within the bloody history of nationalism – a need waiting for recognition and interpretation. He proposed that it's the need for people to feel proud of where they come from, to identify with something beyond merely their own achievements, to anchor their identities beyond the ego. This is an unavoidable and fruitful requirement, he suggested – something that remains valuable even when some particularly awful movements and politicians have exploited this need and driven it in catastrophic directions.

Hegel is a hero of the thought that really important ideas may be in the hands of people you regard as beneath contempt.

EUGENE DELACROIX, *Liberty Leading the People*, 1830

3. Progress is messy

Hegel believed that the world makes progress, but only by lurching from one extreme to another as it seeks to overcompensate for a previous mistake. He proposed that it generally takes three moves before the right balance on any issue can be found, a process that he named the 'dialectic'.

In his own lifetime, he pointed out that governments had improved, but far from directly. The flawed, stifling, unfair 18th-century system of inherited traditional monarchy had been abolished by the French Revolution – whose founding fathers had wanted to give proper voice to the majority of people.

But what should have been the peaceful birth of representative government had ended up in the anarchy and chaos of The Terror. This in turn had led to the emergence of Napoleon, who had restored order and ensured opportun-ity for talent and ability – but who had also overreached himself and had become a military brute, tyrannising the rest of Europe and trampling on the liberty he had professed to love. Eventually, the modern 'balanced constitution' emerged, an arrangement that more sensibly balanced up popular representation with the rights of minorities and a decent centralised authority. But this resolution had taken at least forty years and incalculable bloodshed to reach.

In our own time, think of the slow path towards sensible attitudes to sex. The Victorians had imposed too much repression. Yet the 1960s may have turned out to be too liberal. It might only be by the 2020s that we will find the right balance between extremes.

Hegel takes some of the weight off our backs by insisting that progress will always be slow and troubled. He adds that what happens in history will occur in individuals as well. We too learn slowly and with massive overcorrections. Take the development of our emotional lives. We might, in our twenties, have been with someone so emotionally intense we felt suffocated; we therefore freed ourselves and took up with someone cooler and more reserved; but they might eventually also have become oppressive over time. We may be 52 before we get this aspect more or less right.

This can seem the most appalling waste of time. But Hegel insists the painful stepping from error to error is inevitable, something we must expect and reconcile ourselves to when planning our lives or contemplating the mess in history books or on the nightly news.

4. Art has a purpose

Hegel rejects the idea of 'art for art's sake'. In his most impressive work – the *Introductory Lectures on Aesthetics* – he argues that painting, music, architecture, literature and design all have a major job to do. We need them so that important insights become powerful and helpful in our lives. Art is 'the sensuous presentation of ideas'.

Just knowing a fact often leaves us cold. In theory we believe conflict in Syria is important; in practice we switch off. In principle we know we should be more forgiving to our partners. But this abstract conviction gets forgotten at the least provocation (a crumpled newspaper in the hall, imperfect parking technique).

The point of art, Hegel realises, is not so much to come up with startlingly new or strange ideas, but to make the good, important, helpful thoughts we often already know and make them stick in our minds.

5. We need new institutions

Hegel took a very positive view of institutions and of the power they can wield. The insight of an individual might be profound. But it will be ineffective and transient unless it gets embodied in an institution. Jesus's ideas about suffering and compassion needed the Catholic Church to take them to the world. Freud's ideas about the complexity of childhood didn't become a properly constructive force until they got organised, extended and institutionalised at the Tavistock Clinic in London.

The point is that for ideas to be active and effective in the world, a lot more is needed than that they are correct. This was a point Hegel made again and again in different ways. In order for an idea to be important in a society, it needs employees and buildings, training programmes and legal advisors, for institutions to allow for the scale of time that big projects need – much longer than the maturity of one individual.

The essential function of an institution is to make the major truths powerful in society. (And an institution loses its way when it stops having a profound mission.) So, as new needs of a society get recognised, they should, ideally, lead to the formation of new institutions.

Nowadays, we might say we need major new institutions to focus on relationships, consumer education, career choice, mood management, and how to bring up less damaged children.

Conclusion

Hegel put his finger on a crucial feature of modern life: we long for progress and improvement, yet we are continually confronted by conflict and evidence of setbacks.

His insight is that growth requires the clash of divergent ideas and therefore will be painful and slow. But at least once we know this we don't have to compound our troubles by thinking them abnormal. Hegel gives us a more accurate and hence more manageable view of ourselves, our difficulties, and where we are in history.

Friedrich Nietzsche

1844–1900

The challenge begins with how to pronounce his name. The first bit should sound like 'Knee', the second like 'cher': Knee – cher.

Friedrich Nietzsche was born in 1844 in a quiet village in the eastern part of Germany, where – for generations – his forefathers had been pastors. He did exceptionally well at school and university; and so excelled at ancient Greek (a very prestigious subject at the time) that he was made a professor at the University of Basel when still only in his mid-twenties.

But his official career didn't work out. He got fed up with his fellow academics, gave up his job and moved to Switzerland and Italy where he lived modestly and often alone. He was rejected by a succession of women, causing him much grief ('My lack of confidence is immense'). He didn't get on with his family ('I don't like my mother and it's painful even for me to hear my sister's voice') and, in response to his isolation, grew a huge moustache and took long country walks every day. For many years, his books hardly sold at all. When he was 44, his mental health broke down entirely. He never recovered and died eleven years later.

Nietzsche believed that the central task of philosophy was to teach us how to 'become who we are'. In other words, how to discover and be loyal to our highest potential.

To this end, he developed four helpful lines of thought:

1. Own up to envy

Envy is – Nietzsche recognised – a big part of life. Yet we're generally taught to feel ashamed of our envious feelings. They seem an indication of evil. So we hide them from ourselves and others, so much so that there are people who will sometimes say, with all sincerity, that they don't envy anyone.

This is logically impossible, insisted Nietzsche, especially if we live in the modern world (which he defined as any time after the French Revolution). Mass democracy and the end of the old feudal-aristocratic age had, in Nietzsche's eyes, created a perfect breeding ground for envious feelings, because everyone was now encouraged to feel that they were equal to everyone else. In feudal times, it would never have occurred to the serf to feel envious of the prince. But now everyone compared themselves to everyone else and was exposed to a volatile mixture of ambition and inadequacy as a result.

However, there is nothing wrong with envy, maintained the philosopher. What matters is how we handle it. Greatness comes from being able to learn from our envious crises. Nietzsche thought of envy as a confused but important signal from our deeper selves about what we really want. Everything that makes us envious is a fragment of our true potential, which we disown at our peril. We should learn to study our envy forensically, keeping a diary of envious moments, and then sift through episodes to discern the shape of a future, better self.

The envy we don't own up to will otherwise end up emitting what Nietzsche called 'sulfurous odours.' Bitterness is envy that doesn't understand itself. It is not that Nietzsche believed we always end up getting what we want (his own life had taught him this well enough). He simply insisted that we must become conscious of our true potential, put up a heroic fight to honour it, and only then mourn failure with solemn frankness and dignified honesty.

2. Don't be a Christian
Nietzsche had some extreme things to say about Christianity: 'I call Christianity the one great curse, the one great intrinsic depravity … In the entire New Testament, there is only person worth respecting: Pilate, the Roman governor.'

This was knockabout stuff, but his true target was more subtle and more interesting: he resented Christianity for protecting people from their envy.

Christianity had in Nietzsche's account emerged in the late Roman Empire in the minds of timid slaves, who had lacked the stomach to get hold of what they really wanted (or admit they had failed) and so had clung to a philosophy that made a virtue of their cowardice. Christians had wished to enjoy the real ingredients of fulfilment (a position in the world, sex, intellectual mastery, creativity) but had been too inept to get them. They had therefore fashioned a hypocritical creed denouncing what they wanted but were too weak to fight for – while praising what they did not want but happened to have. So, in the Christian value system, sexlessness turned into 'purity', weakness became 'goodness', submission to people one hated 'obedience' and, in Nietzsche's phrase, 'not-being-able-to-take-revenge' turned into 'forgiveness'.

Christianity amounted to a giant justification for passivity and a mechanism for draining life of its potential.

3. Never drink alcohol
Nietzsche himself drank only water – and, as a special treat, milk. And he thought we should do likewise. He wasn't making a small, eccentric dietary point. The idea went to the heart of his philosophy, as contained in his declaration: 'There have been two great narcotics in European civilisation: Christianity and alcohol.'

He hated alcohol for the very same reasons that he scorned Christianity: because both numb pain, and both reassure us that things are just fine as they are, sapping us of the will to change our lives for the better. A few drinks usher in a transient feeling of satisfaction that can get fatally in the way of taking the steps necessary to improve our lives. It's not that Nietzsche admired suffering for its own sake. But he recognised the unfortunate – but crucial – truth that growth and accomplishment have irrevocably painful aspects:

> What if pleasure and displeasure were so tied together that whoever wanted to have as much as possible of one must also have as much as possible of the other ...
> You have a choice in life: either as little displeasure

EDVARD MUNCH, *Friedrich Nietzsche*, 1906

as possible, painlessness in brief ... or as much dis-
pleasure as possible as the price for an abundance
of subtle pleasures and joys ...

Nietzsche's thought recalibrates the meaning of suffering. If
we are finding things difficult, it is not necessarily a sign of
failure, it may just be evidence of the nobility and arduous-
ness of the tasks we've undertaken.

4. 'God is Dead'

Nietzsche's dramatic assertion about the demise of God is not, as it's often taken to be, some kind of a celebratory statement. Despite his reservations about Christianity, Nietzsche did not think that the end of belief was anything to celebrate.

Religious beliefs were false, he knew; but he observed that they were in some areas very beneficial to the sound functioning of society. Giving up on religion would mean that humans would be left to find new ways of supplying themselves with guidance, consolation, ethical ideas and spiritual ambition. This would be tricky, he predicted.

Nietzsche proposed that the gap left by religion should ideally be filled with culture (philosophy, art, music, literature): culture should replace Scripture.

However, Nietzsche was deeply suspicious of the way his own era handled culture. He believed the universities were killing the humanities, turning them into dry academic exercises, rather than using them for what they were always meant to be: guides to life. He particularly admired the way the Greeks had used tragedy in a practical, therapeutic way, as an occasion for catharsis and moral education – and wished his own age to be comparably ambitious.

He accused university and museum-based culture of retreating from the life-guiding, morality-giving potential of culture, at precisely the time when the 'Death of God' had made these aspects ever more necessary.

He called for a reformation, in which people – newly conscious of the crisis brought on by the end of faith – would fill the gaps created by the disappearance of religion with the wisdom and healing beauty of culture.

Conclusion

Every era faces particular psychological challenges, thought Nietzsche, and it is the task of the philosopher to identify, and help solve, these.

For Nietzsche, the 19th century was reeling under the impact of two developments: mass democracy and atheism. The first threatened to unleash torrents of undigested envy and venomous resentment; the second to leave humans without guidance or morality.

In relation to both challenges, Nietzsche worked up some fascinating solutions – from which our own times have some highly practical things to learn, as he would dearly have wished.

Martin Heidegger

1889–1976

T he field is not without other distinguished contestants, but in the competitive history of incomprehensible German philosophers, Martin Heidegger must, by any reckoning, emerge as the overall victor. Nothing quite rivals the prose of his masterpiece *Being and Time* (1927) in terms of contortions and the sheer number of complex compound German words that the author coined, among them *Seinsvergessenheit* (Forgetfulness of Being), *Bodenständigkeit* (Rootedness-in-soil) and *Wesensverfassung* (Essential Constitution).

At first, it is likely to be puzzling and perhaps irritating, but gradually, one may warm to the style and understand that beneath its vaporous surface, Heidegger is telling us some simple, even at times homespun truths about the meaning of our lives, the sicknesses of our time and the routes to freedom. We should bother.

He was born, and in many ways remained, a rural provincial German who loved picking mushrooms, walking in the countryside and going to bed early. He hated television, aeroplanes, pop music and processed food. Born in 1889 to a poor Catholic family, he became an academic star after the publication of *Being and Time* – but made the fatal misstep of taking Hitler at his word in the mid-1930s (he wasn't alone). He hoped that the Nazis would restore order and dignity to Germany and, to fit in with the mood of the times, he made a few fiery speeches and tried to ban Jewish academics from Freiburg University, where he was rector. One can almost forgive him this period of lunacy, for which he paid dearly. After Germany's defeat in 1945, he was hauled in front of a Denazification Commission and was forbidden to teach until the end of the decade. Amazingly (it was a testimony to the appeal of his ideas), his career gradually revived, though he spent more and more time in a hut he owned in the woods, away from modern civilisation, until his death in 1976.

Throughout his career, he sought to help us live more wisely. He wanted us to be braver about facing up to certain truths, and to lead richer, more thoughtful, happier lives. Philosophy was no academic exercise. It was – as it had been for the ancient Greeks – a spiritual vocation and a form of therapy. He diagnosed modern humanity as suffering from a number of new diseases of the soul:

1. We have forgotten to notice we're alive

We know it in theory, of course, but we aren't day-to-day properly in touch with the sheer mystery of existence, the mystery of what Heidegger called '*das Sein*' or 'Being'. Much of his philosophy is devoted to trying to wake us up to the strangeness of existing on a planet spinning in an otherwise seemingly silent, alien and uninhabited universe.

It's only at a few odd moments, perhaps late at night, or when we're ill and have been alone all day, or are on a walk through the countryside, that we come up against the uncanny strangeness of everything: why things exist as they do, why we are here rather than there, why the world is like this, why that tree or this house are the way they are. To capture these rare moments when the normal state of things wobbles a little, Heidegger talks, with capital letters, of the Mystery of Being. His entire philosophy is devoted to getting us to appreciate, and respond appropriately to, this rather abstract but crucial concept.

For Heidegger, the modern world is an infernal machine dedicated to distracting us from the basic wondrous nature of Being. It constantly pulls towards practical tasks, it overwhelms us with information, it kills silence, it doesn't want to leave us alone – partly because realising the Mystery of Being has its frightening dimensions. Doing so, we may be seized by fear (angst) as we become conscious that everything that had seemed rooted, necessary and oh-so-important may be contingent, senseless and without true purpose. We may ask why we have this job rather than that one, are in a relationship with one person rather than another, are alive when we might so easily be dead ... Much of daily life is designed to keep these odd, unnerving but crucial questions at bay.

What we're really running away from is a confrontation with – and even non-German speakers might respond to the sonorous depth of this key Heideggerian term – *das Nichts* (The Nothing), which lies on the other side of Being.

The Nothing is everywhere; it stalks us, it will swallow us up eventually, but – Heidegger insists – a life is only well lived when one has taken Nothingness and the brief nature of Being on board – as we might do when, for example, a gentle evening light gives way to darkness at the end of a warm summer's day in the foothills of the Bavarian alps.

2. We have forgotten that all Being is connected
We look at the world through the prism of our own narrow interests. Our professional needs colour what we pay attention to and bother with. We treat others and nature as means and not as ends.

But occasionally (and again walks in the country are particularly conducive to this realisation), we may be able to step outside our narrow orbit and take a more generous view of our connection with the rest of existence. We may sense what Heidegger termed the 'Unity of Being', noticing – in a way we hadn't previously – that we, and that ladybird on the bark, and that rock, and that cloud, are all in existence right now and are fundamentally united by the basic fact of Being.

Heidegger values these moments – and wants us to use them as the springboard to a deeper form of generosity, an overcoming of alienation and egoism and a more profound appreciation of the brief time that remains to us before *das Nichts* claims us in turn.

3. We forget to be free and to live for ourselves
Much about us isn't, of course, very free. We are – in Heidegger's unusual formulation – 'thrown into the world' at the start of our lives: thrown into a particular and narrow

social milieu, surrounded by rigid attitudes, archaic prejudices and practical necessities not of our own making.

The philosopher wants to help us to overcome this *Geworfenheit* (Thrownness) by understanding its multiple features. We should aim to grasp our psychological, social and professional provincialism – and then rise above it to a more universal perspective.

In so doing, we'll make the classic Heideggerian journey away from *Uneigentlichkeit* to *Eigentlichkeit* (from Inauthenticity to Authenticity). We will, in essence, start to live for ourselves.

And yet most of the time, for Heidegger, we fail dismally at this task. We merely surrender to a socialised, superficial mode of being what he called 'they-self' (as opposed to 'ourselves'). We follow *das Gerede* (The Chatter), which we hear about in the newspapers, on TV and in the large cities Heidegger hated to spend time in.

What will help us to pull away from the 'they-self' is an appropriately intense focus on our own upcoming death. It's only when we realise that other people cannot save us from *das Nichts* that we're likely to stop living for them; to stop worrying so much about what others think, and to cease giving up the lion's share of our lives and energies to impress people who never really liked us in the first place. 'Angst' about 'The Nothing', though uncomfortable, can save us: awareness of our *Sein-zum-Tode* (Being-toward-death) is the road to life. When, in a lecture in 1961, Heidegger was asked how we might recover authenticity, he replied tersely that we should simply aim to spend more time 'in graveyards'.

4. We treat others as objects
Most of the time, without quite meaning to, we treat people as what Heidegger terms *das Zeug* (Equipment) – as if they were tools, rather than Beings in Themselves.

The cure for this selfishness lies in exposure to great art. It is works of art that will help us to step back from

VINCENT VAN GOGH, *A Pair of Shoes*, 1887

ourselves and appreciate the independent existence of other people and things.

Heidegger elaborated this idea in the course of a discussion of a painting by Van Gogh of a pair of peasant shoes. Normally, we don't pay much attention to shoes; they are merely another bit of 'equipment' that we need to get by. But when they are presented to us on a canvas, we're liable to notice them – as if for the first time – for their own sakes.

The same might happen to us when confronted by other bits of the natural and the man-made world represented by great artists. Thanks to art, we'll feel a new kind of *Sorge* (Care) for Being that lies beyond our selves.

Conclusion
It would be lying to say that Heidegger's meaning and moral is ever very clear. Nevertheless, what he tells us is intermittently fascinating, wise and surprisingly useful. Despite the

extraordinary words and language, in a sense, we know a lot of it already. We merely need reminding and emboldening to take it seriously, which the odd prose style helps us to do. We know in our hearts that it is time to overcome our *Geworfenheit*, that we should become more conscious of *das Nichts* day-to-day, and that we owe it to ourselves to escape the clutches of *das Gerede* for the sake of *Eigentlichkeit* – with a little help from the graveyard.

Jean-Paul Sartre

1905–1980

Jean-Paul Sartre was born in 1905. His father, a navy captain, died when he was a baby – and he grew up extremely close to his mother until she remarried, much to his regret, when he was 12. Sartre spent most of his life in Paris, where he often went to cafés on the Left Bank and sat on benches in the Jardin du Luxembourg. He had a strabismus, a wandering eye, and wore distinctive, heavy glasses. He was awarded the 1964 Nobel Prize in Literature, but refused it on the grounds that the award was capitalist and bourgeois. He was very short (five feet three inches) and frequently described himself as ugly. He wore his hair vigorously brushed back. When he died in 1980 (aged 74), 50,000 people accompanied his coffin through the streets of Paris.

Sartre became famous as the key figure in the philosophical movement known as existentialism. He made thinking and philosophy glamorous. He wrote a dense, hard-to-follow book called *Being and Nothingness*, which enhanced his reputation not so much because people could understand his ideas but because they couldn't quite. Sartre was the beneficiary of a desire, which became widespread in the second half of the 20th century, to revere books for the mystery they appeared to touch, rather than for the clarity of their claims.

Existentialism was built around a number of key insights:

1. Things are weirder than we think

Sartre is acutely attentive to moments when the world reveals itself as far stranger and more uncanny than we normally admit; moments when the logic we ascribe to it day-to-day becomes unavailable, showing things to be highly contingent and even absurd and frightening.

Sartre's first novel – *Nausea*, published in 1938 – is full of evocations of such moments. At one point, the hero, Roquentin, a 30-year-old writer living in a fictional French seaside town, is on a tram. He puts his hand on the seat, but then pulls it back rapidly. Instead of being the most basic and obvious piece of design, scarcely worth a moment's notice, the seat promptly strikes him as deeply strange; the word 'seat' comes loose from its moorings, the object it refers to shines forth in all its primordial oddity, as if he's never seen one before – and its material and slight swell makes him think of the repulsive bloated belly of a dead donkey. Roquentin has to force himself to remember that this thing beside him is something for people to sit on. For a terrifying moment, Roquentin has peered into what Sartre calls the 'absurdity of the world.'

Such a moment goes to the heart of Sartre's philosophy. To be Sartrean is to be aware of existence as it is when it has been stripped of any of the prejudices and stabilising assumptions lent to us by our day-to-day routines. We can try out a Sartrean perspective on many aspects of our own lives. Think of what you know as 'the evening meal with your partner'. Under such a description, it all seems fairly logical, but a Sartrean would strip away the surface normality to show the radical strangeness lurking beneath. Dinner really means that when your part of the planet has spun away from the energy of a distant hydrogen and helium explosion, you slide your knees under strips of a chopped-up tree and put sections of dead animals and plants in your mouth and chew, while next to you, another mammal whose genitals you sometimes touch is doing the same. Or think of your job through Sartrean eyes: you and many others swathe your bodies in cloth and congregate in a large box where you make agitated sounds at one another; you press many plastic buttons with great rapidity in exchange for pieces of paper. Then you stop and go away. The next time the sky gets light, you come back.

2. We are free
These weird moments are certainly disorienting and rather scary, but Sartre wants to draw our attention to them for

one central reason: because of their liberating dimensions. Life is a lot odder than we think (going to the office, having dinner with a friend, visiting our parents – none of this is obvious or remotely normal), but it's also as a consequence far richer in possibilities. Things don't have to be quite the way they are. We're freer than we allow ourselves to imagine amidst the ordinary press of commitments and obligations. It's only late at night, or perhaps when we're ill in bed or taking a long train journey somewhere unfamiliar, that we give our minds licence to daydream in less conventional directions. These moments are at once unsettling and freeing. We could get out of the house, break off a relationship and never see the person we live with again. We might throw in our jobs, move to another country and reinvent ourselves as someone entirely different.

We are usually full of reasons why none of that would be possible. But through his descriptions of moments of disorientation, Sartre wants to give us access to a different way of thinking. He wants to push us away from the normal, settled perspective to liberate our imaginations: we might not have to keep taking the bus to work, saying things we don't mean to people we don't like or sacrificing our vitality for false notions of security.

In the course of fully realising our freedom, we will come up against what Sartre calls the 'anguish' of existence. Everything is (terrifyingly) possible because nothing has any preordained, God-given sense or purpose. Humans are just making it up as they go along and are free to cast aside the shackles at any moment. There is nothing in the non-human order of the world called 'marriage' or 'job'. These are just labels we have put on things and are – as proper existentialists – free to take them off again.

This is frightening, hence the term 'anguish', but Sartre sees anguish as a mark of maturity, a sign that we are fully alive and properly aware of reality, with its freedom, its possibilities and its weighty choices.

3. We shouldn't live in 'bad faith'

Sartre gave a term to the phenomenon of living without taking freedom properly on board. He called it 'bad faith'.

We are in bad faith whenever we tell ourselves that things have to be a certain way and shut our eyes to other options. It is bad faith to insist that we *have* to do a particular kind of work or live with a specific person or make our home in a given place.

The most famous description of bad faith comes in *Being and Nothingness*, when Sartre notices a waiter who strikes him as overly devoted to his role, as if he were first and foremost a waiter rather than a free human being:

> His movement is quick and forward, a little too precise, a little too rapid. He comes towards the patrons with a step that is a little too quick. He bends forward a little too eagerly; his voice, his eyes express an interest a little too solicitous for the order of the customer ...

Sartre diagnoses him as suffering from *bad faith*. The man (he was probably modelled on someone in Saint-Germain's Café de Flore) has convinced himself that he is essentially, necessarily, a waiter rather than a free creature who could be a jazz pianist or a fisherman on a North Sea trawler. The same attitude of ingrained, option-less servitude might today be observed in an IT manager or a parent collecting their child from school. Each of these might also feel: I have to do what I am doing, I have no choice, I am not free, my role makes me do what I do.

Realising one's freedom in an existential sense should not be confused with the American self-help idea that we're all free to be or do anything without suffering pain or sacrifice. Sartre is far gloomier and more tragic than this. He merely wants to point out that we have more options than

we normally believe – even if in some cases the leading option (which Sartre defended vigorously) might be to com-
mit suicide.

4. We're free to dismantle capitalism

The one factor that most discourages people to experience
themselves as free is money. Most of us will shut down a
range of possible options (moving abroad, trying out a new
career, leaving a partner) by saying, 'that's if I didn't have to
worry about money.'

This passivity in the face of money enraged Sartre at a
political level. He thought of capitalism as a giant machine
designed to create a sense of necessity that doesn't in fact
exist in reality: it makes us tell ourselves we have to work
a certain number of hours, buy a particular product or service, pay people a specific low fee for their work. But in this,
there is only the denial of freedom – and a refusal to take as
seriously as we should the possibility of living in other ways.

It was because of these views that Sartre had a lifelong
interest in Marxism (although he was a critic of the USSR
and the French Communist Party). Marxism seemed in
theory to allow people to explore their freedom, by reducing the role played in their lives by material considerations,
money and property.

All this remains a tantalising thought: could we change
politics to regain contact with our fundamental freedoms?
How could our attitudes to capital change? How many
hours a week should one work? How could what's on TV
or where people go on holiday or the school curriculum be
better? How could our toxic, propaganda-soaked media be
changed?

Despite writing a great deal (he was estimated to have
written at least five pages every day of his adult life), Sartre
did not pursue these lines of thoughts. He opened up possibilities, but the tasks remain ours to undertake.

Conclusion

Sartre is inspiring in his insistence that things do not have to be the way they are. He is hugely alive to our unfulfilled potential, as individuals and as a species.

He urges us to accept the fluidity of existence and to create new institutions, habits, outlooks and ideas. The admission that life doesn't have some preordained logic and is not inherently meaningful can be a source of immense relief when we feel oppressed by the weight of tradition and the status quo. Sartre is especially useful to us in adolescence, when parental and social expectations can crush us – and in the darker moments of mid-life, when we recognise there is still a little time to make a change, but no longer quite so much.

Albert Camus

1913–1960

A lbert Camus was an extremely handsome mid-20th-century French-Algerian philosopher and writer, whose claim to our attention is based on three novels, *The Outsider* (1942), *The Plague* (1947), and *The Fall* (1956), and two philosophical essays, *The Myth of Sisyphus* (1942) and *The Rebel* (1951).

Camus won the Nobel Prize in Literature in 1957 – and died at the age of 46, inadvertently killed by his publisher Michel Gallimard, when his Facel Vega sports car they were in crashed into a tree. In his pocket was a train ticket he had decided not to use at the last minute.

Camus's fame began with and still largely rests upon his novel, *The Outsider*. Set in Camus's native Algiers, it follows the story of a laconic, detached, ironic hero called Meursault – a man who can't see the point of love, or work, or friendship – and who one day – somewhat by mistake – shoots dead an Arab man without knowing his own motivations and ends up being put to death – partly because he doesn't show any remorse, but not really caring for his fate one way or the other.

The novel captures the state of mind defined by the sociologist Émile Durkheim as *anomie*, a listless, affectless alienated condition where one feels entirely cut off from others and can't find a way to share any of their sympathies or values.

Reading *The Outsider* has long been an adolescent rite of passage among French and many other teenagers – which isn't a way of doing it down, for a lot of the greatest themes are first tackled at 17 or so.

The hero of *The Outsider*, Meursault cannot accept any of the standard answers for why things are the way they are. He sees hypocrisy and sentimentality everywhere – and can't overlook it. He is a man who cannot accept the normal explanations given to explain things like the education system, the workplace, relationships and the mechanisms of government. He stands outside normal bourgeois life, highly critical of its pinched morality and narrow concerns for money and family.

As Camus put it in an afterword he wrote for the American edition of the book: 'Meursault doesn't play the game … he refuses to lie. … He says what he is, he refuses to hide his feelings, and immediately society feels threatened.'

Much of the unusual mesmerising quality of the book comes from the coolly distant voice in which Meursault speaks to us, his readers.

The opening is one of the most legendary in 20th-century literature and sets the tone: 'Today mother died. Or maybe yesterday, I don't know.'

The ending is as stark and as defiant. Meursault, condemned to death for a murder committed almost off-hand, because it can be interesting to know what it's like to press the trigger, rejects all consolations and heroically accepts the universe's total indifference to humankind: 'My last wish was that there should be a crowd of spectators at my execution and that they should greet me with cries of hatred.'

Even if we are not killers and will ourselves be really quite sad when our mother dies, the mood of *The Outsider* is one we are all liable to have some experience of … when we have enough freedom to realise we're in a cage, but not quite enough freedom to escape it … when no one seems to understand … and everything appears a bit hopeless … perhaps in the summer before we go to college.

Aside from *The Outsider,* Camus's fame rests on an essay, published the same year as the novel, called *The Myth of Sisyphus.*

This book, too, has a bold beginning: 'There is but one truly serious philosophical problem and that is suicide. Judging whether life is or is not worth living, that is the fundamental question of philosophy.'

The reason for this stark choice is, in Camus's eyes, because as soon as we start to think seriously, as philosophers do, we will see that life has no meaning – and therefore we will be compelled to wonder whether or not we should just be done with it all.

To make sense of this rather extreme claim and thesis, we have to situate Camus in the history of thought. His dramatic announcement that we have to consider killing ourselves because life might be meaningless is premised on a previous notion that life could actually be rich in God-given meaning – a concept that would sound remote to many of us today.

And yet, we have to bear in mind that for the last 2,000 years in the West, a sense that life was meaningful was a given, accorded by one institution above any other: the Christian Church.

Camus stands in a long line of thinkers, from Kierkegaard to Nietzsche to Heidegger and Sartre, who wrestle with the chilling realisation that there is in fact no preordained meaning in life. We are just biological matter spinning senselessly on a tiny rock in a corner of an indifferent universe. We were not put here by a benevolent deity and asked to work towards salvation in the shape of Ten Commandments or the dictates of the holy Gospels. There's no road map and no bigger point. And it's this realisation that lies at the heart of so many of the crises reported by the thinkers we now know as existentialists.

A child of despairing modernity, Albert Camus accepts that all our lives are absurd in the grander scheme, but – unlike some philosophers – he ends up resisting utter hopelessness or nihilism. He argues that we have to live with the knowledge that our efforts will be largely futile, our lives soon forgotten and our species irredeemably corrupt and violent – and yet should endure nevertheless.

We are like Sisyphus, the Greek figure ordered by the gods to roll a boulder up a mountain and to watch it fall back down again – in perpetuity.

But ultimately, Camus suggests, we should cope as well as we can at whatever we have to do. We have to acknowledge the absurd background to existence – and then triumph

TITIAN, *Sisyphus*, 1548

over the constant possibility of hopelessness. In his famous formulation: 'One must imagine Sisyphus happy.'

This brings us to the most charming and seductive side of Camus: the Camus who wants to remind himself and us of the reasons why life can be worth enduring – and who in the process writes with exceptional intensity and wisdom about relationships, nature, the summer, food and friendship.

As a guide to the reasons to live, Camus is delightful. Many philosophers have been ugly and cut off from their bodies: think of sickly Pascal, sexually unsuccessful Schopenhauer, or poor peculiar Nietzsche. Camus was, by contrast:

Albert Camus posing at a banquet after he was awarded the
Nobel Prize in Literature, 1957.

· Very good looking.
· Extremely successful with women: for the last ten years
  of his life he never had fewer than three girlfriends on
  the go, and wives as well.
· And he had a great dress sense, influenced by James
  Dean and Humphrey Bogart. It isn't surprising he was
  asked to pose by American *Vogue*.

These weren't all just stylistic quirks. Once you properly
realise that life is absurd, you are on the verge of despair
perhaps – but also, compelled to live life more intensely.

Accordingly, Camus grew committed to, and deeply serious about, the pleasures of ordinary life. He said he saw his philosophy as 'a lucid invitation to live and to create, in the very midst of the desert.'

He was a great champion of the ordinary – which generally has a hard time finding champions in philosophy – and after pages and pages of his denser philosophy, one turns with relief to moments when Camus writes in praise of sunshine, kissing and dancing.

Camus was an outstanding athlete as a young man. Once asked by his friend Charles Poncet which he preferred, football or the theatre, Camus is said to have replied: 'Football, without hesitation.'

Camus played as goalkeeper for the local junior Algiers team, Racing Universitaire d'Alger (which won both the North African Champions Cup and the North African Cup in the 1930s).

The sense of team spirit, fraternity, and common purpose appealed to Camus enormously. When Camus was asked in the 1950s by a sports magazine for a few words regarding his time with the RUA, he said: 'After many years during which I saw many things, what I know most surely about morality and the duty of man I owe to sport.' Camus was referring to the morality he defends in his essays: sticking up for your friends and valuing bravery and fair play.

Camus was a great advocate of the sun. His beautiful essay 'Summer in Algiers' celebrates: 'the warmth of the water and the brown bodies of women.' He writes: 'For the first time in 2,000 years, the body has appeared naked on beaches. For twenty centuries, men have striven to give decency to Greek insolence and naivety, to diminish the flesh and complicate dress. Today, young men running on Mediterranean beaches repeat the gestures of the athletes of Delos.'

He spoke up for a new paganism, based on the immediate pleasures of the body:

I recall … a magnificent tall girl who had danced
all afternoon. She was wearing a jasmine garland
on her tight blue dress, wet with perspiration from
the small of her back to her legs. She was laughing
as she danced and throwing back her head. As she
passed the tables, she left behind her a mingled scent
of flowers and flesh.

Camus railed against those who would dismiss such things
as trivial and long for something higher, better, purer: 'If
there is a sin against life, it consists perhaps not so much in
despairing of life as in hoping for another life and in eluding
the implacable grandeur of this life.'

In a letter, he remarked: 'People attract me in so far as
they are impassioned about life and avid for happiness …'

'There are causes worth dying for, but none worth killing for.'

Camus achieved huge acclaim in his lifetime, but the Parisian intellectual community was deeply suspicious of him.
He never was a Parisian sophisticate. He was a working-
class pied-noir (that is, someone born in Algeria but of European origin), whose father had died of war wounds when he
was an infant and whose mother was a cleaning lady.

It isn't a coincidence that Camus's favourite philosopher
was Montaigne – another very down-to-earth Frenchman,
and someone one can love as much for what he wrote as for
what he was like.

Political
Theory

Niccolò Machiavelli

1469–1527

Our assessment of politicians is torn between hope and disappointment. On the one hand, we have an idealistic idea that a politician should be an upright hero, a man or woman who can breathe new moral life into the corrupt workings of the state. However, we are also regularly catapulted into cynicism when we realise the number of backroom deals and the extent of the lying that politicians go in for. We seem torn between our idealistic hopes and our pessimistic fears about the evil underbelly of politics. Surprisingly, the very man who gave his name to the word 'Machiavellian', a word so often used to describe the worst political scheming, can help us understand the dangers of this tired dichotomy. Machiavelli's writings suggest that we should not be surprised if politicians lie and dissemble, but nor should we think them immoral and simply 'bad' for doing so. A good politician – in Machiavelli's remarkable view – isn't one who is kind, friendly and honest; it is someone – however occasionally dark and sly they might be – who knows how to defend, enrich and bring honour to the state. Once we understand this basic requirement, we'll be less disappointed and clearer about what we want our politicians to be.

Niccolò Machiavelli was born in Florence in 1469. His father was a wealthy and influential lawyer, and so Machiavelli received an extensive formal education and got his first job as a secretary for the city, drafting government documents. But soon after his appointment, Florence exploded politically, expelled the Medici family, who had ruled it for sixty years, and suffered decades of political instability, as a consequence of which Machiavelli experienced a series of career reversals.

Machiavelli was preoccupied by a fundamental problem in politics: is it possible to be a good politician and a good person at the same time? And he has the courage to face the tragic possibility that, given how the world really is, the answer is *no*. He doesn't just think that political advancement comes more easily to the unscrupulous, he gets us to contemplate a darker possibility: that doing rightly and well what a political leader should, and fulfilling the proper duties of political leadership, is at odds with being a good person.

Machiavelli wrote his most famous work, *The Prince* (1513), about how to get and keep power and what makes individuals effective leaders. He proposed that the overwhelming responsibility of a good prince is to defend the state from external and internal threats to stable governance. This means he must know how to fight, but more importantly, he must know about reputation and the management of those around him. People should neither think he is soft and easy to disobey, nor should they find him so cruel that he disgusts his society. He should seem unapproachably strict but reasonable. When he turned to the question of whether it was better for a prince to be loved or feared, Machiavelli wrote that while it would theoretically be wonderful for a leader to be both loved and obeyed, he should always err on the side of inspiring terror, for this is what ultimately keeps people in check.

Machiavelli's most radical and distinctive insight was his rejection of Christian virtue as a guide for leaders. Machiavelli's Christian contemporaries had suggested princes should be merciful, peaceful, generous and tolerant. They thought that being a good politician, in short, was the same as being a good Christian. But Machiavelli argued differently with energy. He asked his readers to dwell on the incompatibility between Christian ethics and good governance via the case of Girolamo Savonarola. Savonarola was a fervent, idealistic Christian who had wanted to build the city of God on earth in Florence. He had preached against the excesses and tyranny of the Medici government, and had even managed for a few years to lead Florence as a peaceful, democratic, and (relatively) honest state. However, Savonarola's success could not last, for – in Machiavelli's view – it was based on the weakness that always attends being 'good'

FRA BARTOLOMEO, *Girolamo Savonarola*, c.1497

in the Christian sense. It was not long before his regime became a threat to the corrupt Pope Alexander, whose hench-
men schemed, captured and tortured him, hung and burned
him in the centre of Florence. This, in Machiavelli's eyes, is
what inevitably happens to the nice guys in politics. Eventually they will be faced with a problem that cannot be solved
by generosity, kindness or decency, because they will be up
against rivals or enemies who do not play by those rules. The

unscrupulous will always have a major advantage. It will be impossible to win decently. Yet it is necessary to win in order to keep a society safe.

Rather than follow this unfortunate Christian example, Machiavelli suggested that a leader would do well to make judicious use of what he called, in a deliciously paradoxical phrase, 'criminal virtue'. Machiavelli provided some criteria for what constitutes the right occasion for criminal virtue: it must be necessary for the security of the state, it must be done swiftly (often at night), and it should not be repeated too often, lest a reputation for mindless brutality builds up. Machiavelli gave the example of his contemporary Cesare Borgia, whom he much admired as a leader – though he might not have wanted to be his friend. When Cesare conquered the city of Cesena, he ordered one of his mercenaries, Remirro de Orco, to bring order to the region, which Remirro did through swift and brutal ways. Men were beheaded in front of their wives and children, property was seized, traitors were castrated. Cesare then turned on De Orco himself and had him sliced in half and placed in the public square, just to remind the townspeople who the true boss was. But then, as Machiavelli approvingly noted, that was enough bloodshed. Cesare moved on to cut taxes, imported some cheap grain, built a theatre and organised a series of beautiful festivals to keep people from dwelling on unfortunate memories.

The Catholic Church banned Machiavelli's works for 200 years because of the force with which he had argued that being a good Christian was incompatible with being a good leader. But even for atheists and those of us who are not politicians, Machiavelli's insights are important. He writes that we cannot be good at or for all things. We must pick which fields we want to excel in, and let the others pass – not only because of our limited abilities and resources, but also because of the conflicts within moral codes. Some of the fields we choose – if not being a prince, then perhaps

business or family life or other forms of loyalty and responsibility – may require what we evasively call 'difficult decisions', by which we really mean ethical trade-offs. We may
have to sacrifice our ideal visions of kindness for the sake of
practical effectiveness. We may have to lie in order to keep a
relationship afloat. We may have to ignore the feelings of the
workforce in order to keep a business going. That – insists
Machiavelli – is the price of dealing with the world as it is,
and not as we feel it should be. The world has continued to
love and hate Machiavelli in equal measure for insisting on
this uncomfortable truth.

Machiavelli is prey to a natural misunderstanding. It
can sound as if he is on the side of thuggish or slightly brutal
people. That he's cheering on those who are mean or callous. But actually, his stern advice – about being ruthless – is
best directed to those who run the risk of losing what they
really care about because at key moments they are not ruthless enough.

Thomas Hobbes

1588–1679

T homas Hobbes was a 17th-century English philosopher who is on hand to guide us through one of the
thorniest issues of politics: to what extent should we
patiently obey rulers, especially those who are not very
good – and to what extent should we start revolutions and
depose governments in search of a better world?

Hobbes's thinking is inseparable from one major event
that began when he was 54 years old – and was to mark him
so deeply, it coloured all his subsequent thinking (remarkably, he died when he was 91 and everything he is remembered for today he wrote after the age of 60).

This event was the English Civil War, a vicious, divisive,
costly and murderous conflict that raged across England for
almost a decade and pitted the forces of king against Parliament, leading to the deaths of some 200,000 people on both
sides.

Hobbes was by nature a deeply peaceful and cautious
man. He hated violence of all kinds, a disposition that began
at the age of 4, when his own father, a clergyman, was disgraced, and abandoned his wife and family, after he'd got
into a fight with another vicar on the steps of his parish
church in a village in Wiltshire.

The work for which we chiefly remember Hobbes,
Leviathan, was published in 1651. It is the most definitive, persuasive and eloquent statement ever produced as
to why one should obey government authority, even of a
very imperfect kind, in order to avoid the risk of chaos
and bloodshed. To understand the background of Hobbes's
conservatism, it helps to realise that across Western Europe
in the 17th century, political theorists were beginning to
ask, with a new directness, on what basis subjects should
obey their rulers.

For centuries, way back into the Middle Ages, there had
been a standard answer to this, contained in a theory called
the Divine Right of Kings. This was a blunt, simple, but
highly effective theory stating that it was none other than

God who appointed all kings and that one should obey these monarchs for one clear reason: because the deity said so – and He would send you to hell if you didn't agree.

But this was no longer proving quite so persuasive to many thoughtful people, who argued that the right to rule ultimately lay not with kings, but with ordinary people, who gave kings power – and therefore should only expect to take orders from kings so long as, but only so long, as things were working out well for them. This was known as the social contract theory of government.

Hobbes could see that the Divine Right of Kings theory was nonsense and, what's more, was going to be increasingly unpersuasive as religious observance declined. He himself was, privately, an atheist. At the same time, Hobbes was deeply scared of the possible consequences of the social contract theory, which could encourage people to depose rulers whenever they felt a little unhappy with their lot.

Hobbes had received a first-hand account of the beheading of King Charles I, on a scaffold in front of the Banqueting House at the Palace of Whitehall in 1649 – and his intellectual labours were directed at making sure that such ghastly, primitive scenes would never be repeated.

So, in *Leviathan*, he put forward an ingenious argument that tried to marry up social contract theory with a defence of total obedience and submission to traditional authority. The way he did this was to take his readers back in time, to a period he called 'the state of nature', before there were kings of any kind, and to get them to think about how governments would have arisen in the first place.

Key to Hobbes's argument was that the state of nature could not have been a pretty place, because humans, left to their own devices, without a central authority to keep them in awe, would quickly have descended into squabbling, infighting and intolerable bickering. It would have been a little like the English Civil War, but with people in bear skins bashing each other around with flint tools. In Hobbes's

THOMAS HOBBES, *Leviathan*, 1651

famous formulation, life in the state of nature would have
been: 'nasty, brutish and short.'

As a result, out of fear and dread of chaos, people were
led to form governments. They had done this willingly, as
social contract theorists maintained, but also under considerable compulsion, fleeing into the arms of strong authority,
which they therefore – Hobbes argued – had a subsequent
duty to keep obeying, with only a few rights to complain if
they didn't like it.

The only right that people might have to protest about an absolute ruler, or Leviathan as he called him, was if he directly threatened to kill them.

However, if the ruler merely stifled opposition, imposed onerous taxes, crippled the economy and locked up dissidents, this was absolutely no reason to take to the streets and demand a change of government.

'Though of so unlimited a power, men may fancy many evil consequences, yet the consequences of the want of it, which is perpetual war of every man against his neighbour, are much worse.'

He admitted that a ruler might come along with an 'inclination to do wicked deeds' but the people would still have a duty to obey as 'human affairs cannot be without some inconvenience.' But this inconvenience is the fault of people, not the sovereign, because: 'if men could rule themselves, there would be no need at all of a common coercive power.' As Hobbes went on: 'He that complaineth of injury from his sovereign, complaineth of that whereof he is the author himself; and therefore ought not to accuse any man but himself.'

Hobbes's theory was dark, cautious and not especially hopeful about government. In our more optimistic moment, we want him to be wrong. But it seems Hobbes's name will always be relevant and fresh again when revolutions motivated by a search for liberty go horribly awry. Hobbes was not against revolution for any sinister motives. He just maintained, as he put it in the preface to *Leviathan*, that he felt compelled: '... to set before men's eyes the mutual relation between protection and obedience.'

Jean-Jacques Rousseau

1712–1778

M odern life is, in many ways, founded around the idea of progress: the notion that as we know more (especially about science and technology), and as economies grow larger, we're bound to end up happier. Particularly in the 18th century, as European societies and their economies became increasingly complex, the conventional view was that mankind was firmly set on a positive trajectory; moving away from savagery and ignorance towards prosperity and civility. But there was at least one 18th-century philosopher who was prepared to vigorously question the 'Idea of Progress' – and who continues to have very provocative things to say to our own era.

Jean-Jacques Rousseau, the son of Isaac Rousseau, an educated watchmaker, was born in Geneva in 1712. Almost immediately, Rousseau suffered the first of what he would later call his 'misfortunes' – just nine days after giving birth, his mother, Suzanne Bernard, died from complications that arose from a traumatic and complicated labour. When Rousseau was 10, his father got into a legal dispute and the family was forced to flee to the city of Bern where Isaac would later marry for a second time. From that point on, Rousseau's life was marked by instability and isolation. Throughout his teenage years and adulthood, he changed homes frequently, sometimes in search of love and acclaim, sometimes just to escape persecution.

As a young man, Rousseau went to Paris and was exposed there to the opulence and luxury that was the order of the day in *ancien régime* Paris; the aspirational bourgeoisie did their best to emulate the tastes and styles exhibited by both royalty and aristocracy, only adding to the competitive spirit that fuelled the burgeoning Parisian social scene. The Paris Rousseau was exposed to was a far cry from his birthplace of Geneva, a city that was sober and deeply opposed to luxury goods.

Rousseau's life was shaped by some key chance turning points. One of the most significant of these occurred in 1749 as he read a copy of a newspaper, the *Mercure de France*, that contained an advert for an essay on the subject of whether recent advances in the arts and sciences had contributed to the 'purification of morals'. Upon reading the note placed there by the Académie de Dijon, Rousseau experienced something of an epiphany. It struck him, seemingly for the first time, that civilisation and progress had not in fact improved people; they had exacted a terrible destructive influence on the morals of human beings who had once been good.

Rousseau took this insight and turned it into the central thesis of what became his celebrated *Discourse on the Arts and Sciences*, which won the first prize in the newspaper competition. In the essay, Rousseau offered a scathing critique of modern society that challenged the central precepts of Enlightenment thought. His argument was simple: individuals had once been good and happy, but as man had emerged from his pre-social state, he had become plagued by vice and reduced to pauperism.

Rousseau went on to sketch a history of the world not as a story of progress from barbarism to the great workshops and cities of Europe, but of regress away from a privileged state in which we lived simply, but had the chance to listen to our needs. In technologically backward prehistory, in Rousseau's 'state of nature' (*l'état de nature*), when men and women lived in forests and had never entered a shop or read a newspaper, the philosopher pictured people more easily understanding their own minds, and so being drawn towards essential features of a satisfied life: a love of family, a respect for nature, an awe at the beauty of the universe, a curiosity about others, and a taste for music and simple entertainments. The state of nature was also moral, guided by *pitié* (pity) for others and their suffering. It was from this state that modern commercial 'civilisation' had pulled us, leaving us to envy and long for and suffer in a world of plenty.

Rousseau was aware of just how controversial his conclusion was – he anticipated 'a universal outcry' against his thesis and the *Discourse* indeed prompted a considerable number of responses. Rousseau had found fame.

What was it about civilisation that he thought had corrupted man and produced this moral degeneracy? Well, at the root of his hostility was his claim that the march towards civilisation had awakened in man a form of 'self-love' – *amour-propre* – that was artificial and centred on pride, jealousy and vanity. He argued that this destructive form of self-love had emerged as a consequence of people moving to bigger settlements and cities where they had begun to look to others in order to glean their very sense of self. Civilised people stopped thinking about what they wanted and felt – and merely imitated others, entering into ruinous competitions for status and money.

Primitive man, noted Rousseau, did not compare himself to others but instead focused solely on himself – his objective was simply to survive. Though Rousseau didn't actually employ the term 'noble savage' in his philosophical writings, his account of natural man unleashed a fascination with this concept. For those who might see this as an impossibly romantic story to be explained away as the fancy of an excitable author with a grudge against modernity, it is worth reflecting that if the 18th century listened to Rousseau's argument, it was primarily because it had before it one stark example of its apparent truths in the shape of the fate of the native Indian populations of North America.

Reports of Indian society drawn up in the 16th century described it as materially simple but psychologically rewarding: communities were small, close-knit, egalitarian, religious, playful and martial. The Indians were undoubtedly backward in a financial sense. They lived off fruits and wild animals, they slept in tents, they had few possessions. Every year, they wore the same pelts and shoes. Even a chief might own no more than a spear and a few pots. But there was a distinct level of contentment amidst the simplicity.

An early depiction of life in a Native American village.

However, within only a few decades of the arrival of the first Europeans, the status system of Indian society had been revolutionised through contact with the technology and luxury of European industry. What mattered was no longer one's wisdom or understanding of the ways of nature, but one's ownership of weapons, jewellery and alcohol. Indians now longed for silver earrings, copper and brass bracelets, tin finger rings, necklaces made of Venetian glass, ice chisels, guns, alcohol, kettles, beads, hoes and mirrors.

These new enthusiasms did not come about by coincidence. European traders deliberately attempted to foster desires in the Indians, so as to motivate them to hunt the animal pelts the European market was demanding. Sadly, their new wealth didn't appear to make the Indians much happier. Certainly the Indians worked harder. Between 1739 and 1759, the 2,000 warriors of the Cherokee tribe were estimated to have killed one and a quarter million deer to satisfy European demand. But rates of suicide and alcoholism rose, communities fractured, factions squabbled. The tribal chiefs didn't need Rousseau to understand what had happened, but they concurred totally with his analysis nevertheless.

Rousseau died in 1778, aged 66, while taking a walk outside Paris. He'd spent the last years as a celebrity, living with his common-law wife. But he also was constantly on the move fleeing persecution in Geneva after some of his more radical ideas, especially about religion, caused controversy (the stress of this had also caused a series of mental breakdowns). He is now buried in the Pantheon in Paris, and the Genevans celebrate him as their most famous native son.

In an age such as our own, one in which opulence and luxury can be deemed both desirable and exceedingly offensive, Rousseau's musings continue to reverberate. He encourages us to sidestep jealousy and competition and instead look solely to ourselves in identifying our self-worth. It is only by resisting the evil of comparison, Rousseau would tell us, that we can avoid feelings of misery and inadequacy. Though difficult, Rousseau was confident that this was not impossible, and he thus leaves behind a philosophy of fundamental criticism, but also one of profound optimism. There is a way out of the misery and corruption produced by the mores and institutions of modern civilisation – the hard part is that it involves looking to ourselves and reviving our natural goodness.

Adam Smith

1723–1790

Adam Smith is our guide to perhaps the most pressing dilemma of our time: how to make a capitalist economy more humane and more meaningful.

He was born in Scotland in Kirkcaldy – a small manufacturing town – near Edinburgh in 1723. He was a hard-working student and very close to his mother. In his childhood, he was briefly kidnapped by gypsies. As an adolescent, though from the middle class, he toured France with the grandest young aristocrat of his time, with whom he'd struck up a close friendship. He then became an academic philosopher, wrote a major book about the importance of sympathy, and lectured on logic and aesthetics. He had a charming smile. His study was usually very messy.

He was also one of the greatest thinkers in the history of economics – in part because his concerns went far beyond the economic. He wanted to understand the money system because his underlying ambition was to make nations and people happier. In his time, that would normally have meant getting interested either in religion or in government. Intellectual debate was dominated by passionate discussions about the role of the church and the foundations of the state. But Smith insisted that what philosophers should really worry about is the economy: how money is earned, how it is spent, and who gets how much for doing what.

Smith remains an invaluable guide to four ideas, which can help us to create a better kind of capitalism:

1. Specialisation
When one considers the modern world of work, two facts stand out:

- Modern economies produce unprecedented amounts of wealth (for the elite).
- Many ordinary people find work rather boring and, a key complaint, meaningless.

The two phenomena are (strangely) intimately related, as Adam Smith was the first to understand through his theory of *specialisation*. He argued that in modern businesses, tasks formerly done by one person in a single day could far more profitably be split into many tasks carried out by multiple people over whole careers.

Smith hailed this as a momentous development: he predicted that national economies would become hugely richer the more specialised their workforces became. A country where people made their own bread for breakfast, had a go at building their own houses in the morning, tried to catch fish for lunch and educated their children themselves in the afternoon was doomed to poverty. Far better to split everything up into individual areas of expertise and encourage people to trade their needs and talents.

One sign our world is now so rich, Smith could tell us, is that every time we meet a stranger, we're unlikely to understand what they do. The mania for incomprehensible job titles – logistics supply manager, packaging coordinator, communications and learning officer – prove the economic logic of Smith's insight.

But there is one huge problem with specialisation: *meaning*. The more jobs are subdivided, the less likely every job is to feel meaningful, because what we call meaning emerges from a visceral impression that one is engaged in something that is making a difference to someone else's life. When businesses are small and their processes contained, this sense of helping others is readily available, even if one's doing nothing grander than running a small clothes shop or a bakery. But when everything is industrialised, one ends up as a tiny cog in a gigantic machine whose overall logic (though present, and available to the management) is liable to be absent from the minds of people lower down in the organisation. A company with 150,000 employees distributed across four continents, making things that take five years from conception to delivery, will struggle to maintain any sense of purpose and cohesion.

So horrified were some thinkers by the implications of specialisation, they argued we should go back to an artisanal economy (the great fantasy of philosophers in the 19th century). But Smith was more inventive. He discerned that what many workers in advanced economies lack is a satisfying story about how their individual efforts fit into the bigger scheme; how they are helping other people and serving society.

Bosses of the specialised corporations of modernity therefore have an additional responsibility to their workers: reminding them of the purpose, role and ultimate dignity of their labour.

2. Consumer capitalism

Smith's age saw the development of what we'd now call consumer capitalism. Manufacturers began turning out luxury goods for a broadening middle class. Shopping arcades sprang up, as did fashion magazines and homeware brands. Some commentators were appalled. The philosopher Jean-Jacques Rousseau wished to ban 'luxury' from his native Geneva and return to a simpler way of life. He was a particular fan of ancient Sparta and argued that his city should copy its austere, martial lifestyle.

Disagreeing violently, Smith pointed out to the Swiss philosopher that luxury goods and stupid consumerism in fact had a very serious role to play in a good society – for it was they that provided the surplus wealth that allowed societies to look after their weakest members. Yes, consumer societies might not have the surface moral rigour of Sparta, but they qualified as properly moral on a different score: that they didn't let young children and the old starve, for they could afford hospitals and poor relief. All those embroidered lace handkerchiefs, jewelled snuffboxes and miniature temples made of cream for dessert were unnecessary and flippant, no doubt, but they encouraged trade, created employment and generated immense wealth – and had to be defended on that score.

If Smith had ended it there, it would have made for an uncomfortable choice (either the silliness of consumer capitalism or the oppressive austerity of Sparta – or North Korea). But Smith held out some fascinating hopes for the future: consumption didn't invariably have to involve idiotic and frivolous things. He observed that humans have many 'higher' needs that are in fact very sensible and good, and yet that currently lie outside of capitalist enterprise: among these, our need for education, for self-understanding, for beautiful cities and for rewarding social lives.

The capitalism of today still hasn't quite got around to resolving the awkward choices Smith and Rousseau circled. But the hope for the future is that we won't forever merely be making money off degrading or superficial consumer needs (pumping out ever more greetings cards or sneakers). We'll also learn to generate sizeable profits from helping people in truly important, ambitious ways. Psychotherapy should, for example, rightly be one of the gargantuan industries of the later 21st century.

3. How to treat the rich

Then as now, the great question was how to get the rich to behave well towards the rest of society. The Christian answer to this was: make them feel guilty; show them the sufferings of the poor and appeal to their consciences. Meanwhile, the radical, left-wing answer was: raise taxes. But Smith disagreed with both approaches: the hearts of the rich were likely to remain cold and high taxes would simply lead the rich to flee the country.

He arrived at more original and more subtle recommendations thanks to a theory about what the rich really want. He proposed that, contrary to what one might expect, it isn't money the rich really care about. It is honour and respect. The rich accumulate money not because they are materially greedy, but because they are emotionally needy. They do so primarily in order to be liked and approved of.

This vanity provides wise governments with a highly useful tool. Rather than taxing the rich, these governments should learn to give the rich plenty of honour and status – in return for doing all the good things that these narcissists wouldn't normally bother with, like funding schools and hospitals and paying their workers well.

As Smith put it: 'The great secret of education is to direct vanity to proper objects.'

4. Educate consumers

Big corporations feel very evil to us now, the natural targets of blame for low-paying jobs, environmental abuse and sickening ingredients. But Adam Smith knew there was an unexpected, and more important, element responsible for these ills: our taste. Collectively, it is we, the consumers, who opt for certain kinds of ease and excitement over others. And once that basic fact is in place, everything else follows in the slipstream. It's not companies that primarily degrade the world. It is our appetites, which they merely serve.

As a result, the reform of capitalism hinges on an odd-sounding, but critical task: the education of the consumer. We need to be taught to want better-quality things and pay a proper price for them, one that reflects the true burden on workers and the environment.

A good capitalist society doesn't therefore just offer customers choice, it also spends a considerable part of its energies educating people about how to exercise this choice in judicious ways. Capitalism needs to be saved by elevating the quality of demand.

Conclusion

The economic state of the world can seem at once so wrong and yet so complicated, we end up collapsing into despair and passivity.

Adam Smith is on hand to lend us confidence and hope. His work is full of ideas about how human values can be reconciled with the needs of businesses. He deserves our ongoing attention because he was interested in an issue that has become a leading priority of our own times: how to create an economy that is at once profitable and civilised.

Karl Marx

1818–1883

Most people agree that we need to improve our economic system somehow. It threatens our planet through excessive consumption, distracts us with irrelevant advertising, leaves people hungry and without healthcare, and fuels unnecessary wars. Yet we're also often keen to dismiss the ideas of its most famous and ambitious critic, Karl Marx. This isn't very surprising. In practice, his political and economic ideas have been used to design disastrously planned economies and nasty dictatorships. Frankly, the remedies Marx proposed for the ills of the world now sound a bit demented. He thought we should abolish private property. People should not be allowed to own things. At certain moments one can sympathise. But it's like wanting to ban gossip or forbid watching television. It's going to war with human behaviour. And Marx believed the world would be put to rights by a dictatorship of the proletariat, which does not mean anything much today. Openly Marxist parties received a total of only 1,685 votes in the 2010 UK general election, out of the nearly 40 million ballots cast.

Nevertheless, we shouldn't reject Marx too quickly. We ought to see him as a guide whose diagnosis of capitalism's ills helps us navigate towards a more promising future.

Karl Marx was born in 1818 in Trier, Germany. He was descended from a long line of rabbis, but his family converted to Christianity when he was 6 in order to assimilate with German society. At the posh and prestigious University of Bonn, he racked up huge debts, was imprisoned for drunkenness and disturbing the peace, and got into a duel. He also wanted to become a drama critic. Displeased, Marx's father sent him to the more serious University of Berlin, where he joined a group of philosophers known as the Young Hegelians, who were extremely sceptical of modern economics and politics.

Soon Marx became involved with the Communist Party, a tiny group of intellectuals advocating for the overthrow of the class system and the abolition of private property. He worked as a journalist and secretly became engaged to a wealthy young woman, Jenny von Westphalen. Due to his political activity, the young couple had to flee Germany and eventually settled in London.

Marx wrote an enormous number of books and articles, sometimes with his friend Friedrich Engels. Some of the most important are *Critique of Hegel's Philosophy of Right* (1843), *The Holy Family* (1845), *Theses on Feuerbach* (1845), *Economic and Philosophic Manuscripts of 1844* (1845), *The Communist Manifesto* (1848), *Critique of the Gotha Program* (1875), and the very long *Capital* (1867–1894).

Mostly, Marx wrote about capitalism, the type of economy that dominates the Western world. It was, in his day, still getting going, and Marx was one of its most intelligent and perceptive critics. These were some of the problems he identified with it:

1. Modern work is 'alienated'

One of Marx's greatest insights, delivered in an early book known as the *Manuscripts of 1844*, is that work can be one of the sources of our greatest joys. It is because Marx had such high hopes for work that he was so angry at the miserable work that most of humanity is forced to endure.

In order to be fulfilled at work, Marx wrote that workers need 'to see themselves in the objects they have created'. At its best, labour offers us a chance to externalise what's good inside us (let's say, our creativity, our rigour, our logic), and to give it a stable, enduring form in some sort of object or service independent of us. Our work should – if things go right – be a little better than we manage to be day-to-day, because it allows us to concentrate and distil the best parts of us.

Think of the person who built this chair: it is straightforward, strong, honest and elegant. Now, its maker would not always have been these things. Sometimes he or she

A handcrafted rosewood chair

might have been bad tempered, despairing, unsure. Yet the chair is a memorial to the positives of his or her character. That's what work is ideally, thought Marx. But he also observed how, in the modern world, fewer and fewer jobs have this characteristic of allowing us to see the best of ourselves in what we do.

Part of the problem with modern work is that it is incredibly specialised. One can tell because people have very weird-sounding job titles: you find packaging technology specialists, beverage dissemination officers, gastronomical hygiene technicians and information architects. These jobs take years of training to master, which makes the modern economy highly efficient, but we end up with a situation where it is seldom possible for one's real nature to find expression in what one is doing day-to-day.

In Marx's eyes, all of us are generalists inside. We were not born to do one thing only. It's merely the economy that – for its own greedy ends – pushes us to sacrifice ourselves to one discipline alone, rendering us (in Marx's words) 'one-sided and dependent' and 'depressed spiritually and physically to the condition of a machine.' It was in the *Manuscripts of 1844* that Marx first argued that modern work leads to 'alienation' – in German, *Entfremdung*.

In our hearts, we are far more multiplicious and promiscuous than the modern economy allows: beneath the calm outward façade of the accountant might lie someone pining to have a go at landscape gardening. Many a poet would want to have a go at working in industry for a few years.

Marx recognises our multiple potentials. Specialisation might be an economic imperative, but it can be a human betrayal.

Marx also wants to help us find work that is more meaningful. Work becomes meaningful, Marx says, in one of two ways. Either it helps the worker directly to reduce suffering in someone else or else it helps them in a tangible way to increase delight in others. A very few kinds of work, like being a doctor or an opera star, seem to fit this bill perfectly.

But often people leave their jobs and say they couldn't see the point in working in sales or designing an ad campaign for garden furniture or teaching French to kids who don't want to learn. When work feels meaningless, we suffer – even if the salary is a decent one. Marx is making a first sketch of an answer to how we should reform the economy; we need an economic system that allows more of us to reduce suffering or increase pleasure. Deep down, we want to feel that we are helping people. We have to feel we are addressing genuine needs – not merely servicing random desires.

Marx was aware of a lot of jobs where a person generates money but can't see their energies 'collected' anywhere. Their intelligence and skills are dissipated. They can't point to something and say: 'I did that, that is me'. It can afflict people doing apparently glamorous jobs – a news reader or a catwalk model. Day-to-day, it is exciting. But over the years it does not add up to anything. Their efforts do not accumulate. There isn't a long-term objective their work is directed towards. After a number of years they simply stop. It's the reverse of an architect who might labour for five years on a large project – but all the millions of details, which might be annoying or frustrating in themselves, eventually add up to an overall, complete achievement. And everyone who is part of this participates in the sense of direction and purpose. Their labours are necessary to bring something wonderful into existence. And they know it.

2. Modern work is insecure

Capitalism makes the human being utterly expendable; just one factor among others in the forces of production and one that can ruthlessly be let go the minute that costs rise or savings can be made through technology. There simply is no job security in capitalism. And yet, as Marx knew, deep inside of us, we long for security with an intensity similar to that which we feel in relationships. We don't want to be arbitrarily let go; we are terrified of being abandoned. Marx knows we are expendable; it all depends on cost and need. But he has sympathy for the emotional longings of the worker. Communism – emotionally understood – is a promise that we always have a place in the world's heart, that we will not be cast out. This is deeply poignant.

3. Workers get paid little while capitalists get rich

This is perhaps the most obvious qualm Marx had with capitalism. In particular, he believed that capitalists shrunk the wages of the labourers as much as possible in order to skim off a wide profit margin. It was very difficult for the labourers to protest or alter their circumstances. Not only were they in desperate need of employment, but their landlords and employers could conspire to keep them desperate by

A mural by the Mexican Marxist artist Diego Rivera shows the workers
inside a vast machine-like system of modern production.

raising the price of living along with any rise in wages. Modern life also brought new challenges that kept the proletariat
weak: crowded quarters, disease, crime-ridden cities, in-
juries in the factory. In short, Marx wrote, the workers
could be almost endlessly exploited.

4. Capitalism is very unstable

Long before the Great Depression or the computer-traded
stock market, Marx recognised that capitalist systems are
characterised by series of crises. This is partly because capitalists seek increasingly big risks in order to make even bigger
profits, and this speculation disrupts prices and employment.
But capitalism isn't just volatile because of competition and
human frailty. In Marx's view, it is inherently unstable – a
force that constantly overpowers itself, a 'sorcerer who is no
longer able to control the powers of the nether world whom
he has called up by his spells.'

Ironically, Marx pointed out, we have crises in capitalism not because of shortages, but because of abundance; we

have too much stuff. Our factories and systems are so efficient we could give everyone on this planet a car, a house, access to a decent school and hospital. Few of us would need to work. But we don't liberate ourselves. Marx thinks this is absurd, the outcome of some form of pathological masochism. In 1700, it took the labour of almost all adults to feed a nation. Today, a developed nation needs hardly anyone to be employed in farming. Making cars needs practically no employees. Unemployment is currently dreadful and seen as a terrible ill. But, in Marx's eyes, it is a sign of success: it is the result of our unbelievable productive powers. The job of a hundred people can now be done by one machine. And yet rather than draw the positive conclusion from this, we continue to see unemployment as a curse and a failure. Yet, logically, the goal of economics should be to make more and more of us unemployed and to celebrate this fact as progress rather than as failure.

Marx believes that because we don't distribute wealth to everyone, nor seek and celebrate unemployment, we are plagued by instability, unhappiness and unrest. 'Society suddenly finds itself put back into a state of momentary barbarism,' he wrote. 'And why? Because there is too much civilisation … too much industry, too much commerce.'

5. Capitalism is bad for capitalists
Although Marx sometimes called the capitalists and bourgeoisie 'vampires' and 'hostile brothers', he did not think they were evil at heart. In fact, he believed that they were also victims of the capitalist system. For example, he was acutely aware of the sorrows and secret agonies that lay behind bourgeois marriage. Affluent people of his day spoke about family in the most reverent and sentimental of ways. But Marx argued that marriage was actually an extension of business. Marriage concentrated money in the hands of men, who used it to control their wives and children. The idealised bourgeois family was in fact fraught with tension,

oppression, and resentment, and stayed together not because of love but for financial reasons. Marx didn't think
the capitalists wanted to live this way. He simply believed
that the capitalist system forces everyone to put economic
interests at the heart of their lives, so that they can no longer
know deep, honest relationships. He called this psychological tendency *Warenfetischismus* (commodity fetishism) because it makes us value things that have no objective value
and encourages us to see our relationships with others primarily in economic terms.

This is another important aspect of Marx's work: he
makes us aware of the insidious, subtle way in which an economic system colours the sort of ideas people will have about
all sorts of matters. The economy generates what Marx
termed an ideology. In his 1845 work *The German Ideology*,
he wrote, 'the ideas of the ruling class are in every epoch the
ruling ideas'. A capitalist society is one where most people,
rich and poor, believe all sorts of things that are really just
value judgements that relate back to the economic system,
for example: that a person who doesn't work is practically
worthless, that if we simply work hard enough we will get
ahead, that more belongings will make us happier and that
worthwhile things (and people) will invariably make money.

In short, one of the biggest evils of capitalism is not that
there are corrupt people at the top – this is true in any human
hierarchy – but that capitalist ideas teach all of us to be anxious, competitive, conformist, and politically complacent.

* * *

Marx wrote remarkably little about what a communist system should look like. He believed his writings were mostly
descriptions, rather than prescriptions, about what was to
come. When criticised for his rather vague predictions (that
there would be a 'dictatorship of the proletariat', for example), he scoffed that he did not wish to write recipes 'for

the cook-shops of the future.' Perhaps he wisely sensed how hard it is to guess future tastes, both culinary and political.

Nevertheless, we do get little glimpses of Marx's utopia hidden in his writings. *The Communist Manifesto* describes a world without private property, without any inherited wealth, with a steeply graduated income tax, centralised control of the banking, communication, and transport industries, and free public education for all children. Marx also expected that communist society would allow people to develop lots of different sides of their natures. In *The German Ideology*, he wrote that 'in communist society ... it [is] possible for me to do one thing today and another tomorrow, to hunt in the morning, fish in the afternoon, rear cattle in the evening, criticise after dinner, just as I have a mind, without ever becoming hunter, fisherman, herdsman or critic.' We'd get to explore all the different parts of ourselves – our creativity, our intellect, our gentleness, and our ferocity – and everyone would have a bit of time to do philosophy.

***

After Marx moved to London, he was supported – rather ironically for an anti-capitalist – by his friend and intellectual partner Friedrich Engels, a wealthy man whose father owned a cotton plant in Manchester. Engels covered Marx's debts, made sure his works were published, and (in order to divert the suspicions of Mrs Marx) even claimed paternity for a baby who was likely Marx's illegitimate child. Moreover, the two men wrote each other adoring poetry.

Marx was not a well-respected or popular intellectual in his day. He spent much of his time puttering around the reading rooms of the British Museum slowly writing an interminable book about capital. He and Engels were always trying to avoid the secret police (including Marx's brother-in-law, who ran the Prussian secret service). When Marx died in 1883, he was a stateless person; fewer than a dozen people attended his funeral.

Respectable, conventional people of Marx's day would have laughed at the idea that his ideas would remake the world. Yet just a few decades later they did: his writings became the keystone for some of the most important ideological movements of the 20th century.

Marx had an unusually broad view of modern problems. He coined fancy-sounding terms like 'dialectical materialism' because he wanted to challenge us to connect our daily experiences and choices to vast historical forces, to help us see ourselves as part of a larger, morally important struggle. His work is sometimes confusing, not only because he changed his mind over the course of his life but also because he wanted to develop his own language to describe modern problems in a way that was neither prescriptive nor strictly scientific.

We should resist a dismissive reading of Marx on the basis of what happened to his ideas in the 20th century, because he is particularly useful to us in this present moment. Like many of us, he wanted to understand why the modern economy seemed to produce so much misery along with its material wealth. He was astounded by the power of capitalism, the way that it allowed for the 'subjection of Nature's forces to man ... clearing of whole continents for cultivation, canalisation of rivers, whole populations conjured out of the ground.' But he also could see that capitalism does not make us happier, wiser, or kinder – it cannot inherently lead us to be more human or more fully developed.

Considering the failures of previous Marxist-inspired regimes, we're unlikely to improve things by implementing the kind of revolutions Marx predicted. But we should think very seriously about what he tells us about the deeper problems of capitalism. For too long, being a Marxist has meant you agree with the least impressive part of Marx's ideas: his solutions to the ills of the world. And because they look so odd, everything else he has to say falls by the wayside.

But Marx was like a brilliant doctor in the early days of medicine. He could recognise the nature of the disease, although he had no idea how to go about curing it. He got fixated on some moves that might have looked plausible in the 1840s but that don't offer much guidance today. At this point in history, we should all be Marxists in the sense of agreeing with his diagnosis of our troubles. But we need to go out and find the cures that will really work.

Tantalisingly, they are truly out there, scattered in this and that research paper and economic book sidelined by the mass media. We need to consider how to build an economy that not only brings us greater prosperity but also a better relationship to nature, to money, to each other, and to ourselves. We don't need a dictatorship of the proletariat, but we do need to reconsider why we value work and what we want to get out of it. We shouldn't get rid of private property, but we do need a more thoughtful, authentic relationship to money and consumption. And we must begin to reform capitalism not by simply deposing heads of banks but by upending the contents of our own minds. Only then will we truly be able to imagine an economy that is not only productive and innovative, but also fosters human freedom and fulfilment. As Marx himself declared: 'philosophers have only interpreted the world in various ways. The point, however, is to change it.'

John Ruskin

1819–1900

John Ruskin was one of the most ambitious and impassioned English social reformers of the 19th century. He was also – at first sight – a deeply improbable reformer, because he seemed to care mostly about one thing – beauty – which has a reputation for being eminently apolitical and removed from 'real life'. And yet the more Ruskin thought about beauty – the beauty of things humans make, ranging from buildings to chairs, paintings to clothes – the more he realised that the quest to make a more beautiful world is inseparable from the need to remake it politically, economically and socially. In a world that is nowadays growing not only ever more polluted and more unequal but also, though we seldom remark upon it, *uglier*, Ruskin's emphasis on beauty and his understanding of its role in political theory make him an unusual yet timely and very necessary figure. Towards the end of his life, Tolstoy very accurately described Ruskin as, 'one of the most remarkable men not only of England and of our generation, but of all countries and times.'

Ruskin was born in London in 1819 into a wealthy and cosseted home. He was an only child of parents who devoted much of their energies to nurturing and developing his precocious talents in art and literature. His father was an immensely successful wine and sherry importer, with a taste for Byron, Shakespeare, Walter Scott and Turner. Ruskin's parents decided to educate him at home, fearing that other children might encourage coarse habits in their son. He spent most of his days alone in his parents' huge garden, drawing flowers. As a treat in the evening he would be allowed to sit quietly in the corner of the drawing room, sketching illustrations for scenes in the Bible. Every year, during his teens, he went with his parents on long tours of France, Switzerland and Italy. They travelled slowly in their own large coach, stopping at every town along the way.

Young Ruskin particularly liked the French Alps (and the delicious trout that they often ate for dinner in Chamonix).

JOHN RUSKIN, *The Doge's Palace, Venice*, 1852

But the place that most impressed him and changed the course of his life was Venice, which he first saw when he was 16 and to which he returned almost every year during long periods of his adult life. In Venice, he spent his days visiting churches, floating in gondolas and looking at paintings. He also loved to make highly accurate drawings of his favourite architectural details.

Venice was, he said, 'the paradise of cities'. And he declared the Doge's Palace to be 'the central building of the world.' He was entranced by its beauty, its dignity and the splendour of its craftsmanship. 'It would be impossible, I believe, to invent a more magnificent arrangement of all that is in building most dignified and most fair.'

On his return to England, Ruskin was struck by the contrast between the glories of Venice and the often dingy realities of British urban life. It's a familiar phenomenon. We too are liable to come back from the Grand Canal to Sauchiehall Street in Glasgow or Acton High Street and feel our spirits

Suburban England

sink. And yet, although we may mutter a few disparaging remarks, on the whole, we leave it at that, feeling that the ugliness that surrounds us is some sort of inviolable phenomenon we would be best to resign ourselves to.

This wasn't Ruskin's way. The more he experienced the contrast between Venice and modern Britain, the more it broke and enraged his heart. He couldn't get over the appalling realisation that, in one place, human effort had led to such delightful results and that elsewhere (in fact, in most places) the same quantity of labour, the same (or more) money and similar human beings had produced dismal and soul-destroying results. Why were modern humans so bad at creating liveable environments? Why was the contemporary world so dispiritingly, monstrously ugly?

Ruskin had begun his career as an art critic. His ambition had been to open his audience's eyes to the beauty of certain paintings and buildings, but in middle age, a more direct and urgent goal came into view. He realised that the ugliness of most things in Britain (from the factories to the railway stations, the pubs to the workers' housing) was the clearest indication of the decadence, cruel economic ideology and rotten moral foundations of his society.

Attempting to change this was to be his life's work. He devoted the remainder of his career to an urgent, vocal fight against the underlying principles of modern capitalism. He attacked property developers for putting profit before the interests of the community. He lambasted industrialists for degrading the lives of their workers. And he laid into the whole of the Victorian bourgeoisie for neglecting their responsibilities towards the poor, for shortening their days and coarsening their spirits.

Partly, his attacks were delivered as lectures. Ruskin spent a good part of every year giving talks up and down Britain. He was always off to harangue some group of industrialists in Birmingham or Sheffield about their crooked value systems and the immense heart-rending superiority of Venice to modern England – a fact that was all the more shocking to his audiences since Britain was, just then, getting into its stride as the workshop of the world.

But he was also interested in practical action. When his father died, he was left an enormous fortune, which he set about spending on good causes. In 1871, he founded The Guild of St George. He had long admired the medieval guild system, where workers were well organised within trades that offered them both job security and pride in their work. Ruskin's Guild was an attempt to reorganise economic life along pre-capitalist lines. He tried to set up a network of farms creating sustainable, unadulterated foodstuffs (for a time, he was a leading maker of apple juice). He built workshops to produce woollen and linen clothes. He encouraged businesses turning out high-quality but affordable pottery, cutlery and furniture. And he wanted the Guild to act as a property development company that could be content with breaking even rather than aiming for the usual profit margins that he believed were incompatible with beauty. And finally, he wanted to set up a network of schools offering evening classes as well as a number of museums for workers, as an alternative to the numbing mass media otherwise pushed their way. Along with diverting the lion's share of his wealth to the Guild, he also encouraged wealthy people around the country to contribute their riches to the project.

The Guild was in some ways a success. Quite a few industrialists gave Ruskin their surplus wealth. Some cottages were bought on the Welsh coast where a group of Ruskin's devotees started a business making jumpers. Near Scarborough, a farm was bought that made a variety of jams. A museum was started in Sheffield. His most devoted disciple, William Morris, set up a highly influential furniture and interior decoration company, William Morris & Sons, whose chairs and wallpapers remain successful.

And the Guild itself has survived today – it can be found at www.guildofstgeorge.org.uk – and still performs some of the work that Ruskin had championed.

But of course, Ruskin did not manage single-handedly to reform capitalism. It seems a general law that people who can think well aren't the most adept at organising change. They aren't good with the accounts, they get impatient with meetings – and because of these procedural flaws, the world doesn't change as much as it should. However, Ruskin is as close to a thinker-activist as the 19th century produced, and he remains an inspiration to anyone who seeks not just to reflect on the world, but also to alter it in the direction of beauty and wisdom.

To zero in on only one of his schemes, in the mid-1870s while he was a professor at Oxford, Ruskin got increasingly bothered that his students didn't understand the meaning and pleasure of work. They went to parties and wrote essays but never did anything very productive with their hands, which he believed had a detrimental effect on their characters. There was a road in a nearby village of Hinksey that had become so filled with ruts and potholes that it was more or less unusable. The carts had to avoid it and make their way over the village green, messing up the grass. The local children didn't have anywhere to play.

So Ruskin got together sixty students and organised them to mend the road and tidy the green. Eyewitnesses described Ruskin on a wintry morning wearing a 'blue cloth cap, with earflaps pulled about his ears, sitting cheerily by the roadside breaking stones not only with a will but with knowledge, and cracking jokes the while.' Mending the road took them a long time, and they made very imperfect progress. There were complaints from the local landlord and a general conviction that Ruskin was a touch unhinged.

But the underlying point is crucial. Out of fear of seeming ridiculous, we often end up not tackling the challenges around us. The road mending was a small instance of a larger idea that animated Ruskin's life: that it is the duty of creative, privileged people to direct their efforts towards making the world more pleasing and tidy, more convenient and beautiful, not just for themselves, but for the greatest good of the greatest number. He also believed that we should not (cannot) leave this to the forces of the market, because they will never get round to planting wildflowers by the edges of roads and making sure that village greens are pretty.

Throughout his life, Ruskin contrasted the general beauty of nature with the ugliness of the man-made world. He set up a useful criterion for any man-made thing: was it in any way the equal of something one might find in nature? This was the case with Venice, with Chartres Cathedral, with the chairs of William Morris … but not with most things being turned out by the factories of the modern world.

So Ruskin thought it helpful for us to observe and be inspired by nature (he was a great believer that everyone in the country should learn to draw things in nature). He wrote with astonishing seriousness about the importance of looking at the light in the morning, of taking care to see the different kinds of cloud in the sky and of looking properly at how the branches of a tree intertwine and spread. He took immense delight in the beautiful structures of nests and beavers' dams. And he loved feathers with a passion.

There was an urgent message here. Nature sets the standard. It provides us with particularly intense examples of beauty and grace. The plumage of a bird, the clouds over the mountains at sunset, the great trees bending in the wind – nature is ordered, beautiful, simple, effective. It is only with us that things seem to go wrong. Why can we not be as it is? There is a humiliating contrast between the natural loveliness of trees by a stream and the bleak griminess of an average street; between the ever-changing interest of the sky and the monotony and dreariness of so much of our lives. Ruskin felt that this painful comparison was instructive. Because we are part of nature we have the capacity to live up to its standard. We should use the emotion we feel at the beauty of nature to energise us to equal its works. The goal of human society is to honour the dignity and grandeur of the natural world.

By championing beauty so intensely, Ruskin rescues bits of our own experiences that we rarely take too seriously. Most of us have at points felt that trees are lovely, that somewhere else (and it could be Venice) is far more beautiful than the place we live in day-to-day, that there are too many shoddy things in the world, that work really isn't enjoyable enough, that often we are misemployed – but we tend to dismiss these thoughts as too personal, minor, not really of significance to anyone other than ourselves. Ruskin argues us into a more ambitious and more serious attitude. It is, he says, just such thoughts and experiences that need to be given proper weight, which need to be analysed and understood. They provide crucial clues as to what is really wrong with the world and can therefore lead us towards moves that may make it genuinely better.

Ruskin's approach to politics was to hold resolutely on to a vision of what a really sane, reasonable, decent and good life would look like – and then to ask rigorously just how a society would need to be set up for that to be the average life, for an ordinary person, and not a rare piece of luck only for the very privileged. For this he deserves our, and posterity's, ongoing interest and gratitude.

Henry David Thoreau

1817–1862

M ost of the time, successful modern life involves lots of technology, constantly being connected with other people, working very hard for as much money as possible, and doing what we are told. These elements are almost a conventional prescription for success. So it may come as a surprise that some of the best advice about modern life comes from an unemployed writer who lived alone in the woods and refused to pay his taxes. Henry David Thoreau (originally David Thoreau), reminds us about the importance of simplicity, authenticity and downright disobedience.

He was born in 1817, in Concord, an unassuming town west of Boston. His father was a pencil-maker and his mother took in boarders. He attended Harvard College in 1833 and graduated in 1837 with good marks. Yet he rejected the ordinary career paths like law, medicine, or the church. He took up teaching for a period, but failed to settle into a job at the local school because he couldn't stand their practice of corporal punishment. He was, in short, dissatisfied with every obvious trajectory.

Then Thoreau struck up a remarkable friendship with the American philosopher, Ralph Waldo Emerson (1803–1882). Emerson believed in transcendentalism, an outlook that holds that the world is divided into two realities: material reality and spiritual reality. Transcendentalists emphasise the importance of the spiritual over the material when it comes to leading a fulfilling life.

Emerson and his transcendentalism had a huge influence on Thoreau. Moreover, Emerson inspired Thoreau to work seriously towards becoming a writer. Thoreau's house was busy and noisy, and he found working at the pencil business tiring and uninspiring. But Emerson owned a plot of land in the woods surrounding the nearby Walden Pond, and in 1845 he allowed Thoreau to build a small cabin (3 by 4.5 metres) there. It had three chairs, one bed, a table, a desk, and a lamp.

Thoreau's cabin at Walden Pond

Thoreau moved in on the Fourth of July with two aims: to write a book, and to ascertain whether it was possible to work one day a week and devote six to his philosophical work.

In his two years in the cabin, Thoreau penned his most notable work: *Walden; or, Life in the Woods*, which was eventually published in 1854. It was a modest commercial and literary success at the time, but it would become an inspirational text about self-discovery. Thoreau argued that his escape to Walden Pond was not simply a relaxing retreat to the forest. He settled there to 'live deep and suck out the marrow of life,' as he put it:

> I went to the woods because I wished to live delib-
> erately, to front only the essential facts of life, and
> see if I could not learn what it had to teach, and not,
> when I came to die, discover that I had not lived.

Thoreau believed that people often 'miss' life – they remain so stuck in their ways that they fail to see that other approaches to fulfilment exist: 'it appears as if men had deliberately chosen the common mode of living because they preferred it to any other. Yet they honestly think there is no choice left.' After some time in the cabin, Thoreau discovered a different, more conscious lifestyle.

To begin with, Thoreau concluded that we actually need very few things. He suggested that we think about our belongings in terms of how little we can get by with, rather than how much we can get. Money, he believed, is largely superfluous, for it does not help us to develop our soul. Work, in the traditional sense, is also unnecessary: 'As for work, we haven't any of any consequence.' Thoreau aimed to labour for only one day a week, and he found this was entirely possible. He pointed out that walking the distance of a 30-mile train journey took a day, but working to earn the money to pay for the same journey would take more than a day. Best of all, walking allows us to view nature and gives us time for contemplation – and that, in Thoreau's view, was what time was for: 'I found that, by working about six weeks in a year, I could meet all the expenses of living. The whole of my winters, as well as most of my summers, I had free and clear for study.'

Like his friend Emerson, Thoreau deeply valued what he called self-reliance. He distrusted society and the 'progress' it seemed to make. 'The civilised man has built a coach,' Emerson said, 'but has lost the use of his feet.' He felt that economic independence from other people and from the government was crucial, and while he understood that we need the company of other people from time to time, he felt that too often we use the company of other people to fill gaps in our inner life that we are afraid to confront ourselves. The task of learning to live alone was, for Thoreau, not so much about carrying out daily chores as it was about becoming a good companion for oneself, relying first and foremost on oneself for companionship and moral guidance: 'Insist on yourself; never imitate. Your own gift you can present every moment with the cumulative force of a whole life's cultivation; but of the adopted talent of another, you have only an extemporaneous, half possession.' Most of all, one should change oneself before seeking to change the world.

Thoreau also saw technology as an often unnecessary distraction. He saw the practical benefits of new inventions, but he also warned that these innovations could not address the real challenge of personal happiness: 'our inventions are wont to be pretty toys, which distract our attention from serious things ... We are in great haste to construct a magnetic telegraph from Maine to Texas; but Maine and Texas, it may be, have nothing important to communicate.' What we need to be happy isn't work or money or technology or even lots of friends, but time.

Thoreau also believed we should look to nature, which is full of deep spiritual significance. He sought 'to be always on the alert to find God in nature.' He thought of animals, forests and waterfalls as inherently valuable both for their beauty and their role in the ecosystem. He said he would be very happy 'if all the meadows on the earth were left in a wild state,' for we are likely to find that 'nature is worth more even by our modes of valuation than our improvements are.' We can best understand ourselves as a part of nature; we should see ourselves as 'nature looking into nature,' rather than an external force or the master of nature.

Most of all, nature provides the meaning that money and technology and other people's opinions cannot, by teaching us to be humble and more aware, by fostering introspection and self-discovery. Thoreau believed that with the right kind of consciousness, human beings could transcend their previous limitations and ideas. This mental state – and not money or technology – would provide real progress. He optimistically declared, 'Only that day dawns to which we are awake. There is more day to dawn. The sun is but a morning star.' If we clear our lives of distractions and make time for a little contemplation, new discoveries await us.

***

Perhaps the best testament of the value of Thoreau's individual contemplation and personal authenticity is that his ideas lead him to powerful political conclusions. He believed that people should behave in a way that would make their governments more moral, prioritising their moral conscience over the dictates of law. In 'Resistance to Civil Government' (1849), Thoreau argued that people are morally obliged to challenge a government that upholds hypocritical or flagrantly unfair laws. The American government of Thoreau's day had, in his view, bullied Mexico into war in 1846 to expand its territory; it also upheld slavery. So Thoreau turned to what he called 'Civil Disobedience' – peacefully resisting immoral laws – in protest. In July 1846, he withheld payment of his poll tax duty to avoid paying for the Mexican–American War and slavery. He spent a night in prison for his troubles, an adventure that led to the writing of his essay 'Resistance to Civil Government'. 'There will never be a really free and enlightened State until the State comes to recognise the individual as a higher and independent power, from which all its own power and authority are derived, and treats him accordingly,' he wrote. 'I ask for, not at once no government, but at once a better government.'

It was not until it was picked up by subsequent reformers that 'Civil Disobedience' – as it was later called – became one of the most influential pieces of American political philosophy in history. Mohandas Gandhi adopted Thoreau's idea of nonviolent disobedience as a model for his fight against

British colonialism, and referred to Thoreau as 'one of the greatest and most moral men America has produced.' In the Second World War, a number of people in Denmark adopted the methods of civil disobedience to resist the Nazi movement, and Thoreau became a hero there. Furthermore, Martin Luther King famously used Thoreau's ideas in his fight for equality for African-Americans. King's first exposure to nonviolent methods of protest came when he read Thoreau's work in 1944; it convinced him that 'noncooperation with evil is as much a moral obligation as is cooperation with good.'

Despite his time as a hermit, Thoreau teaches us how to approach our frighteningly vast, highly interconnected and morally troubling modern society. He challenges us to be authentic not just by avoiding material life and its distractions, but by engaging with the world, and withdrawing our support for the government when we believe it is acting unjustly. This might make us feel uncomfortable: how many of us want to risk our liberty or possessions on one act of defiance? Yet civil disobedience has become one of the most powerful forms of doing 'nothing' (avoiding certain actions) the world has ever seen.

Thoreau remains highly relevant, for we are not far from the problems he sought to address. His emphasis on frugality and turning one's back on the material world is a fresh insight in a world of economic trouble. Indeed, interest in Thoreau peaks around economic crises: during the depression in the 1930s, his philosophy became especially popular in America. Yet – as Thoreau would probably argue – it should not take a severe crisis for us to question a materialistic life.

We can also continue to learn from his appreciation for nature and the psychological possibilities it offers. Thoreau later became a patron saint of the environmental movement; the Sierra Club – one of the largest environmental organisations in America – uses Thoreau's slogan: 'In wildness is the preservation of the world' as their guiding mantra.

After he left Walden, Thoreau travelled widely, spent time working as a surveyor, and published many more essays, especially about the environment. He had struggled with tuberculosis since his college years and fell ill with it yet again after an outing to count tree rings. He died three years later in 1862, aged only 44. However, his works endure, and remind us of just how important it is to remove the distractions of money, technology, and other people's views in order to live according to our inner nature.

Matthew Arnold

1822–1888

M atthew Arnold was the most important educational reformer of the 19th century. He realised that, in the modern world, education would be one of the keys to a good society. But it had to be education of a special kind – and not one that we nowadays necessarily recognise or strive for. Instead of saying that schools should teach more trigonometry or improve the literacy rates in particular socio-economic percentiles, Arnold advocated a strange-sounding, but deeply sane and necessary, agenda. Schools should promote – as he put it – 'sweetness and light'. It was a turn of phrase calculated to irritate his contemporaries, but it neatly captured what he was trying to do – and what we might be inspired to try in turn.

In his lifetime, Arnold was a laughing stock for some of the newspapers of Britain. The *Daily Telegraph* in particular constantly teased him for being pretentious: 'an elegant Jeremiah' as they put it. Whenever there was a strike or a riot, they imagined Arnold earnestly telling people not to fuss so much about vulgar, practical things like unemployment or low wages, and instead to raise their minds to higher ideals and concentrate on sweetness and light. It was a deeply unfair criticism (as we shall see) but there was just enough in Arnold's character to make it stick. It reveals just how easy it is to come across as fey, out of touch and inconsequential when one is trying to stand up for fragile, slightly complicated things.

Matthew Arnold was born in 1822. His father, Thomas Arnold, was a major intellectual celebrity of his times: a tireless, immensely active and stern headmaster of Rugby public school, who had a starring role in *Tom Brown's Schooldays*, one of the bestselling novels of the era.

Matthew was a disappointment, and a puzzle, to his father. He liked to read in bed in the morning, he enjoyed strolling through woods and meadows, he was charmed by young women in Paris, he wrote poetry, he neglected his studies and published – to the world's indifference – a couple of slim volumes of verse. Eventually, he fell in love with a woman called Frances Lucy Wightman – his pet name for her was Flu – the daughter of a judge. But to get married he needed a solid career, so he took up a senior post in the Department of Education as an inspector of schools. For years, he travelled the length and breadth of Victorian England, checking whether children were being properly taught. He earned a very respectable salary; the family grew, they went on interesting holidays and lived comfortably and happily in the West End of London – though Arnold was never quite on top of his finances.

Arnold didn't write a great deal of poetry in these years, but his charm (and his late father's many influential friends) got him elected to the highly prestigious position of Professor of Poetry at Oxford. There was no money attached to the role – but it meant he got to give a series of lectures each year to the opinion formers of the nation. It was to prove the making of him, for it was thanks to his post that he matured into a profound social critic. His best lectures were gathered together into his most important and influential book, *Culture and Anarchy* (1869).

There was a lot that bothered Arnold about the modern world – as it was just beginning to reveal itself. But he summed it up in one embracing idea: anarchy. By 'anarchy', he didn't mean people in black balaclavas breaking shop windows. Rather he meant something much more familiar and closer to home: a toxic kind of freedom. He meant a society where market forces dominate the nation; where the commercial media sets the agenda and coarsens and simplifies everything it touches; where corporations are barely restrained from despoiling the environment; where human beings are treated as tools to be picked up and put down at will; where there is no more pastoral care and precious little sense of community; where hospitals treat the body but no one treats the soul; where no one knows their neighbours anymore; where romantic love is seen as the only bond worth pursuing – and where there is nowhere to turn to at moments of acute distress and inner crisis. It's a world we've come to know well.

Arnold believed that the forces of anarchy had become overwhelming in Europe in the second half of the 19th century. Religion was in terminal decline. Business reigned triumphant. A practical, unpsychological money-making mentality ruled. Newspaper circulation was growing exponentially. And politics was dominated by partisanship, conflict and misrepresentation.

In the past, religion might have served to reign in these anarchic tendencies. But in his best poem, *Dover Beach*, Arnold described how 'the Sea of Faith' had ebbed away, like a tide from the shore, leaving only a 'melancholy, long, withdrawing roar'.

What could replace the function that religion had once played in society? What forces might constrain anarchy and civilise, guide, inspire and humanise instead? Arnold proposed one resounding solution: culture. It must be culture, he proposed, that would overcome the forces of anarchy inadvertently unleashed by capitalism and democracy.

But to play such a role, by culture one could not simply continue to mean what a lot of people then (as today) understood by the term: an interest in going to art galleries on holiday, watching an occasional play and writing some essays about Jane Austen at school.

By culture, Arnold meant a force that would guide, educate, console and teach; in short, in the highest sense, a therapeutic medium. The great works of art weren't to be thought of as mere entertainment, they contained – when interpreted and presented properly (and this is where Arnold thought his society had gone so wrong) – a set of suggestions as to how we might best live and die, and govern our societies according to our highest possibilities.

Arnold's goal was therefore to try to change the way the elite establishment (the museums, the universities, the schools, the learned societies) were teaching works of culture, so that they could become what he felt they had it in their power to be: a proper bulwark against modern anarchy and the agents to deliver appropriate doses of those important qualities, sweetness and light.

By 'light', Arnold meant 'understanding'. The great works of culture have it in their power to clear mental confusion, they give us words for things we had felt but had not previously grasped; they replace cliché with insight. Given their potential, Arnold believed that schools and the mass media had a responsibility to help us get to know as many of these light-filled works as possible. He wanted a curriculum that would systematically teach everyone in the land: 'the best that has been thought and said in the world', so that through this knowledge we might be able to turn 'a stream of fresh and free thought upon our stock notions and habits.'

But Arnold was conscious of how the teaching of works of culture in fact needlessly distances us from their power. Academic commentary grows like ivy around masterpieces, choking the majesty and interest of their message to us. Museums for their part make art sound immensely complicated, abstract and peculiar. As for the big and insightful thoughts that may lie in philosophy, they have frequently been formulated in ways that make it exceptionally difficult to understand them and see their personal import (Arnold had academic culprits like Hegel in mind). So, Arnold tried to impress upon his intellectual contemporaries a project that remains urgent to this day: that of 'carrying from one end of society to the other, the best knowledge and the best ideas of their time; who have laboured to divest knowledge of all that was harsh, uncouth, difficult, abstract, professional, exclusive; to humanise it, to make it efficient outside the clique of the cultivated and learned.'

To make it efficient outside the clique of the cultivated and learned. Note how this ostensibly rarefied and impractical commentator had something deeply practical and very democratic in mind. He recognised that, in a populist, market-driven society, it was no use keeping culture for the few, writing books that only a hundred people could understand. The real task was to know how to popularise. If culture was to be properly powerful, it would have to learn to be popular first.

By 'sweetness', Arnold meant that he wanted works of culture to be presented to the audience in sweet ways. He saw the absolute necessity of sugar-coating things. In a free society, cultural authority could no longer be strict and demanding – people would simply turn away or vote for something less severe. Anyone who wanted to advocate serious (but potentially very beneficial) things would have to learn the art of sweetness. They would have to charm and amuse and please and flatter. Not because they were insincere but precisely because they were so earnest. In Arnold's ideal world, the lessons of advertising – which in his day discovered how to sell expensive watches and fire tongs and special knives for boning chickens – would have to be used by intellectuals and educators. Instead of wondering how to persuade middle-income people to purchase potato peelers or soup dishes, they would ponder how to make Plato's philosophy more impressive or how to find a larger consumer base for the ideas of St Augustine.

By sweetness, Arnold also meant kindness and sympathy. He wanted a world where people would – in the public realm – be nicer to one another. Enough of the brutality and coarseness of the *Daily Telegraph*, a publication that every day took pleasure in gunning down new victims and turning personal tragedies in to the stuff of mockery. He wished culture to help foster a spirit of kind-hearted enquiry, a readiness to suppose that the other person might have a point, even if one didn't quite see it yet. He wanted to promote a tenderness towards people's failings and weaknesses. He saw sweetness as an essential ingredient of a good, humane society.

Culture and Anarchy remains filled with eminently valid answers to the problems of the modern world. With religion gone, it really is only culture that can prevent anarchy. But we still have a way to go before culture has been divested of, to use Arnold's words, all that is 'harsh, uncouth, difficult, abstract, professional, exclusive' about it.

This book is – in its own way – a small contribution to fulfilling Arnold's magisterial vision.

William Morris

1834–1896

The 19th-century designer, poet and entrepreneur William Morris is one of the best guides we have to the modern economy – despite the fact that he died in 1896 (while Queen Victoria was still on the throne), never made a telephone call, and would have found the very idea of television utterly baffling.

Morris was the first person to understand two issues that have become decisive for our times. Firstly: the role of pleasure in work. And, secondly: the nature of consumer demand. The preferences of consumers – what we collectively appreciate and covet and are willing to pay for – are crucial drivers of the economy and hence of the kind of society we end up living in. Until we have better collective taste, we will struggle to have a better economy and society. It's a huge idea.

William Morris was born in 1834 into a well-off family. His father was a financier in the City of London and they lived in a large house near Walthamstow in Essex. His father died young (Morris was only 13) and it turned out he had been involved in a range of highly speculative – and only just legal – ventures. A great deal of the family fortune was lost – although a few secure investments remained that gave young Morris a comfortable (though by no means huge) income for life.

The fact that he was always reasonably well-off did not blunt his empathy for financial hardship. Personally and politically Morris was an instinctively warm and generous man. But it did bring a useful perspective: he was acutely aware that there are some key problems that are not caused by a shortage of money and that more money won't solve. So he could never be persuaded that financial growth in and of itself could be the sure sign of improvement – whether in an individual or a national life.

When he was 18, Morris went to university. He didn't do much of the work he was supposed to but he had a wonderful time. Almost the first day he made friends for life with a fellow student called Edward Burne-Jones, who went on to become one of the most successful artists of the era.

After graduating, Morris spent some time training as an architect. But at this stage a conventional career wasn't his main concern. He saw himself as an artist and a poet. He was simply interested in making things for his own satisfaction and maybe for the enjoyment of a few friends. He was not seeking to sell his paintings or be paid for writing poems. Morris's friends used to call him 'Topsy' – because of his volatile, occasionally fiery, temper.

His favourite model was a young actress with a dramatically beautiful face, Jane Burden. A year later they got married. Morris became obsessed with the project of building and furnishing a family house at Bexleyheath, in southeast London. It was called the Red House, and pretty much everything in it – chairs, tables, lamps, wallpaper, wardrobes, candlesticks, glasses – were designed from scratch either by Morris himself or by his close friend and architectural collaborator Philip Webb. Artistic friends painted murals on the walls.

The experience of building and fitting out his house taught Morris his first big lesson about the economy. It would have been simpler (and maybe cheaper) to have ordered everything from a factory outlet. But Morris wasn't trying to find the quickest or simplest way to set up home. He wanted to find the way that would give him – and everyone involved in the project – maximum satisfaction. And it fired Morris with an enthusiasm for the medieval idea of craft. The worker would develop sensitivity and skill – and enjoy the labour. It wasn't mechanical or humiliating.

He spotted that craft offers important clues to what we actually want from work. We want to know we've done something good with the day. That our efforts have counted towards tangible outcomes that we actually see and feel are worthwhile. And Morris was already noticing that when people really like their work, the issue of exactly how much you get paid becomes less critical. (Though Morris always believed, in addition, that people deserved honourable pay for honest work.) The point is you can absolutely say you are not doing it purely for the money.

Labour could be dignified. It was a timely insight. This was an era of massive industrialisation; workers were pouring into the new factories – even though the conditions were often horrendous. The status of working with your hands, of making physical things, was low. It was then (as now) more prestigious to sit at a desk than to stand at a forge or by a kiln.

The problem, though, was that Morris was not only a craftsman and a labourer at the Red House. He was also the client. Of course – sceptics might point out – he could have a great time because this was basically just pursuing a hobby.

Yet this was precisely what Morris didn't want to do. He was determined to show that the principles of craft and satisfying work (for the worker) could and should be at the heart of the modern world. And that – he realised – meant making them into a business.

So, in 1861 – still in his mid-twenties – Morris started a decorative arts business: Morris, Marshall, Faulkner & Co.; which they liked to call simply 'the Firm'. His colleagues included Burne-Jones, the brilliant poet, painter and charismatic personality Dante Gabriel Rossetti, and the architect Philip Webb.

They set up a factory making wallpaper, chairs, curtains and tables. They were very proud not only of the elegant designs but of the quality of the workmanship that went into all their products. They believed that factories should be attractive places, and they were keen for clients and others to come and take a tour and see for themselves the healthy pleasant environment in which the goods were produced.

The firm soon encountered a very instructive problem. If you make high-quality goods and pay your workers a fair and decent wage, then the cost of the product is going to be higher. It will always be possible for competitors to undercut

Design for wallpaper by William Morris, 1862

the price and offer inferior goods, produced in less humane ways, for less money.

If you ask a comparatively high price – to ensure the dignity of work and quality of materials and so make something that will last – you really risk losing customers.

The factories and machines of the Industrial Revolution had brought mass production. Prices were lower, but there was a loss of quality and a dependence on routine, deadening labour in depressing circumstances. It can seem as if it is inevitable that the low price must triumph. Surely the logic of economics dictates that the lower price will necessarily win. Or does it?

For Morris, the key factor is, therefore, whether customers are willing to pay the just price. If they are, then work can be honourable. If they are not, then work is necessarily going to be – on the whole – degrading and miserable.

So, Morris concluded that the lynchpin of a good economy is the education of the consumer. We collectively need to get clearer about what we really want in our lives and why, and how much certain things are worth to us (and therefore how much we are prepared to pay for them).

An important clue to good consumption, Morris insisted, is that you should 'have nothing in your houses that you do not know to be useful or believe to be beautiful.' This is a crucial attitude. It doesn't involve renunciation, it's not an invitation to bleak renunciation, he's not trying to make anyone feel guilty or ashamed.

Rather than reaching for lots of quick fixes and items of fleeting use and charm, Morris wished for people to see their purchases as investments and buy items sparingly. He would have preferred for someone to spend £1,000 on an intricate, hand-made dining set that would last for decades and grow to become a family heirloom, than for each generation to buy its own cheap alternative, just to be thrown away when fashions changed. This way, people could take pride in and really enjoy the things they bought. There is some sense of satisfaction and pride in buying something you know will last and that can be handed down to future generations.

For Morris himself, the business did not work out terribly well. There was healthy demand from the well-to-do. The Morris lines of furniture, wallpaper, fabrics and lamps continued to sell for many years. But he didn't manage to break into the wider, bigger markets that he aspired to. The point wasn't to provide more elegance and luxury for the rich. The big idea was to bring solid, well-designed, finely produced articles to the mass consumer. Morris wanted to transform the ordinary – not the elite – experience of buying things.

One of his last creations was a utopian story called *News from Nowhere*. In it he imagines how, ideally, a society would develop. He learns a lot from Marxism: this is a society with strong social bonds, in which the profit motive is not dominant. But he pays equal attention to the beauty of life: the expansive woodlands, the lovely buildings, the kinds of clothes people wear, the quality of the furniture, the charm of the gardens.

Morris's health declined in his sixties. In the summer of 1896, he took a health cruise to Norway. But the fjords didn't work and he died of tuberculosis a few weeks after he got home.

Morris directs our attention to a set of centrally important tests that a good economy should pass.

- How much do people enjoy working?
- Does everyone live within walking distance of woods and meadows?
- How healthy is the average diet?
- How long are consumer goods expected to last?
- Are the cities beautiful (generally, not just in a few privileged parts)?

The economy can (with fatal ease) feel as if it is governed by abstract, complex laws concerning discounted cash flows and money supply. His point is that, nevertheless, the economy is intimately tethered to our preferences and choices. And that these are open to transformation. It may not be necessary (as Marx thought) to bring factories and banks and all the corporations into public ownership; and it may not be necessary (as Milton Friedman and others claimed) to wind back government impact on markets. The true task in creating a good economy, Morris shows us, lies much closer to home.

John Rawls

1921–2002

M any of us feel that our societies are a little – or even plain totally – 'unfair'. But we have a hard time explaining our sense of injustice to the powers that be in a way that sounds rational and without personal pique or bitterness.

That's why we need John Rawls, a 20th-century American philosopher who provides us with a foolproof model for identifying what truly might be unfair – and how we might gather support for fixing things.

Born in Baltimore, Maryland, USA in 1921, Rawls – nicknamed Jack – was exposed, and responded, to the injustices of the modern world from a very young age. As a child, he witnessed at first-hand shockingly deprived areas of Maine, where many of his fellow Americans were evidently being denied the opportunities and support his loving attorney father and social activist mother were able to give him. Rawls also saw the arbitrariness of suffering when two of his brothers died from infections unwittingly contracted from *him*. If this was not enough, he saw the horrors and lawlessness of the Second World War in the final stages of the European campaign. All this inspired him to go into academia with a far from arcane mission: he wanted to use the power of ideas to change the unjust world he was living in.

Rawls shone academically at Harvard and Cornell and gravitated towards the more worldly philosophers of his day, including Isaiah Berlin, H.L.A. Hart and Stuart Hampshire: all were out to change the world through their work and all became his friends. It was the publication of *A Theory of Justice* in 1971 that properly made Rawls's name – and is why we continue to revere him now. Having read and widely discussed his book, Bill Clinton was to label Rawls 'the greatest political philosopher of the 20th century'– and had him over to the White House for dinner on a regular basis.

Success never affected Rawls personally. He was a humble and kind man, who took the concerns of others seriously at a political and personal level. He did social work with children and deprived young adults in Boston where he lived. He looked after the financial interests of the children of a colleague who had died prematurely. He had exquisite manners. During a doctoral viva, an elderly Rawls once re-positioned himself directly in front of the sun to ensure that one of his nervous young candidates would be spared any glare and so could best focus on the defence of her thesis.

What, then, does this exemplar of fairness have to tell the modern world?

1. Things as they are now are patently unfair

The statistics all point to the radical unfairness of society. Comparative charts of life expectancy and income projec-tions direct us to a single overwhelming moral. And yet, day-to-day, it can be hard to take this unfairness seriously, especially in relation to our own lives.

That's because so many voices are on hand telling us that, if we work hard and have ambition, we can make it. Rawls was deeply aware of how the American dream seeped through the political system and into individual hearts – and he knew its corrosive, regressive influence. Sure enough, there seem to be lots of people who bear out the morality tale to perfection; presidents who came from nothing, entrepreneurs who were once penniless or-phans ... The media parades them before us with glee. How then can we complain about our lot when they were able to get to the pinnacle?

Rawls never accepted this. Certainly he was aware of the extraordinary success stories, but he was also a statisti-cian who knew that the rags-to-riches tales were overall so negligible as not to warrant serious attention by politi-cal theorists. Indeed, to keep mentioning them was merely a clever political sleight of hand designed to prevent the powerful from undertaking the necessary task of reform-ing society.

President Obama holding an election night event in Chicago.

As Rawls forcibly reminds us, in the modern United States, and many parts of Europe too, if you are born poor, the chances of you remaining poor (and dying young) are simply overwhelming and incontestable.

But what can we do about this? Rawls was politically canny. He understood that debates about unfairness and what to do about it often get bogged down in arcane details and petty squabbling, which mean that, year after year, nothing quite gets done.

What Rawls was therefore after was a simple, economical and polemical way to show people how their societies were unfair and what they might do about it – in ways that could cut through the debate and touch people's hearts as well as minds (for he knew that emotion mattered a lot in politics).

2. Imagine if you were not you
A lot of the reason why societies don't become fairer is that those who benefit from current injustice are spared the need to think too hard about what it would have been like to be born in different circumstances. They resist change

from ingrained bias and prejudice, from a failure of the imagination.

Rawls intuitively understood that he had to get these people on board first – and somehow manage to appeal to their imaginations and their innate moral sense.

So he devised one of the greatest thought experiments in the history of political thought, easily the equal of anything in the work of Thomas Hobbes, Jean-Jacques Rousseau or Immanuel Kant.

This experiment is called 'the veil of ignorance', and through it Rawls asks us to imagine ourselves in a conscious, intelligent state before our own birth, but without any knowledge of what circumstances we were going to be born into; our futures shrouded by a veil of ignorance. Standing high above the planet, we wouldn't know what sort of parents we'd have, what our neighbourhoods would be like, how the schools would perform, what the local hospital could do for us, how the police and judicial systems might treat us and so on ...

The question that Rawls asks us all to contemplate is: if we knew nothing about where we'd end up, what sort of a society would it feel safe to enter? In what kind of political system would it be rational and sane for us to take root – and accept the challenge laid down by the veil of ignorance?

Well, for one thing, certainly not the United States. Of course, the US has a great many socio-economic positions it would be truly delightful to be born into. Vast swathes of the country enjoy good schools, safe neighbourhoods, great access to colleges, fast tracks into prestigious jobs and some highly elegant country clubs ... To be generous, at least 30 per cent of this vast and beautiful nation has privilege and opportunity. No wonder the system doesn't change: there are simply too many people, millions of people, who benefit from it.

But that's where the 'veil of ignorance' comes in handy: it stops us thinking about all those who have done well and draws our attention to the appalling risks involved in entering US society *as if it were a lottery*, behind the veil of ignorance – without knowing if you'd wind up the child of an orthodontist in Scottsdale, Arizona, or as the offspring of a black single mother in the rougher bits of eastern Detroit. Would any sane birth-lottery player really want to take the gamble of ending up in the 70 per cent of people who have substandard healthcare, inadequate housing, poor access to a good legal structure and a sloppy system of education? Or would the sane gambler not insist that the rules of the entire game had to be changed to maximise the overall chances of a decent outcome for any single player?

3. What you know needs to be fixed
Rawls answers the question for us: any sane participant of the veil of ignorance experiment is going to want a society with a number of things in place: they'll want the schools to be very good (even the public ones), the hospitals to function brilliantly (all of them, even the free ones), they'll want the standard access to the law to be unimpeachable and fair, and they'll want decent housing for everyone.

The veil of ignorance forces observers to accept that the country they'd really want to be born randomly into would be a version of Switzerland or Denmark – that is to say, a country where things are pretty good wherever you end up, where the local transport system, schools, hospitals and political systems are decent and fair whether you're at the top or bottom. In other words, you know what sort of a society you want to live in. You just hadn't focused on it properly until now.

Rawls's experiment allows us to think objectively about what a fair society looks like in its details. When addressing major decisions about the allocation of resources, to overcome our own bias, we need only ask ourselves: 'how would I feel about this issue if I were stuck behind the veil of ignorance?' The fair answer emerges directly when we contemplate what we would need in order still to be adequately positioned *in the worst-case scenario*.

4. What to do next

A lot will depend on what's wrong with your society. In this sense, Rawls was usefully undoctrinaire – he recognised that the veil of ignorance experiment would throw up different issues in different contexts: in some, the priority might be to fix air pollution, in others, the school system.

But when he addressed the US of the late 20th century, Rawls could see some obvious things that needed to be done: education would have to be radically improved, the poor as well as the rich would have to be able to run for election, healthcare would have to be made attractive at all levels.

Rawls provides us with a tool to critique our current societies based on a beautifully simple experiment. We'll know we finally have made our societies fair when we will be able to say in all honesty, from a position of imaginary ignorance before our births, that we simply wouldn't mind at all what kind of circumstances our future parents might have and what sort of neighbourhoods we might be born into. The fact that we simply couldn't sanely take on such a challenge now is a measure of how deeply unfair things remain – and therefore how much we still have left to achieve.

Eastern
Philosophy

Buddha

563 BC–483 BC

The story of the Buddha's life, like all of Buddhism, is a story about confronting suffering. He was born between the 6th and 4th century BC, the son of a wealthy king in the Himalayan foothills of Nepal. It was prophesied that the young Buddha – then called Siddhartha Gautama – would either become the emperor of India or a very holy man. Since Siddhartha's father desperately wanted him to be the former, he kept the child isolated in a palace with every imaginable luxury: jewels, servants, lotus ponds, even beautiful dancing women.

For twenty-nine years, Gautama lived in bliss, protected from even the smallest misfortunes of the outside world: 'a white sunshade was held over me day and night to protect me from cold, heat, dust, dirt, and dew.' Then, at the age of 30, he left the palace for short excursions. What he saw amazed him: first he met a sick man, then an ageing man, and then a dying man. He was astounded to discover that these unfortunate people represented normal – indeed, inevitable – parts of the human condition that would one day touch him, too. Horrified and fascinated, Gautama made a fourth trip outside the palace walls – and encountered a holy man who had learned to seek spiritual life in the midst of the vastness of human suffering. Determined to find the same enlightenment, Gautama left his sleeping wife and son and walked away from the palace for good.

Gautama tried to learn from other holy men. He almost starved himself to death by avoiding all physical comforts and pleasures, as they did. Perhaps unsurprisingly, it did not bring him solace from suffering. Then he thought of a moment when he was a small boy: sitting by a river, he'd noticed that when the grass was cut, the insects and their eggs were trampled and destroyed. Seeing this, he'd felt compassion for the tiny insects.

Reflecting on his childhood compassion, Gautama felt a profound sense of peace. He ate, meditated under a fig tree, and finally reached the highest state of enlightenment:

'nirvana', which simply means 'awakening'. He became the Buddha, 'the awakened one'.

The Buddha awoke by recognising that all of creation, from distraught ants to dying human beings, is unified by suffering. Recognising this, the Buddha discovered how to best approach suffering. First, one shouldn't bathe in luxury, nor abstain from food and comforts altogether. Instead, one ought to live in moderation (the Buddha called this 'the middle way'). This allows for maximal concentration on cultivating compassion for others and seeking enlightenment. Next, the Buddha described a path to transcending suffering called 'the four noble truths.'

The first noble truth is the realisation that prompted the Buddha's journey – that there is suffering and constant dissatisfaction in the world: 'Life is difficult and brief and bound up with suffering.' The second is that this suffering is caused by our desires, and thus 'attachment is the root of all suffering.' The third truth is that we can transcend suffering by removing or managing all of our attachments. The Buddha thus made the remarkable claim that we must change our outlook, not our circumstances. We are unhappy not because we don't have a raise or a lover or enough followers, but because we are greedy, vain and insecure. By reorienting our mind, we can grow to be content.

The fourth and final noble truth the Buddha uncovered is that we can learn to move beyond suffering through what he termed 'the eightfold path'. The eightfold path involves a series of aspects of behaving 'right' and wisely: right view, right intention, right speech, right action, right livelihood, right effort, right mindfulness, and right concentration. What strikes the Western observer is the notion that wisdom is a habit, not merely an intellectual realisation. One must exercise one's nobler impulses. Understanding is only part of becoming a better person.

Seeking these correct modes of behaviour and awareness, the Buddha taught that people could transcend much

Young Prince Siddhartha with his bride and servants.

of their negative individualism – their pride, their anxiety, and the desires that made them so unhappy – and in turn they would gain compassion for all other living beings who suffered as they did. With the correct behaviour and what we now term a 'mindful attitude', people can invert negative emotions and states of mind, turning ignorance into wisdom, anger into compassion, and greed into generosity.

The Buddha travelled widely throughout northern India and southern Nepal, teaching meditation and ethical behaviour. He spoke very little about divinity or the afterlife. Instead, he regarded the state of living as the most sacred issue of all.

After the Buddha's death, his followers collected his 'sutras' (sermons or sayings) into scripture and developed texts to guide followers in meditation, ethics and mindful living. The monasteries that had developed during the Buddha's lifetime grew and multiplied throughout China and East Asia. For a time, Buddhism was particularly uncommon in India itself, and only a few quiet groups of yellow-clad monks and nuns roamed the countryside, meditating

Art being invited to support philosophy: a beautifully carved
eight-spoke wheel commonly used as a Buddhist symbol. The eight spokes
represent the eightfold path.

quietly in nature. But then, in the 3rd century BC, an Indian king named Ashoka grew troubled by the wars he had fought and converted to Buddhism. He sent monks and nuns far and wide to spread the practice.

Buddhist spiritual tradition spread across Asia and eventually throughout the world. Buddha's followers divided into two main schools: Theravada Buddhism, which colonised Southeast Asia, and Mahayana Buddhism, which took hold in China and Northeast Asia. The two groups sometimes distrust each other's scriptures and prefer their own, but they follow the same central principles passed down over two millennia. Today, there are between a half and one and a half billion Buddhists following the Buddha's teachings and seeking a more enlightened and compassionate state of mind.

Intriguingly, the Buddha's teachings are important regardless of our spiritual identification. Like the Buddha, we are all born into the world not realising how much suffering it contains, and unable to fully comprehend that misfortune, sickness and death will come to us too. As we grow older, this reality often feels overwhelming, and we may seek to avoid it altogether. But the Buddha's teachings remind us of the importance of facing suffering directly. We must do our best to liberate ourselves from our own tyrannous desires, and recognise suffering as our common connection with others, spurring us to compassion and gentleness.

Lao Tzu

6th/5th century BC–5th/4th century BC

L ittle is truly known about the Chinese philosopher Lao Tzu (sometimes also known as Laozi or Lao Tze), who is a guiding figure in Daoism (also translated as Taoism), a still popular spiritual practice. He is said to have been a record keeper in the court of the central Chinese Zhou Dynasty in the 6th century BC, and an older contemporary of Confucius. This could be true, but he may also have been entirely mythical – much like Homer in Western culture. It is certainly very unlikely that (as some legends say) he was conceived when his mother saw a falling star, or was born an old man with very long earlobes – or lived 990 years.

Lao Tzu is said to have tired of life in the Zhou court as it grew increasingly morally corrupt. So he left and rode on a water buffalo to the western border of the Chinese Empire. Although he was dressed as a farmer, the border official recognised him and asked him to write down his wisdom. According to this legend, what Lao Tzu wrote became the sacred text called the *Tao Te Ching*. After writing this, Lao Tzu is said to have crossed the border and disappeared from history, perhaps to become a hermit. In reality, the *Tao Te Ching* is likely to be the compilation of the works of many authors over time. But stories about Lao Tzu and the *Tao Te Ching* have passed down through different Chinese philosophical schools for over 2,000 years and have become wondrously embellished in the process.

Today there are at least 20 million Daoists, and perhaps even half a billion, living around the world, especially in China and Taiwan. They practise meditation, chant scriptures, and worship a variety of gods and goddesses in temples run by priests. Daoists also make pilgrimages to five sacred mountains in eastern China in order to pray at the temples and absorb spiritual energy from these holy places, which are believed to be governed by immortals.

Daoism is deeply intertwined with other branches of thought like Confucianism and Buddhism. Confucius is often believed to have been a student of Lao Tzu. Similarly, some believe that when Lao Tzu disappeared, he travelled to India and Nepal and either taught or became the Buddha. Confucianist practices to this day not only respect Lao Tzu as a great philosopher but also try to follow many of his teachings.

There is a story about the three great Asian spiritual leaders (Lao Tzu, Confucius, and Buddha). All were meant to have tasted vinegar. Confucius found it sour, much like he found the world full of degenerate people, and Buddha found it bitter, much like he found the world to be full of suffering. But Lao Tzu found the taste sweet. This is telling, because Lao Tzu's philosophy tends to look at the apparent discord in the world and see an underlying harmony guided by something called the 'Dao'.

The *Tao Te Ching* is somewhat like the Bible: it gives instructions (at times vague and generally open to multiple interpretations) on how to live a good life. It discusses the 'Dao', or the 'way' of the world, which is also the path to virtue, happiness and harmony. This way isn't inherently confusing or difficult. Lao Tzu wrote, 'the great Dao is very even, but people like to take by-ways.' In Lao Tzu's view, the problem with virtue isn't that it is difficult or unnatural, but simply is that we resist the very simple path that might make us most content.

In order to follow the Dao, we need to go beyond simply reading and thinking about it. Instead we must learn *wu wei* ('flowing' or 'effortless action'), a sort of purposeful acceptance of the way of the Dao, and live in harmony with it. This might seem lofty and bizarre, but most of Lao Tzu's suggestions are actually very simple.

First, we ought to take more time for stillness. 'To the mind that is still,' Lao Tzu said, 'the whole universe surrenders.' We need to let go of our schedules, worries and complex thoughts for a while and simply experience the world. We spend so much time rushing from one place to the next in life, but Lao Tzu reminds us 'nature does not hurry, yet

Buddha, Confucius and Lao Tzu as the 'Three Vinegar Tasters'.

everything is accomplished.' It is particularly important that we remember that certain things – grieving, growing wiser, developing a new relationship – only happen on their own schedule, like the changing of leaves or the blossoming of bulbs.

When we are still and patient, we also need to be open. 'The usefulness of a pot comes from its emptiness,' Lao Tzu said. 'Empty yourself of everything. Let your mind become still.' If we are too busy, too preoccupied with anxiety or ambition, we will miss a thousand moments of the human experience that are our natural inheritance. We need to be awake to the way light reflects off of ripples on a pond, the way other people look when they are laughing, the feeling of the wind playing with our hair. These experiences reconnect us to parts of ourselves.

This is another key point of Lao Tzu's writing: we need to be in touch with our real selves. We spend a great deal of time worrying about who we ought to become, but we should instead take time to be who we already are at heart. We might rediscover a generous impulse, or a playful side we had forgotten. Our ego is often in the way of our true self, which must be found by being receptive to the outside world rather than focusing on some critical, too-ambitious internal image. 'When I let go of what I am,' Lao Tzu wrote, 'I become what I might be.'

What is the best book about philosophy one could look at? For Lao Tzu, it wasn't a volume (or a scroll) but the book of nature. It is the natural world, in particular its rocks, water, stone, trees and clouds, that offers us constant, eloquent lessons in wisdom and calm – if only we remembered to pay attention a little more often.

In Lao Tzu's eyes, most of what is wrong with us stems from our failure to live 'in accordance with nature'. Our envy, our rage, our manic ambition, our frustrated sense of entitlement, all of it stems from our failure to live as nature suggests we should. Of course, 'nature' has many moods, and one can see in it almost anything one likes depending on one's perspective. But when Lao Tzu refers to nature, he is thinking of some very particular aspects of the natural world; he focuses in on a range of attitudes he sees in it which, if we manifested them more regularly in our own lives, would help us find serenity and fulfilment.

Lao Tzu liked to compare different parts of nature to different virtues. He said, 'The best people are like water, which benefits all things and does not compete with them. It stays in lowly places that others reject. This is why it is so similar to the Way (Dao).' Each part of nature can remind us of a quality we admire and should cultivate ourselves – the strength of the mountains, the resilience of trees, the cheerfulness of flowers.

Daoism advises us to look to trees as case studies in graceful endurance. They are constantly tormented by the elements, and yet because they are an ideal mixture of the supple and the resilient, they respond without some of our customary rigidity and defensiveness and therefore survive and thrive in ways we often don't. Trees are an image of patience too, for they sit out long days and nights without complaint, adjusting themselves to the slow shift of the seasons – showing no ill temper in a storm, no desire to wander from their spot for an impetuous journey; they are content to keep their many slender fingers deep in the clammy soil, metres from their central stems and far from the tallest leaves, which hold the rainwater in their palms.

Water is another favourite Daoist source of wisdom, for it is soft and seemingly gentle, and yet, when it is given sufficient time, is powerful enough to mould and reshape stone. We might adopt some of its patient, quiet determination when dealing with certain family members or frustrating political situations in the workplace.

Daoist philosophy gave rise to a school of Chinese landscape painting still admired today for awakening us to the virtues of the natural world.

At one level, it seems strange to claim that our characters might evolve in the company of a waterfall or a mountain, a pine tree or a celandine, objects that, after all, have no conscious concerns, and so, it would seem, cannot either encourage or censor behaviour. And yet an inanimate object may, to come to the lynchpin of Lao Tzu's claim for the beneficial effects of nature, still work an influence on those around it. Natural scenes have the power to suggest certain values to us – mountains: dignity; pines: resolution; flowers: kindness – and, in unobtrusive ways, may therefore act as inspirations to virtue.

The idea that the contemplation of nature is a source of perspective and tranquillity is well known in theory, but so easy to overlook because we take it for granted and never give it the time and focus required.

Often our heads are filled with unhelpful phrases and ideas: things that have wormed their way into our imaginations and, by stirring up anxieties, make it harder for us to cope. For example: 'Have the courage to live out your dreams', 'Never compromise', 'Fight until you win ...' These can (in certain cases) be a kind of poison, for which Lao Tzu's words – combined with natural scenes – are the ideal antidote.

Nature does not hurry
yet everything is accomplished.

Life is a series of natural and spontaneous changes.
Do not resist them.
That only causes sorrow.

The words of Lao Tzu set a mood. They are peaceful, reassuring and gentle. And this is a frame of mind we often find it difficult to hold onto, though it serves us well for many tasks in life: getting the children off to school, watching one's hair go grey, accepting the greater talent of a rival, realising that one's marriage will never be very easy ...

Be content with what you have.
Rejoice in the way things are.

It would be a mistake to take Lao Tzu's sayings literally in all cases. To rejoice in the way everything happens (a mediocre first draft, a car crash, a wrongful imprisonment, a brutal stabbing ...) would be foolish. But what he says is, on certain occasions, extremely helpful: when your child has a different view of life from you but one that is full of unexpected insight nevertheless; when you are not invited out but have a chance to stay home and examine your thoughts for a change; when your bicycle is perfectly nice – even though it's not made of carbon fibre.

We know that nature is good for our bodies. Lao Tzu's contribution has been to remind us that it is also full of what deserves to be called philosophical wisdom: lessons that can make a particular impression on us because they reach us through our eyes and ears, rather than just our reason.

Of course, there are issues that must be addressed by action, and there are times for ambition. Yet Lao Tzu's work is important for Daoists and non-Daoists alike, especially in a modern world distracted by technology and focused on what seem to be constant, sudden and severe changes. His words serve as a reminder of the importance of stillness, openness and reconciliation with inevitable natural forces.

Confucius

551–479 BC

W e know very little for certain about the life of the Chinese philosopher Confucius (a westernised version of his name, which means 'Master Kong'). He is said to have been born in 551 BC in China; he may have been a student of the Daoist master Lao Tzu. According to tradition, he began government service aged 32 and served many roles, including Minister of Crime under Duke Ding in the state of Lu. However, when Confucius was 56, he and the duke fell out over the duke's excesses, and so Confucius left the court and wandered for twelve years.

Confucius presented himself as a 'transmitter who invented nothing', because he believed he was teaching the natural path to good behaviour passed down from older, divine masters. Around the 2nd century BC, Confucius's works were collected into the *Analects* (Lunyu), a collection of sayings written down by his followers. These are not always commandments, because Confucius didn't like prescribing strict rules. Instead, he believed that if he simply lived virtuously, he would inspire others to do the same. For example, one of the short passages in the *Analects* is:

> The stable burned down when Confucius was at court. On his return, he said, 'Has any man been hurt?' He did not ask about the horses.

In this simple three-sentence story, we are able to contemplate the implied value of human lives over objects or horses, and to wonder if we would have done the same.

Some of the morals Confucius taught are easily recognisable – most notably his version of the 'Golden Rule': 'Do not do to others what you do not want done to yourself'. But some of them also sound very strange or old-fashioned to modern ears (especially to Western ones). We need his advice all the more for this; it serves as an antidote to the troubles we currently face. Here are a few examples of what Confucius helps us remember:

Silk painting (probably Sung Dynasty) showing Chinese philosopher and teacher Confucius lecturing students in the *Classics of Filial Piety* around 500 BC.

1. Ceremony is important

The *Analects* are a long and seemingly disorganised book of short events, filled with strange conversations between Confucius and his disciples, like this one:

> Tsze-kung wished to do away with the offering of a sheep connected with the inauguration of the first day of each month. The master said, 'Tsze, you love the sheep; I love the ceremony.'

At first this is baffling, if not also humorous. But Confucius is reminding Tsze – and us – about the importance of ceremony.

In the modern world we tend to shun ceremony and see this as a good thing – a sign of intimacy, or a lack of pretension. Many of us seek informality and would like nothing more than to be told 'just make yourself at home!' when visiting a friend. But Confucius insisted on the importance of rituals. The reason he loved ceremonies more than sheep is that he believed in the value of *li*: etiquette, tradition and ritual.

This might seem very outdated and conservative at first glance. But in fact many of us long for particular rituals – that meal mum cooked for us whenever we were sick, for example, or the yearly birthday outing, or our wedding vows. We understand that certain premeditated, deliberate and precise gestures stir our emotions deeply. Rituals make our intentions clear, and they help us understand how to behave. Confucius taught that a person who combines compassion (*ren*) and rituals (*li*) correctly is a 'superior man', virtuous and morally powerful.

2. We should treat our parents with reverence

Confucius had very strict ideas about how we should behave towards our parents. He believed that we should obey them when we are young, care for them when they are old, mourn at length when they die and make sacrifices in their memory thereafter. 'In serving his parents, a son may remonstrate with them, but gently', he said. 'When he sees that they do not incline to follow his advice, he shows an increased degree of reverence, but does not abandon his purpose; and should they punish him, he does not allow himself to murmur'. He even said that we should not travel far away while our parents are alive and should cover for their crimes. This attitude is known as *filial piety* (*xiào*).

This sounds strange in the modern age, when many of us leave our parents' homes as teenagers and rarely return to visit. We may even see our parents as strangers, arbitrarily thrust upon us by fate. After all, our parents are so out of touch, so pitifully human in their shortcomings, so difficult, so judgemental – and they have such bad taste in music. Yet

Confucius recognised that in many ways moral life begins in the family. We cannot truly be caring, wise, grateful and conscientious unless we remember mum's birthday,

3. We should be obedient to honourable people

Modern society is very egalitarian. We believe that we're born equal, each uniquely special, and should ultimately be able to say and do what we like. We reject many rigid, hierarchical roles. Yet Confucius told his followers, 'Let the ruler be a ruler, the subject a subject, a father a father, and a son a son.'

This might sound jarring, but it is in fact important to realise that there are people worthy of deep veneration. We need to be modest enough to recognise the people whose experience or accomplishments outweigh our own. We also should practise peaceably doing what these people need, ask, or command. Confucius explained, 'The relation between superiors and inferiors is like that between the wind and the grass. The grass must bend, when the wind blows across it.'

4. Cultivated knowledge can be more important than creativity

Modern culture places a lot of emphasis on creativity – unique insights that come to us suddenly. But Confucius was adamant about the importance of the universal wisdom that comes from years of hard work and reflection. He listed compassion (*ren*) and ritual propriety (*li*) among three other virtues: justice (*yi*), knowledge (*zhi*) and integrity (*xin*). These were known as the 'Five Constant Virtues'. While Confucius believed that people were inherently good, he also saw that virtues like these must be constantly cultivated like plants in a garden. He told his followers:

> At fifteen, I had my mind bent on learning. At thirty, I stood firm. At forty, I had no doubts. At fifty, I knew the decrees of Heaven. At sixty,

my ear was an obedient organ for the reception
of truth. At seventy, I could follow what my heart
desired, without transgressing what was right.

He spoke about moral character and wisdom as the work of
a lifetime.

Of course, a burst of inspiration may well be what we
need to start our business or redo our rough draft or even
reinvent our life. But we also need to devote more energy to
slowly changing our habits, for the core of who we are is
determined by ingrained patterns of behaviour.

***

After travelling for many years, Confucius returned to his
homeland at the age of 68 and devoted himself to teaching. He is said to have died in 479 BC at the age of 72 – an
auspicious and magical number. He died without reforming
the duke and his officials. But after his death, his followers
created schools and temples in his honour across East Asia,
passing his teachings along for over 2,000 years. (They also
kept his genealogy, and more than 2 million people alive
today claim to be his direct descendants.) At first, Confucian scholars were persecuted in some areas during the Qin
Dynasty (3rd century BC). But in the later Han Dynasty (3rd
century BC to 3rd century AD), Confucianism was made the
official philosophy of the Chinese government and remained
central to its bureaucracy for nearly 2,000 years. For a time,
his teachings were followed in conjunction with those of Lao
Tzu and the Buddha, so that Daoism, Confucianism, and
Buddhism were held as fully compatible spiritual practices.
Perhaps most importantly, Confucian thought has been a
huge influence on Eastern political ideas about morality,
obedience and good leadership.

Today, millions of people still follow Confucius's
teachings as a spiritual or religious discipline, and observe

Confucian rituals in temples and at home. He is called by many superlatives, including 'Laudably Declarable Lord Ni', 'Extremely Sage Departed Teacher', and 'Model Teacher for Ten Thousand Ages'. He remains a steadfast spiritual guide.

We might find Confucian virtues strange or old-fashioned, but this is what ultimately makes them all the more important and compelling. We need them as a corrective to our own excesses. The modern world is almost entirely un-Confucian – informal, egalitarian and full of innovation. So we are conversely at risk of becoming impulsive, irreverent and thoughtless without a little advice from Confucius about good behaviour – and sheep.

Sen no Rikyū

1522–1591

I n the West, philosophers write long non-fiction books, often using incomprehensible words, and limit their involvement with the world to lectures and committee meetings. In the East, and especially in the Zen tradition, philosophers write poems, rake gravel, go on pilgrimages, practise archery, write aphorisms on scrolls, chant and, in the case of one of the very greatest Zen thinkers, Sen no Rikyū, involve themselves in teaching people how to drink tea in consoling and therapeutic ways.

Sen no Rikyū was born in 1522 in the wealthy seaport of Sakai, near present-day Osaka. His father, Tanaka Yohyoue, was a warehouse owner who worked in the fish trade and wished his son to join him in business. But Rikyū turned away from commercial life and went in search of wisdom and self-understanding instead. He became fascinated by Zen Buddhism, apprenticed himself to a few masters and took to a life of wandering the countryside with few possessions. We remember him today because of the contributions he made to the reform and appreciation of the *chanoyu*, the Japanese tea ceremony.

The Japanese had been drinking tea since the 9th century, the practice having been imported from China by merchants and monks. The drink was considered healthy as well as calming and spiritual. But it was Rikyū's achievement to put the tea ceremony on a more rigorous and profound philosophical footing. Thanks to his efforts, which were both practical and intellectual, drinking tea in highly ritualised and thoughtful ways, in particular buildings that he helped to design, became an integral part of Zen Buddhist practice; as central to this spiritual philosophy as poetry or meditation.

The Japan of his era had grown image-conscious and money-focused. Rikyū promoted an alternative set of values that he termed *wabi-sabi* – a compound word combining *wabi,* or simplicity, with *sabi,* an appreciation of the imperfect. Across fields ranging from architecture to interior

The Tai-an tearoom in Kyoto, designed by Rikyū.

design, philosophy to literature, Rikyū awakened in the Japanese a taste for the pared down and the authentic, for the undecorated and the humble.

His particular focus was the tea ceremony, which Rikyū believed to hold a superlative potential to promote *wabi-sabi*. He made a number of changes to the rituals and aesthetics of the ceremony. He began by revolutionising the space in which the tea ceremony was held. It had grown common for wealthy people to build extremely elaborate teahouses in prominent public places, where they served as venues for worldly gatherings and displays of status. Rikyū now argued that the teahouse should be shrunk to a mere two metres square, that it should be tucked away in secluded gardens and that its door should be made deliberately a little too small, so that all who came into it, even the mightiest, would have to bow and feel equal to others. The idea was to create a barrier between the teahouse and the world outside. The very path to the teahouse was to pass around trees and stones, to create a meander that would help break ties with the ordinary realm.

Properly performed, a tea ceremony was meant to promote what Rikyū termed *wa*, or harmony, which would emerge as participants rediscovered their connections to nature: in their garden hut, smelling of unvarnished wood, moss and tea leaves, they would be able to feel the wind and hear birds outside – and feel at one with the non-human sphere. Then might come an emotion known as *kei*, or sympathy, the fruit of sitting in a confined space with others and being able to converse with them free of the pressures and artifice of the social world. A successful ceremony was to leave its participants with a feeling of *jaku*, or tranquillity, one of the most central concepts in Rikyū's gentle, calming philosophy.

Rikyū's prescriptions for the ceremony extended to the instruments employed. He argued that tea ceremonies shouldn't henceforth rely on expensive or conventionally beautiful cups or teapots. He liked worn bamboo tea scoops that made a virtue of their age. Because in Zen philosophy everything is impermanent, imperfect and incomplete, objects that are themselves marked by time and haphazard marks can, suggested Rikyū, embody a distinct wisdom and promote it in their users.

It was one of Rikyū's achievements to take an act that in the West is one of the most routine and unremarkable activities and imbue it with a solemnity and depth of meaning akin to a Catholic Mass. Every aspect of the tea ceremony, from the patient boiling of the water to the measuring out of green tea powder, was coherently related to Zen's philosophical tenets about the importance of humility, the need to sympathise with and respect nature, and the sense of the importance of the transient nature of existence.

It's open-ended where this approach to everyday life might go. It leaves open the possibility that many actions and daily habits might, with sufficient creative imagination, become similarly elevated, important and rewarding in our lives. The point isn't so much that we should take part in tea ceremonies, rather that we should make aspects of our everyday spiritual lives more tangible by allying certain materials and sensuous rituals.

Rikyū reminds us that there is a latent sympathy between big ideas about life and the little everyday things, such as certain drinks, cups, implements and smells. These are not cut off from the big themes; they can make those themes more alive for us. It is the task of philosophy not just to formulate ideas, but also to work out mechanisms by which they may stick more firmly and viscerally in our minds.

Matsuo Bashō

1644–1694

n the West, we have a vague sense that poetry is good for our 'souls', making us sensitive and wiser. Yet we don't always know how this should work. Poetry has a hard time finding its way into our lives in any practical sense. In the East, however, some poets – like the 17th-century Buddhist monk and poet Matsuo Bashō – knew precisely what effect their poetry was meant to produce: it was a medium designed to guide us to wisdom and calm, as these terms are defined in Zen Buddhist philosophy.

Matsuo Bashō was born in 1644 in Ueno, in the Iga province of Japan. As a child he became a servant of the nobleman Tōdō Yoshitada, who taught him to compose poems in the 'haiku' style. Traditionally, haikus contain three parts, two images and a concluding line that helps to juxtapose them. The best known haiku in Japanese literature is called 'Old Pond', by Bashō himself:

Old pond ...
A frog leaps in
Water's sound.

It is all (deceptively) simple – and, when one is in the right, generous frame of mind, very beautiful.

After Yoshitada died in 1666, Bashō left home and wandered for many years before moving to the city of Edo, where he became famous and widely published. However, Bashō grew melancholy and often shunned company, and so until his death in 1694, he alternated between travelling widely on foot and living in a small hut on the outskirts of the city.

Bashō was an exceptional poet, but he did not believe in the modern idea of 'art for art's sake'. Instead, he hoped that his poetry would bring his readers into special mental states valued by Zen. His poetry reflects two of the most important Zen ideals: *wabi* and *sabi*. *Wabi*, for Bashō, meant satisfaction with simplicity and austerity, while *sabi* refers to a contented solitude. (These are the same mindsets sought in the

Zen tea ceremony defined by Rikyū). It was nature, more than anything else, that was thought to foster *wabi* and *sabi*, and it is therefore, unsurprisingly, one of Bashō's most frequent topics. Take this spring scene, which appears to ask so little of the world, and is attuned to an appreciation of the everyday:

> First cherry
> budding
> by peach blossoms.

Bashō's poetry is of an almost shocking simplicity at the level of theme. There are no analyses of politics or love triangles or family dramas. The point is to remind readers that what really matters is to be able to be content with our own company, to appreciate the moment we are in and to be attuned to the very simplest things life has to offer: the changing of the seasons, the sound of our neighbours laughing across the street, the little surprises we encounter when we travel. Take this gem:

> Violets –
> how precious on
> a mountain path.

Bashō also used natural scenes to remind his readers that flowers, weather and other natural elements are – like our own lives – ever-changing and fleeting. Time and the changing of weathers and scenes need to be attended to, as harbingers of our own deaths:

> Yellow rose petals
> thunder –
> a waterfall.

This transience of life may sometimes be heartbreaking, but it is also what makes every moment valuable.

Bashō liked to paint as well as write, and many of his works still exist, usually with the related haikus written alongside them.

In literature, Bashō valued *karumi*, or lightness. He wanted it to seem as if children had written it. He abhorred pretension and elaboration. As he told his disciples, 'In my view a good poem is one in which the form of the verse, and the joining of its two parts, seem light as a shallow river flowing over its sandy bed.'

The ultimate goal of this 'lightness' was to allow readers to escape the burdens of the self – one's petty peculiarities and circumstances – in order to experience unity with the world beyond. Bashō believed that poetry could, at its best, allow one to feel a brief sensation of merging with the natural world. One may become – through language – the rock, the water, the stars, leading one to an enlightened frame of mind known as *muga*, or a loss-of-awareness-of-oneself.

We can see Bashō's concept of *muga*, or self-forgetting, at work in the way he invites us almost to inhabit his subjects, even if they are some rather un-poetic dead fish:

Fish shop
how cold the lips
of salted bream.

In a world full of social media profiles and crafted resumes, it might seem odd to want to escape our individuality – after all, we carefully groom ourselves to stand out from the rest of the world. Bashō reminds us that *muga*, or self-forgetting, is valuable because it allows us to break free from the incessant thrum of desire and incompleteness that otherwise haunts all human lives.

Bashō suffered for long periods from deep melancholy; he travelled the dangerous back roads of the Japanese countryside with little more than writing supplies, and he spent some truly unglamorous nights:

Fleas and lice biting;
awake all night
a horse pissing close to my ear.

Yet *muga* freed Bashō – and it can also free us – from the tyranny of glum moments of individual circumstance. His poetry constantly invites us to appreciate what we have, and to see how infinitesimal and unimportant our personal difficulties are in the vast scheme of the universe.

Bashō's poetry was a clever tool for enlightenment and revelation – through the artfully simple arrangement of words. The poems are valuable not because they are beautiful (though they are this too) but because they can serve as a catalyst for some of the most important states of the soul. They remind both the writer and the reader that contentment relies on knowing how to derive pleasure from simplicity, and how to escape (even if only for a while) the tyranny of being ourselves.

Sociology

St Benedict

AD 480–543

The fiercely individualistic spirit of our age tends to take a dim view of two big ideas: having any sort of rules governing everyday life; and pooling resources to live together in a communal way.

We've come to see ourselves as, each one of us, needing to invent our own unique way of life, governed by our instincts and what we most feel like doing in the moment. As for the idea of community, though it might cross our minds every now and then (especially when we contrast how fun it was at college and how rather arduous and lonely it might be now), nothing in modern capitalism enables us to imagine how we'd ever manage to make the group, rather than the 'I', the centre of things. Everything from domestic appliances to mortgages to romantic love enforces the idea of the lone or couple-based unit. We're influenced by an ideology of personal freedom, where pursuing private ends is seen as the only path to happiness – though the results do not necessarily match the hopes. The joys of being part of a gang are simply not on the radar.

These attitudes, which we take for granted today, contrast so strongly with an idea that flourished for very long periods in many parts of the world and continue to have much to teach us about our real longings: monasticism. Monasticism puts forward the bold thesis that people can actually lead the most fruitful, productive and happy lives when they get together into controlled, organised groups of friends, have some clear rules, and direct themselves towards a few big ambitions. Even if you're not planning on setting up a secular version of a monastery any time soon (though we believe – as you'll see – that this would be no bad idea), monasticism deserves to be studied for the lessons it yields about the limits to modern individualism.

One of the earliest and most influential figures in the history of monasticism – in its Christian, Western guise – was a Roman nobleman living at the end of the 5th century, by the name of Benedict. In his twenties, Benedict studied philosophy in Rome. For a time, he shared the dissipation, wastefulness and lack of genuine ambition of his wealthy fellow students, until he suddenly became weary and ashamed and went off to the mountains in search of a better way of living. Other people soon joined him, and he naturally found his way to starting a few small communities. From there, it was a natural step to write an instruction manual for his followers, with a simple and emphatic title: *Rule*.

Within his lifetime, hundreds of people signed up to live in communities governed by his principles. And for over a thousand years, hugely impressive institutions founded in his name played a central role in European civilisation.

Benedict was an intensely devoted Christian. But it's not necessary to share his beliefs in order to recognise that his recommendations tapped into something fundamental about human nature. His insights into communities are – in fact – detachable from the particular religious environment in which they were originally developed.

1. The pleasures of rules

The rules for living drawn up by Benedict were beautifully precise and detailed. His starting point is a pessimistic view of human nature. He's acutely aware of how readily our lives go off the rails in big and little ways when we just do whatever comes to mind.

His rules include instructions on:

a. Eating

Rule 39: Except the sick, who are very weak, let all abstain entirely from eating the flesh of four-footed animals.

Benedict was very concerned about eating the sort of foods that make you sluggish, self-pitying and slow. He recommended that one should consume modest but nutritious meals only twice a day. (An occasional glass of wine was allowed.) Lamb and beef were to be avoided, but chicken and fish in small quantities were ideal. Benedict was wise enough to see that being an intellectual was entirely compatible with thinking a lot about what one should eat – and his search was for the sort of food that would best nourish and nurture our minds. He thought that everyone should sit together at long tables, but he was also aware of how much idle banter there can be at meals, so he advised that diners should generally listen to someone reading from an important and interesting book while they made their way through lemon chicken with courgettes and beans. If they needed something, they should make a signal with their hands.

b. Silence
Benedict knew the benefits of silence. When you've got a big task on, concentration is key. He knew all about distraction: how easy it is to want to keep checking up on the latest developments, how addictive the gossip of the city can be … That's why his communities tended to be set up in remote locations, often close to mountains, and his buildings featured heavy walls, quiet courtyards and beautifully serene living quarters.

c. Hair and clothing
Fashion was, in Benedict's time, as in ours, a huge source of interest, expense and attention. Benedict was himself a handsome man, but he was keen to put a limit on how much he or anyone else would think about what they had to wear every day. That's why he recommended that everyone in his community wear the same clothes: plain and useful, not too expensive, and easy to wash. What's more, everyone should have their hair cut the same way – very, very short.

d. Balance
Rule 35: Let the brethren serve one another, and let no one be excused from the kitchen service except by reason of sickness.

If you are going to be concentrating quite a lot on ideas and intellectual activities, Benedict knew it could be really helpful also to do some physical activity every day; something repetitive and soothing might be ideal, like sweeping the floor or weeding a row of lettuces. You might also occasionally take your turn preparing a meal or doing the washing up – everyone does. But mostly it will be other people's turns, so you'll be free – and guilt-free.

e. Early nights
You have to go to bed early and get up very early, Benedict knew that. Routine is crucial. You don't suddenly want to be engaging in a conversation that starts at 11 p.m., gets rather heated around midnight and leaves you tossing and unable to sleep at 1 a.m. Get used to winding down systematically, focusing your thoughts and arranging your mind for the next day (a lot of good thinking happens when we're asleep).

f. No porn addiction
Benedict knew that sex gets in the way. But it's no use thinking endlessly, in repetitive cycles, about naked people when you've got really key things to get on with. He wasn't a prude, and had a great deal of fun as a student, but he knew how short life was and how much he had to do. That's why he recommended that in the ideal community everyone should dress in a fairly demure way and that there should be no encouragement given to sexual feelings. Sex simply plays havoc with any attempts to concentrate.

g. Art/architecture
At many strategic points in Benedict's buildings, you'll see beautiful or dramatic works of art that remind you of some important idea or help you get into a useful mood. Benedict didn't think that good art and architecture were luxuries: these were vital supports for our inner lives. He understood that we were likely to take our cue about how to be inside

Bedroom, designed by John Pawson,
Benedictine Monastery of Novy Dvur, Czech Republic.

ourselves by looking around at the moods emanating from
the walls around us. That's why Benedictine monasteries
have long employed the best architects and artists, from Palladio and Veronese to John Pawson in our own times. If
you're going to live together, it makes sense to create a home
that is as uplifting and as calming as can be.

The point isn't so much that we should particularly embrace
the specific rules drawn up by Benedict; rather he is showing
us something more general: the potential for rules to help us
live well.

There are periods in life (and history) when it seems as
if *gaining* freedom is the key to a great time. To a 4-year-
old, who has always been told when to get up, when bath
time is and when the lights go out, it's natural to suppose
that it's wonderful to be old enough to decide for oneself.
But rules about how to live – and the authority to get us to
stick with them – start to look more important, even wise,
when we have a more urgent sense of the *problems* to which
wise rules are possible *solutions*, when we realise how prone

we are to distraction, dissipation, weakness of will and late-night squabbles. At that point, we may learn that rules – far from being interruptions of our native good selves – are really the restraints that safeguard our best possibilities. They make us truer to who we want to be than a system that allows us to do anything whatsoever.

2. The highlights of community

Benedict established his first monastery at Monte Cassino – about halfway between Rome and Naples. It's still there (although it had to be rebuilt after it was damaged by Allied bombing in 1944).

The lofty – and rather inaccessible – location wasn't an accident. The point of going to a monastery was to avoid the distractions that might take one's attention away from what's really important. We might not share Benedict's idea of what's important, but we deeply share the underlying concern: how to focus effectively on what we really want to accomplish and not get distracted all the time.

Benedict acknowledges that it's hard for creatures like us to ponder the nature of God, examine our own failings or decode the meaning of some obscure Biblical passage – when our natural instincts draw us to eating too much, having sex, scratching our bottoms, getting drunk and gossiping.

Under Benedict's inspiration, monasteries made a range of dazzling innovations in the field of non-distraction studies. Benedict proposed that, to avoid distraction, one might need to live far removed from towns and cities. The architecture should be rather grand and imposing – as a continual reminder of the importance of what one is doing. One should live on-site and not commute in. The walls are going to have to be high and thick. There can't be lots of doors or big picture windows looking out onto the wider world. Walls, cloisters and being a good few miles from the local tavernas certainly help in the fight against distraction.

The ideal of the monastic community is that living collectively enables people to accomplish more than would be possible by individual effort.

Some aspects of how Benedict imagined that going – like the segregation of the sexes – don't seem so compelling. But we still need some of the advantages of communal living.

It's something we can see in action in the housing market. The Royal Crescent in Bath, for instance, is an example of collaboration around accommodation and architecture. Today, around 200 people live in this building, mostly in modestly sized flats. By pooling the fabric of their homes, they collectively share one of the world's greatest urban structures. Individually, they all have to deal with phone plans, Wi-Fi systems, electricity bills, council taxes, plumbing emergencies. But quite possibly one administrator could do it all for them – with an immense saving in terms of frustration. We'd all gain so much by giving up a little of our famed, but actually rather exhausting, individualism.

Monasteries frequently evolved into successful business centres, operating the major industries of the day: farming and mining, schools, hospitals and the early versions of hotels.

We think we understand collaboration in business. But actually we are generally only looking at quite a limited range of options. We still assume that in a medium-sized company, 157 people will all need to travel in by slightly different routes, all park their cars, and, in the evenings, all spend their money individually on chicken noodles, rent, a sofa bed and going to a bar.

Many big undertakings of the modern world could be pursued so much more effectively from within a monastery: a great graphic design company, a biotech corporation, a television production firm.

Conclusion
Communal life can be much more enjoyable and less stressful than the nuclear family, with all its disappointments and

pressures. We keep imagining that happiness lies in finding one other very special person (then rail against them for not being perfect enough) or else that it must be about becoming something extraordinary ourselves – rather than joining lots of other very ordinary people to make something superlative. We'd generally be so much better off joining a team. We'd be able to do things on a grander scale and get them done more easily – and more often have our minds in proper focus. That's why Benedict remains a provocative and useful thinker.

Alexis de Tocqueville

1805–1859

Democracy was achieved by such a long, arduous and heroic struggle that it can feel embarrassing – even shameful – to feel a little disappointed by it. We know that at key historical moments people have made profound sacrifices so that we can, every now and then, place a cross next to the name of a candidate on a ballot sheet. For generations, across large parts of the world, democracy was a secret, desperate hope. But today, we're likely to go through periods of feeling irritated and bored by our democratically elected politicians. We're disappointed by the parties and sceptical that elections make a difference. And yet, not to support democracy, to be frankly against democracy, is not a possible attitude either. We appear to be utterly committed to democracy and yet constantly disappointed and frustrated by it.

Perhaps the best guide to some of these feelings, and to modern democracy in general, is a French 19th-century aristocrat, Alexis de Tocqueville, who – in the early 1830s – travelled around the United States studying the political culture of the world's first truly democratic nation and then compiled his thoughts in one of the greatest works of political philosophy, *Democracy in America*, published in France in 1835. For Tocqueville, democracy was a highly exotic and novel political option. He'd been born in 1805, when Napoleon was the populist dictator of half of Europe. After Waterloo, the Bourbon kings came back – and while there were elections, the franchise was extremely limited. But, Tocqueville presciently believed, democracy was going to be the big idea of the future all over the world. What, he wanted to know, would that be like? What would happen when societies that had been governed for generations by small aristocratic elites and who inherited their wealth and power, started to choose their leaders in elections in which pretty much the whole adult population could vote?

That's why Tocqueville went to America: to see what the future would be like. He got there courtesy of a grant from the French government, who wanted him to study the American prison system and compile a report from which it could learn some lessons. But Tocqueville wasn't so interested in prisons and made it clear in letters to friends that his real reason for going was to study American morals, mentalities and economic and political processes. He arrived in New York, together with his friend Gustave de Beaumont, a magistrate, in May of 1831 – and then embarked on a long journey around the new nation that was to last until February 1832.

Tocqueville and Beaumont went as far west as Michigan, which was then frontier country, and there got a sense of the vastness of the American Midwestern landscape. They also went down to New Orleans, but most of their time was spent in Boston, New York and Philadelphia. They met everyone: presidents, lawyers, bankers, cobblers, hairdressers ... and even shook hands with the last surviving signatory of the Declaration of Independence, a man called Charles Carroll.

The observations that Tocqueville made on America are droll, often funny and frequently very acerbic.

1. On New York:

To a Frenchman the aspect of the city is bizarre and not very agreeable. One sees neither dome, nor bell tower, nor great edifice, with the result that one has the constant impression of being in a suburb.

2. On native pride:

I doubt if one could extract from Americans the smallest truth unfavourable to their country. Most of them boast about it without discrimination, and with an impertinence disagreeable to strangers ... Generally speaking there is a lot of small-town pettiness in their makeup ... We have not yet met a really outstanding man.

3. On the middle-class spirit:

This country illustrates the most complete external development of the middle classes, or rather that the whole of society seems to have turned into one middle class. No one seems to have the elegant manners and refined politeness of the upper classes in Europe. ... One is at once struck by something vulgar, and a disagreeable casualness of behaviour ...

4. On attitudes to the Native Americans:

In the midst of this American society, so well policed, so sententious, so charitable, a cold selfishness and complete insensibility prevails when it is a question of the natives of the country.

The Americans of the United States do not let their dogs hunt the Indians as do the Spaniards in Mexico, but at the bottom it is the same pitiless feeling which here, as everywhere else, animates the European race. This world here belongs to us, they tell themselves every day: the Indian race is destined for final destruction which one cannot prevent and which it is not desirable to delay. Heaven has not made them to become civilised; it is necessary that they die. Besides I do not want to get mixed up in it. I will not do anything against them: I will limit myself to providing everything that will hasten their ruin. In time I will have their lands and will be innocent of their death.

Satisfied with his reasoning, the American goes to church where he hears the minister of the gospel repeat every day that all men are brothers, and that the Eternal Being who has made them all in like image, has given them all the duty to help one another.

GEORGE CATLIN, *Stu-mick-o-súcks, Buffalo Bull's Back Fat, Head Chief, Blood Tribe*, 1832

5. Then again, he wasn't so keen on Native Americans himself:

> I was full of recollections of M. de Chateaubriand and of Cooper, and I was expecting to find the natives of America savages, but savages on whose face nature had stamped the marks of some of the proud virtues which liberty brings forth. I expected to find a race of men little different from Europeans, whose bodies had been developed by the strenuous exercise of hunting and war, and who would lose nothing by being seen naked.
>
> Judge my amazement at seeing the picture that follows. The Indians whom I saw that evening were small in stature, their limbs, as far as one could tell under their clothes, were thin and not wiry, their skin instead of being red as is generally thought, was dark bronze and such as at first sight seemed very like that of Negroes. Their black hair fell with singular stiffness on their neck and sometimes on their shoulders. Generally their mouths were disproportionately large, and the expression on their faces ignoble and mischievous.
>
> There was however a great deal of European in their features, but one would have said that they came from the lowest mob of our great European cities. Their physiognomy told of that profound degradation which only long abuse of the benefits of civilisation can give, but yet they were still savages.

But there was a lot to admire in America as well: the prettiness of the women, the healthy simplicity of the food, the jovial frankness of conversations, the comfort of the hotels. Above all, Tocqueville loved the wilderness of America:

> It is impossible to imagine anything more beautiful than the North or Hudson River. The great width of

the stream, the admirable richness of the north bank and the steep mountains which border its eastern margins make it one of the most admirable sights in the world ... We are envying every day the first Europeans who two hundred years ago discovered for the first time the mouth of the Hudson and mounted its current, when its two banks were covered with numberless forests and only the smoke of the savages was to be seen ...

When Tocqueville arrived in New York he was setting foot in the only large-scale, reasonably secure democracy on the planet. And he saw himself as advancing a highly nuanced and helpful enquiry: what are the social consequences of democracy? What should one expect a democratic society to be like?

Tocqueville was particularly alive to the problematic and potentially dark sides of democracy. Five issues struck him in particular:

1. Democracy breeds materialism

In the society that Tocqueville knew from childhood, making money did not seem to be at the forefront of most people's minds. The poor (who were the overwhelming majority) had almost no chance of acquiring wealth. So while they cared about having enough to eat, money as such was not part of how they thought about themselves or their ambitions: there was simply no chance. On the other hand, the tiny upper stratum of landed aristocrats did not need to make money – and regarded it as shameful to work for money at all, or to be involved in trade or commerce. As a result, for very different reasons, money was not the way to judge a life.

However, the Americans Tocqueville met all readily believed that through hard work it was possible to make a fortune and that to do so was wholly admirable and right. There was hence no suspicion whatever of the rich, a certain moral judgement against the poor, and an immense respect for the capacity to make money. It seemed, quite simply, the only achievement that Americans thought worth respecting. For example, in America, observed Tocqueville, a book that does not make money – because it does not sell well – cannot be good, because the test of all goodness is money. And anything that makes a profit must be admirable in every way. It was a flattened, unnuanced view that made Tocqueville see the advantages of the relatively more subtle, multipolar status systems of Europe, where one might (on a good day) be deemed good, but poor – or rich, but vulgar.

Democracy and capitalism had created a relatively equitable, but also very flat and oppressive way for humans to judge each other.

2. Democracy breeds envy and shame

Travelling around the United States, Tocqueville discerned an unexpected ill corroding the souls of the citizens of the new republic. Americans had much, but this affluence did not stop them from wanting ever more and from suffering whenever they saw someone else with assets they lacked. In a chapter of *Democracy in America* entitled 'Causes Of The Restless Spirit Of Americans In The Midst Of Their Prosperity', he sketched an enduring analysis of the relationship between dissatisfaction and high expectation, between envy and equality:

When all the privileges of birth and fortune are abolished, when all professions are accessible to all, and a man's own energies may place him at the top of any one of them, an easy and unbounded career seems open to his ambition, and he will readily persuade himself that he is born to no vulgar destinies. But this is an erroneous notion, which is corrected by daily experience. The same equality which allows every citizen to conceive these lofty hopes, renders all the citizens less able to realize them … To these causes must be attributed that strange melancholy which oftentimes will haunt the inhabitants of democratic countries in the midst of their abundance, and that disgust at life which sometimes seizes upon them in the midst of calm and easy circumstances. Complaints are made in France that the number of suicides increases; in America suicide is rare, but insanity is said to be more common than anywhere else.

Familiar with the limitations of aristocratic societies, Tocqueville had no wish to return to the conditions that had existed prior to 1776 or 1789. He knew that inhabitants of the modern West enjoyed a standard of living far superior to that of the lower classes of medieval Europe. Nevertheless, he appreciated that these deprived classes had also benefited from a mental calm that their successors were forever denied:

> While the power of the Crown, supported by the aristocracy, peaceably governed the nations of Europe, society possessed, in the midst of its wretchedness, several different advantages which can now scarcely be appreciated or conceived. ... The people never having conceived the idea of a social condition different from its own, and entertaining no expectation of ever ranking with its chiefs, received benefits from them without discussing their rights. It grew attached to them when they were clement and just, and it submitted without resistance or servility to their exactions, as to the inevitable visitations of the arm of God. Custom, and the manners of the time, had moreover created a species of law in the midst of violence, and established certain limits to oppression. As the noble never suspected that anyone would attempt to deprive him of the privileges which he believed to be legitimate, and as the serf looked upon his own inferiority as a consequence of the immutable order of nature, it is easy to imagine that a

mutual exchange of good-will took place between
two classes so differently gifted by fate. Inequality
and wretchedness were then to be found in society;
but the souls of neither rank of men were degraded.

Democracies, however, had dismantled every barrier to expectation. All members of the community felt themselves
theoretically equal, even when they lacked the means to
achieve material equality. 'In America,' wrote Tocqueville,
'I never met a citizen too poor to cast a glance of hope and
envy toward the pleasures of the rich'. Poor citizens observed
rich ones at close quarters and trusted that they too would
one day follow in their footsteps. They were not always
wrong. A number of fortunes were made by people from
humble backgrounds. However, exceptions did not make a
rule. America still had an underclass. It was just that, unlike
the poor of aristocratic societies, the American poor were
no longer able to see their condition as anything other than
a betrayal of their expectations.

The different conceptions of poverty held by members
of aristocratic and democratic societies was particularly evident, Tocqueville felt, in the attitude of servants to their masters. In aristocracies, servants often accepted their fates with
good grace. They could have, in Tocqueville's words, 'high
thoughts, strong pride and self-respect'. In democracies,
however, the atmosphere of the press and public opinion
relentlessly suggested to servants that they could reach the
pinnacles of society, that they could become industrialists,
judges, scientists or presidents. Though this sense of unlimited opportunity could initially encourage a surface cheerfulness, especially in young servants, and though it enabled
the most talented or lucky among them to fulfil their goals,
as time passed and the majority failed to raise themselves,
Tocqueville noted that their mood darkened, that bitterness
took hold and choked their spirits, and that their hatred of
themselves and their masters grew fierce.

The rigid hierarchical system that had held in place in almost every Western society until the 18th century, and had denied all hope of social movement except in rare cases, was unjust in a thousand all too obvious ways, but it offered those on the lowest rungs one notable freedom: the freedom not to have to take the achievements of quite so many people in society as reference points – and so find themselves severely wanting in status and importance as a result.

3. The tyranny of the majority

Typically, we think of democracy as being the opposite of tyranny. It should, in a democracy, no longer be possible for a clique to lord it over everyone else by force; leaders have to govern with the consent of the governed. But Tocqueville noticed that democracy could easily create its own specialised type of tyranny: that of the majority. The majority group could, in principle, be very severe and hostile to minorities. Tocqueville wasn't simply thinking of overt political persecution, but of a less dramatic, but still real, kind of tyranny in which simply being 'in a minority' as regards prevailing ideologies starts to seem unacceptable, perverse – even a threat.

Democratic culture, he thought, could easily end up demonising any assertion of difference, and especially of cultural superiority or high mindedness, which could be perceived as offensive to the majority – even though such attitudes might be connected with real merit. In a tyranny of the majority, a society grows ill at ease with outstanding merit or ambition of any kind. It has an aggressively levelling instinct in which it is regarded as a civic virtue to cut down to size anyone who seems to be getting above themselves.

This, he thought, was part of the natural price one could expect to pay for living in a democracy.

4. Democracy turns us against authority

Tocqueville saw democracy as encouraging strong ideas about equality, to an extent that could grow harmful and dispiriting. He saw that democracy encourages 'in the human heart a depraved taste for equality, which impels the weak to want to bring the strong down to their level'.

It's a line of thought that sounds almost brutal today because we instinctively see equality as desirable. But what disturbed Tocqueville was the way in which, in the United States, people of no distinction, in terms of education, skill, experience or talent, would refuse to defer to what Tocqueville called their 'natural superiors', as he put it. They were inspired – he believed – by an unwillingness to bow before any kind of authority. They refused to think that someone could be better than them just because they had trained to be a doctor, studied the law for two decades or had written some good books. A healthy and admirable reluctance to defer to people fatally encouraged a deeply unhelpful refusal to accept any kind of submission to anyone of any sort. And yet, as he saw it, it simply must be the case that some people are wiser, more intelligent, kinder, or more mature than others and for these very good reasons should be listened to with special attention. Democracy was, he thought, fatally biased towards mediocrity.

5. Democracy undermines freedom of mind
Instinctively, you'd suppose that democracy would encourage citizens to have an open mind. Surely democracy encourages debate and allows disagreements to be resolved by voting, rather than by violence? We think of openness of mind as being the result of living in a place where lots of opinions get an airing.

However, Tocqueville came to the opposite conclusion: that in few places could one find 'less independence of mind, and true freedom of discussion than in America'.

Trusting that the system was fair and just, Americans simply gave up their independence of mind and put their faith in newspapers and so-called 'common sense'. The scepticism of Europeans towards public opinion had given way to a naive faith in the wisdom of the crowd.

Furthermore, as this was a commercial society, people were very conscious of not wanting to step too far out of line with their neighbours (who might also be customers). It was better to trot out clichés than to try to be original – and never more so than when there was something new to sell.

***

Back in France, Tocqueville pursued a political career. Although France was nominally a democracy at this point, the electorate was very tightly restricted – less than 5 per cent of adult males were entitled to vote. He was a deputy and, for a few not very glorious months, minister for foreign affairs. But in 1851, the elected president, Louis Napoleon, declared himself emperor and tore up the constitution. Tocqueville, then in his mid-forties, left the political field and led a quieter life on his family estates. He suffered long bouts of tuberculosis and died in 1859, aged 53.

***

Although he says a lot of quite grim things about democracy, Tocqueville isn't anti-democratic. He's not trying to tell us that we shouldn't have democracy. On the contrary, he was convinced that democracy would prevail over all other forms of political organisation. Rather, his aim was to get us to be realistic about what this would mean. Democracies would be very good at some things and really rather terrible at others.

By highlighting the inherent drawbacks of democracy, he was showing why living in a democracy would be, in some key ways, deeply annoying and frustrating. He is teaching the Stoic lesson that certain pains need to be the expected; they are the likely accompaniments of political progress. He's preaching an anti-provincial, worldly lesson: of course there are going to be quite bad things about democratic politics and society, don't be too surprised or shocked; don't come with the wrong expectations ...

Frustration and irritation are secretly fuelled by hope (that is, by the conviction that things really could be very different). By telling us soberly and calmly that democracy has major defects, Tocqueville is trying to get us to be strategically pessimistic. Of course, politics is going to be pretty awful in major ways. It's not that we're doing anything terribly wrong. It's the price you pay (and should be willing to pay) when you give ultimate authority to everyone.

Max Weber

1864–1920

Max Weber is one of the four philosophers best able to explain to us the peculiar economic system we live within called capitalism (Émile Durkheim, Karl Marx and Adam Smith are the others).

Born in Erfurt in Germany in 1864, Weber grew up to see his country convulsed by the dramatic changes ushered in by the Industrial Revolution. Cities were exploding in size, vast companies were forming, a new managerial elite was replacing the old aristocracy. Weber's father, successful in business and politics, prospered greatly from this new era, leaving his son with a fortune that would allow him the independence to be a writer. His mother was a sober, withdrawn figure, who mostly stayed at home practising an extremely pious and sexually strict version of Christianity.

Weber became a successful academic at a young age. But when he was in his mid-thirties, during a family get-together, he fell into a grave quarrel with his father over the latter's treatment of his mother. Weber senior died shortly after and the son believed he might inadvertently have killed him. This catapulted him into severe depression and anxiety. Weber had to give up his university job and lay more or less mute on a sofa for two years.

His wife, Marianne, turned out to be unhelpfully similar to his mother. The marriage was unconsummated and filled with neurotic complaints on both sides. Weber's path to intellectual recovery began after he had a liberating affair with a sexually progressive 19-year-old student, Else von Richthofen (whose sister, Frida, comparable in temperament, was married to the novelist D.H. Lawrence). Max Weber had the sort of life that his contemporary, Freud, was born to address.

Weber was largely unknown during his lifetime. But his fame has grown exponentially ever since – because he originated some key ideas with which to understand the workings and future of capitalism.

1. Why does capitalism exist?

Capitalism might feel normal or inevitable to us but, of course, it isn't. It came into existence only relatively recently, in historical terms, and has successfully taken root in just a limited number of countries.

The standard view is that capitalism is the result of developments in technology (particularly, the invention of steam power).

But Weber proposed that what made capitalism possible was a set of *ideas*, not scientific discoveries – and in particular religious ideas.

Religion made capitalism happen. Not just any religion; a very particular, non-Catholic kind of the sort that flourished in Northern Europe where capitalism was – and continues to be – particularly vigorous. Capitalism was created by Protestantism, specifically Calvinism, as developed by John Calvin in Geneva and by his followers in England, the Puritans.

In his great work, *The Protestant Ethic and the Spirit of Capitalism*, published in 1905, Weber laid out some of the reasons why he believed Protestant Christianity had been so crucial to capitalism:

a. Protestantism makes you feel guilty all the time

Catholics have it – relatively – easy in Weber's analysis. Believers who have strayed are able to confess their transgressions at regular intervals and can be 'cleansed' by priests and thereby recover a sense of their good name in the eyes of God. But no such purifications are available to Protestants, for only God is thought able to forgive, and He won't make his intentions known until the Day of Judgement. Until then, Weber alleged, Protestants are left with heightened feelings of anxiety as well as lifelong guilty desires to prove their virtue before a severe, all-seeing but silent God.

b. God likes hard work

In Weber's eyes, Protestant guilt feelings were diverted into an obsession with hard work. The sins of Adam could only be expunged through constant toil. To rest, relax and go hunting – as the old Catholic aristocracy liked to do – was to ask for divine trouble. Not coincidentally, there were far fewer festivals and days of rest in Protestantism. God didn't like time off. Money earnt wasn't to be blown in feasts celebrating the here and now. It was always and only to be re-invested for tomorrow.

c. All work is holy
Catholics had limited their conception of holy work to the activities of the clergy. But now Protestants declared that work of any kind could and should be done in the name of God, even jobs like being a baker or an accountant. This lent new moral energy and earnestness to all branches of professional life. Work was no longer just about earning a living; it was to be part of a religious vocation connected with proving one's virtue to God. The clerk was meant to approach his work at the office with all the seriousness and piety of a monk.

d. It's the community, not the family, that counts
In Catholic countries, the family was (and often still is) everything. One would regularly give jobs to relatives, help out indolent uncles and lightly swindle the central authorities for family gain without too much compunction. But Protestants took a less benevolent view of family. The family could be a haven for selfish and egoistic motives, running counter to Jesus's injunctions that a Christian should be concerned with the family of all believers, not his or her specific family. For early Protestants, one was meant to direct one's selfless energies to the community as a whole, the public realm where everyone deserved fairness and dignity. To stick up for one's family over and against the claims of the wider group was nothing less than a sin; it was time to do away with narrow vested interests and clan loyalties.

e. There aren't miracles

Protestantism turned its back on miracles. God wasn't thought to be lever-pulling behind the scenes day-to-day. One couldn't get prayers directly answered. Heavenly power didn't intervene in a fantastical, childish way. Weber called this the 'disenchantment of the world.' Instead, in the Protestant philosophy, the emphasis fell on human action: the day-to-day world was ruled by facts, by reason and by the discoverable laws of science. And therefore, prosperity was not mysteriously ordained by God and couldn't be won through imploring prayers. It could only be the result of thinking methodically, acting honestly, and working industriously and sensibly over many years.

Taken together, these five factors created, in Weber's eyes, the crucial catalytic ingredients for capitalism to take hold. In this analysis, Weber was in direct disagreement with Karl Marx, for Marx had proposed a *materialist* view of capitalism (where technology was said to have created a new capitalist social system), whereas Weber now advanced an *idealist* one (suggesting that it was in fact a set of ideas that had created capitalism and given the impetus for its newfound technological and financial arrangements).

The argument between Weber and Marx pivoted around the role of religion. Marx had argued that religion was 'the opium of the masses', a drug that induced passive acceptance of the horrors of capitalism. But Weber turned this dictum on its head. It was religion that was in fact the cause and foremost supporter of capitalism. People didn't tolerate capitalism because of religion, they only became capitalists *as a result of* their religion.

2. How do you develop capitalism around the world?

There are about 35 countries where capitalism is now well developed. It probably works best in Germany, where Weber first observed it. But in the remaining 161 nations, it arguably isn't working well at all.

This is a source of much puzzlement and distress. Billions of dollars in aid are transferred every year from the rich to the poor world and are spent on malaria pills, solar panels and grants for irrigation projects and women's education.

But a Weberian analysis tells us that these materialist interventions will never work, because the problem isn't really a material one to begin with. One has to start at the level of ideas.

What the World Bank and the IMF should be giving sub-Saharan Africa is not money and technology but ideas.

In the Weberian analysis, certain countries fail to succeed at capitalism because they don't feel anxious and guilty enough, they trust too much in miracles, they like to celebrate now rather than reinvest for tomorrow, and their members feel it's acceptable to steal from the community in order to enrich their families, favouring the clan over the nation.

Weber didn't believe that the only way to be a successful capitalist country was actually to convert to Protestantism. He argued that Protestantism had merely brought to their first fruition ideas that could now subsist outside of religious ideology.

Today, Weber would counsel those who wish to spread capitalism to concentrate on our equivalent of religion: culture. It is a nation's attitudes, hopes and sense of what life is about that produces an economy that either flourishes or flounders. The path to reforming an economy shouldn't therefore wind through material aid, it should go through cultural assistance. The decisive question for an economy is not what the rate of inflation is, but what is on TV tonight.

3. Why is capitalism not going so well in the Democratic Republic of the Congo (the poorest country on earth)?

Because, Weber would tell us, this unfortunate nation has the wrong mentality, one far removed from that of Rhineland Germany. They believe in clans, they have magical thinking, they don't believe that God would Himself command them to be an honest mechanic or hairdresser ...

Weber's point is that if capitalism is going to take root in developing nations – and bring the advantages of higher productivity and greater wealth – then we will need to look to changing mentalities, instilling something akin to an updated version of the attitudes of Calvinism.

Weber's views on global development emerged in two books he wrote on two religions that he felt were extremely unhelpful to capitalism, *The Religion of India* and *The Religion of China*. For Weber, the caste system of the Hindus assigns everyone to a status they can't escape and therefore makes any sustained commercial effort futile. The belief in samsara – the transmigration of souls – also inspires the view that nothing substantial can change until the next life. At the same time, a Hindu ideology of the clan takes pressure off individual responsibility and encourages nepotism rather than meritocracy. These ideas have economic consequences; they are why, nowadays, Weberians would argue, there are many excellent public hospitals in Geneva and Erfurt and not too many in Chennai or Varanasi.

Weber noted similarly unhelpful factors in China. There, Confucianism gives too much weight to tradition. No one feels able to rethink how things are done. The devotion to bureaucracy encourages a static society – whereas entrepreneurship arises from a fruitful mixture of anxiety and hope.

4. How can we change the world?

Weber was writing in an age of revolution. Lots of people around him were trying to change things: communists, socialists, anarchists, nationalists, separatists.

He too wanted things to change, but he believed that one first had to work out how political power operated in the world.

He believed that humanity had gone through three distinct types of power across its history. The oldest societies operated according to what he called 'traditional authority'.

This was where kings relied on appeals to folklore and divinity to justify their hold on power. Such societies were deeply inert and only rarely allowed for initiative.

These societies had subsequently been replaced by an age of 'charismatic authority', where a heroic individual – most famously a Napoleon – could rise to power on the back of a magnetic personality and change everything around him through passion and will.

But, Weber insisted, we were now long past this period of history, having entered a third age of 'bureaucratic authority'. This is where power is held by vast labyrinthine bureaucracies whose workings are entirely baffling to the average citizen. It's not obvious what all the functionaries actually do in meetings and at their desks. Bureaucracy achieves its power via knowledge: only the bureaucrats know how stuff works, and it will take an outsider years to work it out (for example, how housing policy or the educational curriculum are actually structured). Most simply give up – usefully for the powers that be …

The dominance of bureaucracy has major implications for anyone trying to change a nation. There is often an understandable, but misguided, desire to think one just has to change the leader, who is imagined as a kind of super-parent personally determining how everything goes. But in fact, removing the leader almost never has the degree of impact that is hoped for. (The replacement of Bush by Obama did not lead, for example, to all the changes some people expected; Weber would not have been surprised.)

Weber knew that today one can't bring about significant social change just by charisma. It can feel as if political change should be driven by fiery rhetoric, marches, fury, and grand, exciting gestures, like publishing a bestselling revolutionary book. But Weber is pessimistic about all such hopes, for they are misaligned with the reality of how the modern world works. The only way to overcome the power lodged within bureaucracy is through knowledge and systematic organisation.

Weber encourages us to see that change is not so much impossible as complicated and slow. If we are to get things to go better, much of it will have to come through outwardly very undramatic processes. It will be through the careful marshalling of statistical evidence, patient briefings to ministers, testimonies to committee hearings and minute studies of budgets.

Conclusion

Weber, though personally a cautious man, is an unexpected source of ideas on how to change things. He tells us how power works now and reminds us that ideas may be far more important than tools or money in changing nations. It is a hugely significant thesis. We learn that so much that we associate with vast impersonal external forces (and that hence feels entirely beyond our control) is, in fact, dependent upon something utterly intimate and perhaps more malleable: the thoughts in our own heads.

Émile Durkheim

1858–1917

É mile Durkheim is the philosopher who can best help us to understand why capitalism makes us richer and yet frequently more miserable; even – far too often – suicidal.

He was born in 1858 in the little French town of Épi-nal, near the German border. His family were devout Jews. Durkheim himself did not believe in God, but he was always fascinated by, and sympathetic to, religion. He was a clever student. He studied at the elite École Normale Supérieure in Paris, travelled for a while in Germany, then took a university job in Bordeaux. He got married and there were two children: Marie and André. Before he was 40, Durkheim was appointed to a powerful and prestigious position as a professor at the Sorbonne. He had status and honours, but his mind remained unconventional and his curiosity insatiable. He died of a stroke in 1917.

Durkheim lived through the immense, rapid transformation of France from a largely traditional agricultural society to an urban, industrial economy. He could see that his country was getting richer, that capitalism was extraordinarily productive and, in certain ways, liberating. But what particularly struck him, and became the focus of his entire career, were the psychological costs of capitalism. The economic system might have created an entire new middle class, but it was doing something very peculiar to people's minds. It was – quite literally – driving them to suicide in ever increasing numbers.

This was the immense insight unveiled in Durkheim's most important work, *Suicide*, published in 1897. The book chronicled a remarkable and tragic discovery: that suicide rates seem to shoot up once a nation becomes industrialised and consumer capitalism takes hold. Durkheim observed that the suicide rate in the Britain of his day was double that of Italy; but in even richer and more advanced Denmark, it was four times higher than in the UK. Furthermore, suicide rates were much higher among the educated than the uneducated;

ÉDOUARD MANET, *Le Suicide*, 1887

much higher in Protestant than in Catholic countries; and much higher among the middle classes than among the poor.

Durkheim's focus on suicide was intended to shed light on a more general level of unhappiness and despair at large in society. Suicide was the horrific tip of the iceberg of mental distress created by capitalism.

Across his career, Durkheim tried to explain why people had become so unhappy in modern societies, even though they had more opportunities and access to goods in quantities that their ancestors could never have dreamt of. He isolated five crucial factors:

1. Individualism
In traditional societies, people's identities are closely tied to belonging to a clan or a class. Their beliefs and attitudes, their work and status, follow automatically from the facts

of their birth. Few choices are involved: a person might be a baker, a Lutheran, and married to their second cousin – without ever having made any self-conscious decisions for themselves. They could just step into the place created for them by their family and the existing fabric of society.

But under capitalism, it is the individual (rather than the clan, or 'society' or the nation) that now chooses everything: what job to take, what religion to follow, who to marry … This 'individualism' forces us to be the authors of our own destinies. How our lives pan out becomes a reflection of our unique merits, skills and persistence.

If things go well, we can take all the credit. But if things go badly, it is crueller than ever before, for it means there is no one else to blame. We have to shoulder the full responsibility. We aren't just unlucky anymore; we have chosen and have messed up. Individualism ushers in a disinclination to admit to any sort of role for luck or chance in life. Failure becomes a terrible judgement upon oneself. This is the particular burden of life in modern capitalism.

2. Excessive hope

Capitalism raises our hopes. Everyone – with enough effort – can become the boss. Everyone should think big. You are not trapped by the past – capitalism says – you are free to remake your life. Advertising stokes ambition by showing us limitless luxury that we could (if we play our cards right) secure very soon. The opportunities grow enormous … as do the possibilities for disappointment.

Envy grows rife. One becomes deeply dissatisfied with one's lot, not because it is objectively awful but because of tormenting thoughts about all that is almost (but not quite) within reach.

The cheery, boosterish side of capitalism attracted Durkheim's particular ire. In his view, modern societies struggle to admit that life is often quite simply painful and sad. Our tendencies to grief and sorrow are made to look like signs of failure rather than, as should be the case, a fair response to the arduous facts of the human condition.

3. We have too much freedom

One of the complaints against traditional societies – strongly voiced in Romantic literature – was that people needed more 'freedom'. Rebellious types complained there were far too many social norms: telling you what to wear, what you were supposed to do on Sunday afternoons, what parts of an arm it was respectable for a woman to reveal ...

Capitalism – following the earlier efforts of Romantic rebels – relentlessly undermined social norms. States became more complex, more anonymous and more diverse. People didn't have so much in common with each other anymore. The rules or norms that one had internalised stopped applying.

What kind of career should you have? Where should you live? What kind of holiday should you go on? What is a marriage supposed to be like? How should you bring up children? Under capitalism, the collective answers get weaker, less specific. There's a lot of reliance on the phrase: 'whatever works for you.' Which sounds friendly but also means that society doesn't much care what you do and doesn't feel confident it has good answers to the big questions of your life.

In very confident moments, we like to think of ourselves as fully up to the task of reinventing life, or working everything out for ourselves. But, in reality, as Durkheim knew, we are often simply too tired, too busy, too uncertain – and there is nowhere to turn.

4. Atheism

Durkheim was himself an atheist, but he worried that religion had become implausible just as its communal side would have been most necessary to repair the fraying social fabric. Despite its factual errors, Durkheim appreciated the sense of community that religion offered: 'Religion gave men a perception of a world beyond this earth where everything would be rectified; this prospect made inequalities less noticeable, it stopped men from feeling aggrieved.'

Marx had disliked religion because he thought it made people too ready to accept inequality. It was an 'opiate' that dulled the pain and sapped the will. But this criticism was founded on a conviction that it would not actually be too difficult to make an equal world and therefore that the opiate could be lifted without trouble.

Durkheim took the darker view that inequality would be very hard to eradicate (perhaps impossible), so we would have to learn, somehow, to live with it. This led him to a warmer appreciation of any ideas that could soften the psychological blows of reality.

Durkheim also saw that religion created deep bonds between people. The king and the peasant worshipped the same God, they prayed in the same building using the same words. They were offered precisely the same sacraments. Riches, status and power were of no direct spiritual value.

Capitalism had nothing to replace this with. Science certainly did not offer the same opportunities for powerful shared experiences. The periodic table might well possess transcendent beauty and be a marvel of intellectual elegance – but it couldn't draw a society together around it.

Durkheim was especially taken with elaborate religious rituals that demand participation and create a strong sense of belonging. A tribe might worship its totem; men might undergo a complex process of initiation. The tragedy – in Durkheim's eyes – was that we had done away with religion at precisely the time when we most needed its collective consoling dimensions and had nothing much to put in its place.

5. Weakening of the nation and of the family

In the 19th century, it had looked, at certain moments, as if the idea of the nation might grow so powerful and intense that it could take up the sense of belonging and shared devotion that once had been supplied by religion. Admittedly there were some heroic moments. In the war against Napoleon, for instance, the Prussians had developed a dramatic all-encompassing cult of the Fatherland. But the excitement of a nation at war had, Durkheim saw, failed to translate into anything very impressive in peacetime.

Family might similarly seem to offer the experience of belonging that we needed. But Durkheim was unconvinced. We do indeed invest hugely in our families, but they are not as stable as we might hope. And they do not provide access to a wider community.

Increasingly, the 'family' in the traditional expansive sense has ceased to exist. It boils down to the couple agreeing to live in the same house and look after one or two children for a while. But in adulthood these children do not expect to work alongside their parents; they don't expect their social circle to overlap with their parents very much and don't feel that their parent's honour is in their hands.

Our looser, more individual sense of family isn't necessarily a bad thing. It just means that it's not well placed to take up the task of giving us a larger sense of belonging – of giving us the feeling that we are part of something more valuable than ourselves.

Conclusion

Durkheim is a master diagnostician of our ills. He shows us that modern economies put tremendous pressures on individuals but leave us dangerously bereft of authoritative guidance and communal solace.

He didn't feel capable of finding answers to the problems he identified but he knew that capitalism would have to uncover them, or collapse. We are Durkheim's heirs – and still have ahead of us the task he accorded us: to create new ways of belonging, to take some of the pressure off the individual, to find a correct balance between freedom and solidarity and to generate ideologies that allow us not to take our own failures so personally and sometimes so tragically.

Margaret Mead

1901–1978

W hen we use 'modern' to describe something, it's usually a positive. We are very appreciative and even a little smug about the miracles of modern science, the benefits of modern technology, and even the superiority of modern viewpoints. But what if, in speeding towards a new and ever-better future, we've left some important truths about ourselves behind? One of the people who best helped us explore this problem was Margaret Mead, perhaps the most famous anthropologist of the 20th century.

Margaret Mead was born in 1901, the oldest of five children. Her father was a professor of finance, and her mother was a sociologist who studied Italian immigrants. When Margaret was little, her family moved frequently, and she alternated between attending traditional schools and home-schooling. She also shopped different religions (because her family members had different faiths) and eventually chose Episcopalian Christianity. Her experience sampling different beliefs and navigating new schools may have influenced her decision to study the wildly different ways people think and interact.

After studying psychology as an undergraduate at De-Pauw University and then Barnard College (at a time when higher education was very unusual for a woman), Mead began a PhD at Columbia University in the relatively new field of anthropology. Her supervisor, Franz Boas, was essentially the founder of the discipline in the United States. Unlike earlier anthropologists, who had imagined that civilisation was progressing in a linear fashion from 'barbarism' to 'savagery' to 'civilisation', Boas argued that the world was teeming with separate cultures, each with their own unique perspectives, insights and deficiencies. The modern Western world was not the pinnacle of human achievement, but simply one specific example of what humans could achieve.

Boas suggested that Mead travel to Samoa, a few tiny volcanic, tropical islands in the centre of the Pacific Ocean, for her fieldwork. At the time Samoa was governed

The Samoan Islands

by America in the east and New Zealand in the west, and was slowly being converted to Christianity. Boas hoped the trip would allow her to study a 'primitive' culture that was still relatively undisrupted by the technologically developed world, and to show that it had its own insights and a highly developed culture. Much in line with Boas's concerns, Mead was particularly interested in primitive communities because she believed that such isolated cultures could serve as 'laboratories' that would reveal which cultural norms were most helpful and healthy. She also believed it was critical to do this quickly; she feared that primitive cultures were slipping away, soon to be lost forever.

Starting in 1925, and lasting until the beginning of the Second World War, Mead travelled to Samoa and then to other islands in the south seas of the Pacific Ocean. She lived among native people there as an anthropologist, recording their ways of life. The groups Mead studied included many fishermen and farmers, and few literate people. Mead learned to carry babies around by having them cling to her neck and to dress in native dress. She had no access to

recording devices other than still cameras, so she mostly relied on her memory and written notes – and, of course, her
ability to quickly learn native languages and become popular with native people. On one island, she lived on the front
porch of the navy pharmacist's dispensary (which had more
privacy than a native house). People came to visit her at all
hours of the day and night, often just to chat. She learned to
be a foreigner locals didn't mind confiding in.

Mead's work demonstrated a particular weakness in
modern society related to sexual life. Mead herself led an
unconventional life, simultaneously involved with successive
husbands and her ever-present female lover – another famous
anthropologist named Ruth Benedict. She believed that 'one
can love several people and that demonstrative affection has
its place in different types of relationship.' Perhaps because
Mead's own life was neither heterosexual nor monogamous,
she emphasised the ease with which other cultures allowed
such practices, and the healthy relationship towards love and
sex that could be maintained with these behaviours.

In her 1928 book *Coming of Age in Samoa*, Mead described Samoan culture as more open and comfortable with
sex. The book was her first and most famous research project, for which she studied girls only a bit younger than herself: adolescents navigating their transition to adulthood.
She wanted to understand whether their experiences were
very different than those of American teenagers, and, if so,
whether their experiences could be learned from. Most of
all she wanted to test whether 'societies could be changed
by changing the way children were brought up.' What she
found was that little children knew all about masturbation
and learned about intercourse and other acts through first-
hand observation, but thought of it as no more scandalous
or worthy of comment than death or birth. Homosexual-
ity was incidental but also not a matter of shame, and
people's orientations fluctuated naturally throughout their
lives without defining them.

Many of the differences Mead found were not simply curiosities, but replicable practices. Divorce was common and not shameful – a relationship was simply said to have 'passed away'. Loving more than one person was accepted and understood to be common. Adultery might lead to divorce, but it wouldn't have to; Mead describes how, in Samoan culture, the lover of a person's husband or wife might gain the forgiveness of the wronged spouse:

> He goes to the house of the man he has injured, accompanied by all the men of his household ... the suppliants seat themselves outside the house, fine mats spread over their heads ... bent in attitude of deepest dejection and humiliation ... Then towards the evening [the betrayed husband] will say at last: 'Come, it is enough. Enter the house and drink the kava. Eat the food which I will set before you and we will cast our trouble into the sea.'

Mead argued that because Samoan culture had an understanding of sex and all of its complexities and difficulties as part of the natural life cycle, and because their culture had developed useful, meaningful responses to address these difficulties, their personal sexual lives were much easier. For example, she found that such norms made adolescence much less difficult for Samoan girls than for American girls, because Samoan girls had relatively few responsibilities and there was little pressure for them to conform to a particular kind of sexual life. They were neither pressured to abstain from sex nor to achieve particular milestones like having boyfriends or getting married. The converse of this situation meant that being an American teenager was stressful largely because of the nature of being American, rather than being teenaged.

Here Mead tapped into a deeper criticism of her own culture. She saw life for Americans of her time as one in which people are brought up 'denied all first-hand knowledge of birth and love and death, harried by a society which will not let adolescents grow up at their own pace, imprisoned in the small, fragile, nuclear family from which there is no escape and in which there is little security.' Although much has changed in America and in the Western world since this time, her insights still apply in many ways. Our adolescents are still pressured to conform to particular models of human sexual behaviour, and these pressures, along with the pressures that we experience long into adulthood, make our lives more difficult and empty than they would otherwise be. Our modern life does not allow us to be as freely loving and sexual, as complex and full of change, as other cultures allow.

Mead also discovered that human behaviour in relation to gender varied widely from culture to culture, far more than Americans at the time could imagine. For example, Americans thought of men as productive, sensible and more aggressive, while women were more frivolous, peaceful and nurturing. But in her 1935 book, *Sex and Temperament in Three Primitive Societies*, Mead studied tribes in Papua New Guinea and found radically different results. She recorded that in the Arapesh tribe both men and women were peaceful and nurturing, while among Mundugumor, men and women were both ruthless and aggressive. Perhaps most striking was Mead's description of the people of the Chambri region, where the women were dominant and far more aggressive than men, while the men were dependents and in need of emotional support. In short, Mead suggested that none of these traits were 'human nature': they were all instead simply possibilities, which were either taught, encouraged, or shunned by native culture.

Mead's striking conclusion was, of course, that culture determined an individual's personality far more than people had previously expected. It was not sex that made women curl their hair or listen to people's feelings, or 'race' that made some nations regularly attack their neighbours.

Rather, it was the social expectations and norms that had developed slowly for centuries, and that laid the groundwork for each individual's psychological makeup. 'We must recognise,' she reminded her readers, 'that beneath the superficial classifications of sex and race the same potentialities exist, recurring generation after generation, only to perish because society has no place for them.'

Modern American culture also had no place for certain potentialities – in this it was no more successful than any primitive culture. We might think, for example, that men like football because they are the more warlike sex, but in fact they have been the more warlike sex because (for some arbitrary reasons or matter of convenience) they have been the sex at war. Similarly, we may believe that women have tended to children because they are nurturing, but actually they have been guided to be nurturing because they were assigned the task of raising children. In making these assumptions, we forget about human potential for gentleness and roughness that other cultures have forgotten.

In making this criticism, Mead followed in a long line of thinkers who recognised that modern civilisation, with all of its technological advantages and rapid developments, had left some aspects of human experience behind – either unrecognised, misunderstood or poorly tended to. In this sense, she was much like the Genevan philosopher Jean-Jacques Rousseau (1712–1778), who had described human beings as originally having a very different and far more solitary nature. Rousseau suggested that as civilisation developed, human nature was moulded by society – often for the worse; this artificial construction of social order (often through violence and oppression), he argued, limits human potential.

Mead's point, in turn, was that even now we wrongly assume the conventions that Rousseau describes as unnatural, and in doing so we miss out on greater possibilities, both for how to behave as individuals and how to reorganise societies. She believed that by studying other cultures, especially primitive ones that had developed apart from our own, we could better explore these possibilities. Perhaps, for example, we can choose when to be loving and when to be aggressive, when to demand a certain standard of sexual behaviour and when to learn how to gracefully and conscientiously accommodate our differing needs.

Mead strongly believed that it was important to consider cultural norms because people needed their culture to help guide them towards healthier emotional lives. She imagined that each culture, like a tribe cast out from the Tower of Babel and given a unique language, had something unique to contribute culturally as well: 'Each primitive people has selected one set of human gifts, one set of human values, and fashioned for themselves an art, a social organisation, a religion, which is their unique contribution to the history of the human spirit.' The beauty of these differences was not that the people she studied always had it better figured out than Americans (sometimes she could be very critical of the people she studied), but rather that both groups could learn from each other: 'from this contrast we may be able to turn, made newly and vividly self-conscious and self-critical, to judge anew and perhaps fashion differently the education we give our children.'

Indeed, Mead herself had learned much from her anthropological subjects. For example, she brought up her daughter, Mary Catherine Bateson, on some of the parenting of the primitive people she worked with. Mead enlisted a new physician, Dr Benjamin Spock, as the child's doctor, in part because he allowed unconventional practices like breastfeeding on demand, which Mead had learned from her research subjects (and which is now commonplace in Western culture, thanks in part to Dr Spock).

During World War Two, access to the South Pacific was impossible, so Mead began to study more 'complex' cultures like her own. She was also asked to turn her research to war purposes, first by studying how to maintain morale during wartime, and then by studying the social complexities of food distribution. She even wrote a book on American national character entitled *And Keep Your Powder Dry* (1942). With the help of her husband Gregory Bateson, she founded the Institute for Intercultural Studies in order to establish further study of other cultures.

After the war, Mead also worked for the US military, studying Russian responses to authority in order to try to predict what the Soviets might do during the cold war. She grew increasingly famous, travelling widely, giving lectures, and teaching at universities. For fifty years, from 1928 until her death in 1978, she worked for the American Museum of Natural History in New York City as a curator for their projects. She wrote twenty books, was made a fellow of the American Academy of Arts and Sciences, was awarded twenty-eight honorary degrees, and was posthumously awarded the Presidential Medal of Freedom.

Mead was a supporter of many political causes, fighting against poverty and racism and supporting women's rights. She wrote a book showing how many of the differences in intelligence between 'races' that psychologists had measured were instead the result of cultural knowledge and convention. She encouraged her readers and listeners to also think of social problems as culturally conditioned, issues that could be overcome by new efforts and ideas. She is famous for having (probably) said, 'Never doubt that a small group of committed people can change the world. Indeed, it is the only thing that ever has.'

Mead's own committed work helped generations of Americans and people everywhere see greater possibilities for individuals and for modern values. She suggested that we see human nature less as a singular and universal fact and more as an ever-changing landscape, one through which we should travel in order to become wiser. 'As the traveller who has once been from home is wiser than he who has never left his own doorstep,' she suggested, 'so a knowledge of one other culture should sharpen our ability to scrutinise more steadily, to appreciate more lovingly, our own.' In doing so, she suggested, we could uncover and support undeveloped human potential forgotten in our rush towards 'modernity'.

Theodor Adorno

1903–1969

Theodor Wiesengrund Adorno was born in Frankfurt in 1903 into a wealthy and cultured family. His father, a wine merchant, was of Jewish origin but had converted to Protestantism at university. Teddy (as his closest friends called him) was an extremely fine pianist from a young age. Until his twenties, he planned for a career as a composer, but eventually focused on philosophy. In 1934, he was barred, on racial grounds, from teaching in Germany. So he moved to Oxford and later to New York and then Los Angeles. He was both fascinated and repelled by Californian consumer culture – and thought with unusual depth about suntans and drive-ins. After the war, he returned to West Germany, where he died in 1969, at the age of 65.

Adorno believed that intellectuals should band together to change society, and he was closely connected with the pioneering Institute of Social Research, which had been founded and funded by his friend Felix Weil (whose father was a hugely successful commodities trader). The Institute aimed to develop a psychological understanding of the problems thrown up by modern capitalism. It focused not so much on the hard economic aspects of life so much as on the culture and mindset of capitalism.

Adorno drew attention to three significant ways in which capitalism corrupts and degrades us:

1. Leisure time becomes toxic

Although Adorno didn't overlook issues like working legislation and the revision of the taxation system, he believed that the primary focus for progressive philosophers should be the study of how the working and middle classes of developed nations think and feel – and in particular, the manner in which they spend their evenings and weekends.

Adorno had a highly ambitious view of what leisure time should be for. It was not to relax and take one's mind off things. Adorno argued that leisure had a great purpose to serve: free time – and the cultural activities we might pursue in it – was our prime opportunity to expand and develop ourselves, to reach after our own better nature, and to acquire the tools with which to change society. It was a time when we might see certain specific films that would help us to understand our relationships with new clarity, or to read philosophy and history books that could give us fresh insights into politics or to listen to the kinds of music that would give us courage to reform ourselves and our collective life.

But, in the modern world, Adorno bemoaned that leisure had fallen into the hands of an omnipresent and deeply malevolent entertainment machine he called 'the culture industry', which occupied the same demonic place in his philosophy as religion had occupied in Marx's. Modern films, TV, radio, magazines and now social media seemed for Adorno to be designed to keep us distracted, unable to understand ourselves and without the will to alter political reality. This was a new and catastrophically dangerous opium for the masses.

For example, the news, while ostensibly updating us on everything that is 'important', is – in Adorno's view – simply there to feed us a mixture of salacious nonsense and political stories that scramble any possibility of understanding the open prison within which we exist. Journalists will self-righteously claim that they are giving us 'the truth', but they are themselves too busy, too scared of their bosses and too thoughtless to be in any position to offer such an elixir. Films for their part excite fears and desires wholly disconnected from the real challenges we face. We might spend two hours of our lives following the adventures of an alien invasion – while the real calamities of our world go unattended. Museums display works of art without allowing them to speak to the needs and aspirations of their audiences. We wander through galleries, silently admiring so-called 'masterpieces', while privately unsure what they really mean and why we should care. The culture industry likes to keep us like that: distracted, pliant, confused and intimidated. As for pop music, this focuses relentlessly on the emotions around romantic love, selfishly suggesting to us that happiness can only come from meeting one very special person, rather than awakening us to the pleasures of community and of a more broadly distributed human sympathy.

Adorno was so strict on the cultural output of his age because he believed in the highest possibilities for culture. It wasn't there to help us pass the time, impress the neighbours or drug us into momentary cheerfulness. It was to be nothing less than a therapeutic tool to deliver consolation, insight and social transformation. No wonder he perceptively described Walt Disney as the most dangerous man in America.

2. Capitalism doesn't sell us the things we really need

Because of the huge range of consumer goods available in modern capitalism, we naturally suppose that everything we could possibly want is available. The only problem, if there is one, is that we can't afford it.

But Adorno pointed out that our real wants are carefully shielded from us by capitalist industry, so that we end up forgetting what it is we truly need and settle instead for desires manufactured for us by corporations without any interest in our true welfare. Though we think we live in a world of plenty, what we really require to thrive – tenderness, understanding, calm, insight – is in painfully short supply and utterly disconnected from the economy.

Instead, capitalism's tool of mass manipulation – advertising – exploits our genuine longings to sell us items that will leave us both poorer and psychologically more depleted. An advert will show a group of friends walking along a beach chatting amiably, or a family having a picnic and laughing warmly together. It does this because it knows we crave community and connection. But the industrial economy is not geared to helping us get these things; it would indeed prefer to keep us lonely and consuming. So at the end of the advert, we'll be urged to buy some 25-year-old whisky or a car so powerful no road would ever let us legally drive it at top speed.

3. There are proto-fascists everywhere

Adorno was writing at the dawn of the age of the psychological questionnaire. These were widely in use in the United States where they measured consumer attitudes and commercial behaviour.

Adorno was intrigued by the underlying concept of the questionnaire and, together with colleagues, devoted himself to designing a rather different kind of questionnaire: one designed to spot fascists – rather than possible purchasers of new washing powders.

The questionnaire asked contributors to assess their level of agreement with statements like:

· Obedience and respect for authority are the most important virtues children should learn.
· A person who has bad manners, habits and breeding can hardly expect to get along with decent people.
· If people would talk less and work more, everybody would be better off.
· When a person has a problem or worry, it is best for him not to think about it, but to keep busy with more cheerful things.

After a battery of such enquiries, Adorno felt confident that he would be able to detect the fascists lingering in the new generation. Given the traumas Germany had just been through, it is no surprise that Adorno gave his questionnaire – and what he called 'the F-scale' – such attention.

But a more widely applicable lesson to be drawn from this experiment concerns the need to change politics not just through legislation and agitation, but also through psychology. Psychology precedes politics. Long before someone is racist, homophobic or authoritarian, they are – Adorno skilfully suggested – likely to be suffering from psychological fragilities and immaturities which it is the task of society as a whole to get better at spotting and responding to.

Rather than leaving problems to fester so long that there is eventually no way to deal with them other than through force (exerted by the police or the military), we should learn to understand the psychology of everyday insanity from the earliest moments. Adorno and his team sent the F-scale to every school in West Germany. Freud should have been able to get to Hitler before the Red Army and General Patton did. Psychotherapy wasn't a rarefied, private, middle-class indulgence. For Adorno, it should rightly take its place at the vanguard of progressive social transformation.

Conclusion

Adorno recognised, very unusually, that the primary obstacles to social progress are cultural and psychological rather than narrowly political and economic. In truth, we already have the money, the resources, the time and the skills to make sure everyone sleeps in an attractive house, stops destroying the planet, is given a fulfilling job and feels supported by the community. The reason why we continue to suffer and hurt one another is first and foremost because our minds are sick. This is the continuing provocation offered by the beguiling and calmly furious work of Theodor Adorno.

Rachel Carson

1907–1964

There's nothing very natural about caring for nature. The standard impulse has often been to conquer and tame the natural world: to clear the forest, hunt the animals, drain the marshes and extract whatever materials we can from the depths of the earth. For a very long time this seemed heroic and benign. Human efforts were on a puny scale in comparison with the apparently boundless abundance of the world. It's only very recently that we have become capable – collectively – of damaging the planet and exhausting some of its resources.

We learn to care for nature when someone is on hand to guide our emotions: to point out the beauty and intricacy of the butterfly, the awesome force and purity of the sea, the economy and grace of the oak tree ...

In the most destructive and polluting country mankind has ever known, that person was – for a generation – Rachel Carson. A scientist and writer, almost single-handedly, Carson taught her fellow Americans to respect nature and recognise that they were in the process of destroying it at a faster rate than any previous civilisation – and would be in dire trouble if they did not alter their arrogant ways at the earliest opportunity.

At first glance, Carson's work seems to be a simple and urgent warning against the dangers of new agricultural technologies (especially noxious chemicals), but her writing is far from being a dry polemic against environmental degradation. Carson understood – like too few environmentalists before and after – that in order for her cause to gain traction in a democratic consumer society, she had to charm her audience into loving nature. It wasn't enough to make them feel guilty about what their consumerism and greed were doing to the world; what she had to do was to make them fall in love with the seas, the forests and the prairies in order that they would stand any chance of wanting to alter their ways.

At the very end of her life, Carson wrote a book specifically for children, beautifully illustrated with photographs of nature. She called it *The Sense of Wonder*, and tried to guide parents to teach their children to feel close to the earth and its miraculous creations from the earliest age:

> A child's world is fresh and new and beautiful, full of wonder and excitement. It is our misfortune that for most of us that clear-eyed vision, that true instinct for what is beautiful and awe-inspiring, is dimmed and even lost before we reach adulthood. If I had influence with the good fairy who is supposed to preside over the christening of all children I should ask that her gift to each child in the world be a sense of wonder so indestructible that it would last throughout life, as an unfailing antidote against the boredom and disenchantments of later years, the sterile preoccupation with things that are artificial, the alienation from the sources of our strength.

Rachel Louise Carson was born and raised on a small family farm in Pennsylvania, where she learned to love animals and nature from her earliest years. In a time when it was unusual for women to have further education, she went to Chatham University and studied a distinctive mixture of English and biology. She then began a PhD at Johns Hopkins University, where, after some frustrating and fruitless studies involving pit vipers and squirrels, she finally published a master's dissertation on the excretory systems of fish. However, she had to leave this topic (and higher education altogether) in order to support her struggling family – after first her father, then her sister, and finally her niece all died tragically young in quick succession.

This was at the time of the Great Depression, when many United States government agencies were creating new jobs – some of them quite peculiar – to shorten unemployment lines. By chance, Carson secured a job writing radio broadcasts for the US Bureau of Fisheries. The series was called *Romance under the Waters* and was designed to educate Americans about marine biology and the importance of the work of the bureau itself. Carson soon discovered an exceptional knack for making the lives of aquatic animals sound interesting to the general public. She wrote about eels, whelks and crabs, about the Atlantic stargazer, the gulf pipefish and the Remo flounder – and gripped her audiences. 'If there is poetry in my book about the sea, it is not because I deliberately put it there,' she wrote modestly, 'but because no one could write truthfully about the sea and leave out the poetry.'

But poetry there certainly was – and it was her genius to know how to express it:

> Who has known the ocean? Neither you nor I, with our earth-bound senses, know the foam and surge of the tide that beats over the crab hiding under the seaweed of his tide-pool home; or the lilt of the long, slow swells of mid-ocean, where shoals of wandering fish prey and are preyed upon, and the dolphin breaks the waves to breathe the upper atmosphere. Nor can we know the vicissitudes of life on the ocean floor ... where swarms of diminutive fish twinkle through the dusk like a silver rain of meteors, and eels lie in wait among the rocks. Even less is it given to man to descend those six incomprehensible miles into the recesses of the abyss, where reign utter silence and unvarying cold and eternal night.

Eventually, Carson wrote three books about the sea. One was a particularly poetic meditation (*Under the Sea Wind*, 1941); a second (*The Sea Around Us*, 1951) looked at the migratory and seasonal patterns of sea creatures; another focused on coastal ecosystems and their resilience and importance (*The Edge of the Sea*, 1955). She had a talent for encouraging readers to abandon their normal myopic human points of view so as to learn to consider existence

Cropduster over a cornfield

from the perspective of a painted goby or an ocean pout.
She understood that scientific facts would never be enough
to stir a population distracted by commercial television and
demanding jobs, that she needed the gifts of a great writer
to help to save the planet.

She wanted to promote identification with the whole of
the earth: so that humans would learn to consider themselves a part of something unfathomable, beautiful and fragile, rather than merely the appointed masters and destroy-
ers of 'resources'. Her gifts reached their climax in her most
subtle, impassioned and moving book, *Silent Spring* (1962).

The book's main topic was – from a distance – rather
unpromising: pesticides. Yet this was a book that would sell
20 million copies and change the course of history.

In the late 1950s, the United States Federal Government
had begun mass-producing chemical pesticides developed in
military-funded laboratories. The most popular was dichlo-
rodiphenlytrichloroethane (DDT), originally designed to rid
Pacific islands of malaria-carrying bugs during the Second
World War. DDT was so effective and apparently so beneficial that its inventor, Paul Hermann Müller, was awarded a
Nobel Prize.

However, DDT turned out to be a Frankenstein-ian invention. It gradually emerged that it killed not only malaria-bearing insects, but also, for months afterwards, any kind of insect whatsoever. Moreover, DDT ran off with rainwater, drained into streams and aquifers and poisoned fish, moles, rats, foxes, rabbits and pretty much anything else alive. Applications of DDT had the power to contaminate the world's food supply, as well as collect in carcinogenic ways in the fatty tissues of humans.

The book caused outrage. Although Carson was an established author, magazines and newspapers shunned her arguments. Scientists who had helped develop DDT and the companies they worked for angrily disputed the dangers of the pesticide. Companies like Monsanto published polemics against the work and launched snide rumours about its author. The executive of one company raged, 'If man were to faithfully follow the teachings of Miss Carson, we would return to the Dark Ages, and the insects and diseases and vermin would once again inherit the earth.' Ezra Taft Benson, the US secretary of agriculture, wrote to President Eisenhower that, since Carson was physically attractive yet unmarried, she was 'probably a communist.' (In fact, she may simply have been too busy writing scientific texts, or – possibly – had a romantic friendship with a close female friend.)

Despite the efforts of corporations and their political allies, *Silent Spring* broke through. Expecting criticism from the chemical industry, Carson had prepared the book as though it were a lawsuit, and included fifty-five pages of notes at the end to prove her points. Her arguments were bulletproof.

The title, *Silent Spring*, provided a terrifying image of a world without songbirds, or almost any kind of natural life whatsoever. It opened with a depiction of a nameless small American town, full of consumer conveniences, slick gadgets and cheap food outlets, but without robins or ladybirds, larks or squirrels. A world ostensibly altered for the convenience of human beings would end up being no world for humans at all.

Carson urged us to leave nature alone: when abandoned to its own devices, nature would itself fight against insect overpopulation. But if man intercepted, unwanted populations would eventually become resistant to all poisons and then balloon rapidly, because the insects that kept pests in check would unwittingly also have been killed.

Carson concluded that scientists (and modern human beings generally) are philosophically naive enough to assume that nature is a force to be controlled at will, rather than a fierce, complex and vast entity that responds unpredictably to any human action. She suggested that human beings should think more creatively about how to prevent insect damage, for example, by sterilising insects, or using the same chemical 'lures' insects use to catch each other, or by using sound at a specific frequency to destroy larvae. Turning towards the larger issue of humans and their environment, she then reminded readers that dealing with nature would always require an appreciation, respect, and awe of nature, and an understanding that it is a force largely beyond human control and full comprehension.

With her lyrical style of writing, her defence of the primitive and her love of nature, Carson was – for a scientific age – an heir to David Henry Thoreau. Like Thoreau, Carson's work was guided by a sense of responsibility towards the earth, the seas and the skies. Like Thoreau, Carson saw them as sources of psychological health and wisdom. By learning to live more closely attuned to their cycles, to their subtle processes, and to their very simplicity, humans would have access to a nourishing wisdom and an inoculation against the psychological ills of modern life.

Carson died from breast cancer shortly after the publication of *Silent Spring*, yet her work has endured. The book quickly became a critical influence on the nascent environmental movement. Not only was DDT strictly controlled and eventually banned (both in the US and abroad), Carson's views on nature became part of our common consciousness. We are, thanks in large part to her, now able to think of ourselves as part of a larger ecosystem that is sharply imperilled by our activities and needs to be treated with the utmost humility and care.

Carson revealed that what might have seemed like an arcane technical matter (getting rid of pests in Midwestern corn fields) was ultimately a metaphysical and moral issue. At heart, good stewardship of the earth requires us to understand both our scientific strength and our distinctive moral stupidity and imaginative blindness.

In her posthumously published book for children, *The Sense of Wonder*, Carson shook off the mantle of the scientist to speak to us in the plainest, most moving terms about how to love the small blue mothership that sustains us:

> One stormy autumn night when my nephew Roger was about twenty months old I wrapped him in a blanket and carried him down to the beach in the rainy darkness. Out there, just at the eve of where-we-couldn't-see, big waves were thundering in, dimly seen white shapes that boomed and shouted and threw great handfuls of froth at us. Together we laughed for pure joy – he a baby meeting for the first time the wild tumult of Oceanus, I with the salt of half a lifetime of sea love in me. But I think we felt the same spine-tingling response to the vast, roaring ocean and the wild night around us.

It is perhaps her most radical idea of all: that it is love, rather than guilt, which is the key to transforming humanity's relationship to nature.

Psychotherapy

Sigmund Freud

1856–1939

H e described himself as an obsessional neurotic. Although the father of modern psychology told us so much about our inner lives, he was touchingly vulnerable himself.

Sigmund Schlomo Freud was born to a middle-class Jewish family in 1856, in what is now the Czech Republic. He had a deep love for his mother, who called him her 'golden Sigi', and an equally deep hostility to his father, who may have threatened to cut off little Sigi's penis if he didn't stop touching it.

His professional life was not an immediate success. As a young medical student, he dissected hundreds of male eels in a vain attempt to locate their reproductive organs, and ultimately failed to publish on the topic. He then turned his attention to a new, exciting anaesthetic drug, trumpeting its amazing properties. But unfortunately cocaine turned out to be dangerous and addictive, and Freud had to stop advocating its medical use.

A few years later, he began at last to outline the discipline that would ultimately make his name: a new psychological medicine he called psychoanalysis. The landmark study was his 1900 book *The Interpretation of Dreams*. Many others followed, most importantly *The Psychopathology of Everyday Life* (1901), *The Cases of 'Little Hans' and the 'Rat Man'* (1909), *Beyond the Pleasure Principle* (1920) and *Civilisation and its Discontents* (1930).

Despite his success as a doctor, author and psychological expert, he was often unhappy. He was a workaholic and confided to a friend, 'I cannot imagine life without work as really comfortable.' During a particularly strenuous part of his research he recorded, 'The chief patient I am preoccupied with is myself ...'

He could be very jealous of his colleagues. He once fainted watching Carl Jung give a talk, and he forbade nearly all his students from even seeing Alfred Adler. He was convinced he would die between 61 and 62 and had great

Freud (bottom left) with some of his colleagues.
He was especially jealous of Carl Jung (bottom right).

phobias about those numbers. He once panicked during a
stay in Athens when his hotel room number was 31, half of
62. He soothed himself with his beloved cigar, but he was
also very self-conscious about it, because he thought it was a
replacement for his earlier masturbatory habits.

Yet his private sorrows and anxieties were in fact part of
his greatest contribution: his investigation into the strange
unhappiness of the human mind. His work shows us that
the conscious, rational part of the mind is, in his words, 'not
even master in its own house.' Instead, we are governed by
competing forces, many beyond our conscious perception.
We should attend to him – however strange, off-putting, or
humorous some of his theories may seem – because he gives
us a wonderfully enlightening account of why being human
is very difficult indeed.

1. Pleasure vs reality

Freud first put forward a theory about this inner conflict in his essay 'Formulations on the Two Principles of Mental Functioning', written in 1911. Here, he described the 'pleasure principle', which drives us towards pleasurable things like sex and panna cotta and away from unpleasurable things like drudgery and annoying people. Our lives begin governed by this instinct alone; as infants we behave more or less solely according to the pleasure principle. As we grow older, our unconscious continues to do the same, for 'the unconscious is always infantile.'

The problem, Freud said, is that we can't simply follow the pleasure principle, as it would make us do crazy things like sleep with members of our own family, steal other people's money, and kill people who annoy us. We need to take into account what he called 'the reality principle'.

Ideally, we adjust to the demands of the reality principle in a useful, productive way: 'a momentary pleasure, uncertain in its results, is given up, but only in order to gain along the new path an assured pleasure at a later time.' This is the

Babies are slaves to the pleasure principle.

underlying principle of so much of religion, education and science: we learn to control ourselves and put away short-term pleasure to achieve greater (and usually more socially acceptable) pleasure in the long run.

But Freud noticed that, in practice, most of us struggle with this. He believed that there were better and worse kinds of adaptations to reality; he called the troublesome ones 'neuroses'. In cases of neuroses, we put aside – or re-press – the pleasure drive, but at a cost. We become unhappy without understanding our own symptoms of distress.

For example, we might struggle to repress our attraction to people who are not our partner. However, this struggle is too painful to experience directly all the time, so we'll unconsciously repress it. Instead, we'll experience delusions of jealousy about our partner, and become convinced they are cheating on us. This is a projection of our true anxiety. It will quell some of our guilt about our wandering eye, but it may also drive our partner mad. It's an adaptation to the challenges we face – but, of course, it isn't really a very good one.

Freud thought that life was full of these kinds of neuroses, brought on as the result of a conflict between our 'id', driven by the pleasure principle, and the 'ego', which rationally decides what we should do about the drives of the id. At times, neuroses come about because of a struggle between the ego and the superego, which is our moralistic side.

In order to understand these dynamics, we'll usually need to think back to the time in our lives that generated so many of our neuroses.

2. Childhood
Childhood is really the time when we learn different adaptations to reality, for the better or (often) for the worse. As babies, we emerge full of raw, unprincipled desires. As we are raised, however, we are 'civilised' and thus brought into line with social reality. If we don't adjust well, trouble will emerge.

First in our psychological history comes what Freud termed the 'oral phase', where we deal with eating. We're born wanting to drink from the breast whenever we want. Yet over time, we have to be weaned. This is very difficult for us. If our parents aren't careful (or worse, if they're a little sadistic) we might pick up all kinds of neuroses: internalised self-denial, using food to calm ourselves down, or hostility to the breast. Most of all, we struggle with dependence. If our mothers wait too long, we may grow up to be very demanding and surprised when the outside world doesn't provide everything we want. Or, we may learn to distrust dependence on others altogether.

Then comes the 'anal phase' (more commonly known as 'potty-training') where we face the challenges of defecation. Our parents tell us what to do and when to go – they tell us how to be good. At this phase we begin to learn about testing the limits of authority. We might, for example, choose to withhold out of defiance. We may then, as adults, become 'anally retentive' and resistant. We also might hold back from spending money. Alternatively, if our parents are too permissive, we may test authority and other people's boundaries too frequently. This leads not only to 'making messes' as a toddler, but also to being spendthrift and inconsiderate when we are older.

Freud says that the way our parents react matters a great deal. If they shame us when we fail to comply, we may develop all kinds of fears and anxieties. But at the same time we need to learn about boundaries and socially appropriate behaviour. In short, potty-training is the prime time for navigating the conflict between our own pleasure-seeking and the demands of our parents. We have to adapt to these demands appropriately, or we'll end up with serious problems.

Next comes the 'phallic phase' (it goes until about the age of 6), where we address the problems of genital longings and newly emerged, impossible sexual wishes. Freud shocked his contemporaries by insisting that little children are sexual: they have sexual feelings, they get erections, they masturbate, they want to rub themselves on various objects and people (even now, the idea makes people uncomfortable). In Freud's time, the kid would be told to stop it, violently; now we tell them this gently. But the point is the same: we can't permit childhood sexuality. For the child, this means that a very powerful part of their young self is firmly repressed.

This is even more complicated because children direct their sexual impulses towards their parents. Freud described what he called the Oedipus complex (named after the Greek tragic figure), in which we are all unconsciously predisposed towards 'being in love with the one parent and hating the other.'

It starts like this: as children, most of us are very attached to our mothers. In fact, Freud says that little boys automatically direct their primitive sexual impulses towards her. Yet no matter how much she loves us, mum will always have another life. She probably has a relationship (most likely with our dad) or if not, a number of other priorities that leave us feeling frustrated and abandoned as children. This makes our infant selves feel jealous and angry – and also ashamed and guilty about this anger. A small male child will particularly feel hatred towards the person who takes mum away and also be afraid that that person might kill him. This entire complex – now the word makes sense – provides a huge amount of anxiety for a small child already. (In Freud's view, little girls have it no easier – they just have a slightly different complex.)

Then comes the problem of actual incest. Adults should not have sex with children; this is a very serious incest taboo on which society depends. We're not supposed to have sex with people we're related to either. But even though we claim to all be horrified by it, as if incest were simply the last thing on our mind, Freud reminds us that things are never made into a taboo unless quite a lot of people are keen on breaking the taboo in their unconscious. This explains all the hysteria around incest and sex with children – the idea of it is lurking somewhere in the back of our minds.

In order to prevent sex in the family, the child has to be weaned off the desire to have sex with mum or dad. Mum or dad need also to be kind and not make them feel guilty about sex. But all kinds of things can go terribly wrong.

Most of us experience some form of sexual confusion around our parents that later ties into our ideas of love. Mum and dad both give us love, but they mix it in with various kinds of troubling behaviour. Yet because we love them and depend on them, we remain loyal to them and also to their destructive patterns. So for example, if our mother is cold and makes belittling comments, we will be apt nevertheless to long for her or even find her very nice. As a result, however, we may be prone to always associate love with coldness.

3. Adulthood

Ideally, we should be able to have genital sex without trouble, and, in the long term, fuse love and sex together with someone who is kind. Of course, it rarely happens.

Typically, we can't fuse sex and love: we have a sense that sex doesn't belong with tender feelings. 'A man of this kind will show a sentimental enthusiasm for women whom he deeply respects but who do not excite him to sexual activities,' noted Freud, 'and he will only be potent with other women whom he does not "love" but thinks little of or even despises.'

Neuroses aren't just created within individuals. The whole of society keeps us neurotic. In his book *Civilisation and its Discontents* (1930), Freud wrote that a degree of repression and psychological dysfunction is simply the cost of living in a society. Society insists on regulating sex, imposes the incest taboo, requires us to put off our immediate desires, demands that we follow authority and makes money available only through work. A non-repressive civilisation is a contradiction.

4. Analysis

Freud attempted to invent a cure for neurosis: psychoanalysis. But from the outset, the offering was very limited. He thought the patient should be under 50, or else their minds would be too rigid. It was very expensive, especially since he thought his patients should come four times a week. And he was quite pessimistic about the outcome: he believed that at best he could transform hysterical unhappiness into everyday misery. Nevertheless, he thought that with a little proper analysis, people could uncover their neuroses and better adjust to the difficulties of reality.

Here are some of the things Freud sought to 'analyse' in his sessions:

a. Dreams

Freud believed that sleep was a chance for us to relax from the difficulties of being conscious, and especially to experience what he called wish-fulfilment. It might not seem obvious at first. For example, we might think we dream about failing our A levels simply because we're stressed at work. But Freud tells us that we actually get these kinds of dreams because some part of us wishes that we'd failed our A levels, and thus didn't have all the responsibilities of adulthood, our job, and supporting our family. Of course, we also have more intuitive wish-fulfilment dreams, like the ones where we sleep with a beguiling co-worker we had never, in the day, known we liked.

Once we wake, we must return to the world and the dictates of our moralistic superego – so we usually repress our dreams. This is why we quickly forget the really exciting dreams we had.

b. Parapraxes

Freud loved to notice how his patients used words. He thought it was particularly telling when they had a slip of the tongue, or a parapraxis (we now call these revealing

Freud's office in London, with a couch for his patients to sit or lie on
as they were analysed.

mistakes ('Freudian slips'). For example, Freud wrote of a
man who asked his wife (whom he didn't like very much)
to come and join him in America, where he had emigrated.
The man meant to suggest that she should take the ship the
Mauretania, but in fact he wrote that she should come on
the *Lusitania* – which had sunk off the coast of Ireland,
torpedoed by a German submarine in the First World War,
resulting in the loss of all on board.

c. Jokes

Freud thought that humour was a psychological survival
mechanism. In his *Jokes and their Relation to the Unconscious* (1905), he explained: '[Jokes] make possible the satisfaction of an instinct (whether lustful or hostile) in the face
of an obstacle that stands in its way.' In short, jokes – like
dreams – allow us to bypass authority and satisfy wishes.

* * *

In 1933, the Nazis rose to power. 'What progress we are making,' Freud told a friend. 'In the Middle Ages they would have burnt me; nowadays they are content with burning my books.' Even he failed to see what the world was up against with the Nazis. Elite friends and a sympathetic Nazi officer helped him and his family escape to London, where he lived for the rest of his life. He died in 1939 of jaw cancer.

Following in Freud's footsteps, other analysts developed new psychoanalytic techniques and eventually the wide and varied field of modern psychiatry. Much of modern therapy is very different from Freud's, but it began with his premise of discovering the dark and difficult parts of our inner lives and unwinding them, slowly, under the guidance of a trained and kindly listener.

We may think we've outgrown him, or that he was ridiculous all along. There's a temptation to say he just made everything up, and life isn't quite as hard as he makes it out to be. But then one morning we find ourselves filled with inexplicable anger towards our partner, or running high with unrelenting anxiety on the train to work, and we're reminded all over again just how elusive, difficult, and Freudian our mental workings actually are. We could still reject his work, of course. But as Freud said, 'No one who disdains the key will ever be able to unlock the door.'

Anna Freud

1895–1982

Anna Freud walking with her father, Sigmund, 1913.

'D'efensive' behaviour is at the root of a lot of the trouble we have with ourselves and others. It leads us to direct blame inaccurately, to hear reasonable criticisms as cruel attacks and to resort to sarcasm and irony as an alternative to sincerity.

The finest guide to the origins of defensive behaviour was the psychoanalyst, and daughter of Sigmund, Anna Freud. Anna was the youngest of the family's six children. She was born in Vienna in 1895 – when her father's radical theories of sex and the mind were starting to make him famous across *fin de siècle* Europe. Anna was regarded as a 'plain' child and she struggled at school, where she acquired a dire nickname – 'black devil'. But later she became a school teacher and then a psychoanalyst – and pioneered the treatment of children.

In 1934, she published *The Ego and Mechanisms of Defence* – the book that laid out for the first time the core idea that we instinctively try to protect our 'ego' (our acceptable picture of who we are) with a variety of defences. A defence mechanism is a method of response intended to spare us pain; the problem is that in the act of defending ourselves in the immediate term, we harm our longer-term chances of dealing with reality and therefore of developing and maturing as a result.

Anna Freud highlighted ten key types of defence mechanism.

1. Denial

We don't admit there is a problem. We think things like: 'I enjoy drinking a lot and I sometimes get quite bad hangovers. But I don't drink too much.' Or: 'I spend quite a bit of money. But no more than other people. I wouldn't say I am a financially irresponsible person.' If other people (relatives, friends, a partner) try to get us to admit there is an issue, we tend to react very badly.

The immediate survival mechanism – the short-term instinct to feel all right about oneself – is to refuse to recognise there is a problem because admitting it means we're going to have to do all sorts of difficult and awkward things about it. But denial gets in the way of long-term coping.

Sometimes, pure denial doesn't quite feel safe enough. One creates a bit of evidence on the other side. A 9-year-old boy – who'd sometimes very much like a cuddle from his mother but is reluctant to admit this to himself – might say that she's mean and annoying. He's 'proving' to himself that he doesn't need her, so when he feels a bit weepy and lonely, it can't possibly be because he needs his mummy.

Denial isn't a lie. This defence mechanism is like a smokescreen that makes it very hard for us to see what's going on in our own lives.

2. Projection
This involves recognising a negative feeling, but instead of seeing that it is one's own dark emotion, the feeling is given to (or projected onto) someone else. This can sound weird and complicated, but it happens a lot.

You get a note saying the boss wants to see you personally about something serious. Your first instinct might be to imagine that they are going to fire you, explain how they've found out some terrible facts about you. You've got a picture in your head of this person being cold, forceful and very angry. When you get to the meeting, you just hear some useful guidance about an important new contract that's coming up. So, all the emotions – the terror, the coldness, the vindictive anger – are actually coming from you. You projected them onto your senior colleague. You have given the negative feelings, which you don't want to recognise in yourself, to someone else.

Or, you feel that your partner is going to be extremely critical if you don't make more money this year than last year. You fret a lot about this; you imagine the cutting remarks they're going to make, the withering looks. But in reality they don't have these feelings. They may be genuinely understanding and sympathetic (though, yes, of course, it would be nice if your income was on the rise). The harsh, bitter thoughts are not in your partner. They are in you – and they came from your mother, let's say. But you project them onto the nearest candidate.

Therefore, instead of being very frustrated with yourself (a highly uncomfortable feeling), you can feel hard done by (a slightly easier feeling). After all, you've got – at least, in your head – such a pushy, never-satisfied partner. Instead of facing the painful and difficult question of why you can't make more – or why it isn't OK for you that you make what you do – you create a diversion: your 'annoying' partner.

3. Turning against the self
We turn to defence mechanisms to protect ourselves from psychological suffering. So it sounds paradoxical to say (as Anna Freud insisted) that hurting oneself – being angry with, or loathing oneself – could be a defence. It's a matter of what we find most frightening. There may be many things that scare us much more than disliking ourselves.

Defences can be traced back to childhood. And a child abandoned, or harmed by, a parent might well seek refuge in a thought that, though grim, is less awful than the alternatives. 'I (feels the child) must be bad and worthless. I'm an awful person – that's why my parent is behaving this way.' So, really – the thought goes – I still have a good parent. It's painful – but it may be less catastrophic than the truth: one is actually in the hands of someone who doesn't care.

4. Sublimation
This involves redirecting unacceptable thoughts or emotions into 'higher' and ideally more constructive channels.

Many musicians have turned negative life experiences – drug addiction, social ills, family problems, and so on – into popular and resonating performances and songs, which have served to energise and inspire many people. A troubled artist such as Vincent van Gogh, who struggled with an absinth addiction that famously led him to cut off his ear, was able to channel his problems into his artwork and create intensely memorable images.

Art gives us the most conspicuous examples of a more widespread possibility. An aggressive impulse to tell everyone what to do and to impose one's will without restraint may be sublimated into a determination to make one's work accurate and impressive. A fascistic impulse may be redirected into a socially beneficial aspiration for order and coherence.

5. Regression

Often enough, childhood seems – in retrospect at least – a time of safety. As a child one was shielded from responsibility. One was not expected to understand, to take difficult decisions, to be consistent, to be good at explaining what the matter was.

In regression – as a defence – one becomes childish in some crucial way. One might, for instance, dither a great deal, rather than take a decision and bear responsibility for the consequences.

A core feature of regression is the conviction that troubles are always the fault of other people. It's a strategic return to the child's belief that the parents rule the world and can do anything, so if anything goes wrong they could and should put it right. And the one person who cannot possibly be blamed is, of course, the child.

A tantrum is a characteristic regressive defence mechanism. Rather than try to work out a solution to a problem, one tries (in the logic of childhood) to solve it by getting upset. In the adult world this can look crazy. But babies really do have to signal for help by crying, screaming and banging their fists. It's absolutely the best they can do. So the tantrum means, in effect – I cannot be responsible for this situation: you must help me because I am only a baby.

6. Rationalisation

Rationalisation is a smart-sounding excuse for our actions (or what happens to us). But it's carefully tailored to get the conclusion we feel we need: that we are innocent, nice, worthy.

One key type of rationalisation involves doing down the things one does not have but secretly would like. After being rejected for a job, the defensive rationaliser will say: 'it was a boring company' or 'I never wanted the job anyway'. They may have very much desired the job. But it can be agonising and deeply humiliating to admit this to oneself. So, a more acceptable sense of oneself is preserved by creating the reasonable, careful – rational – sounding fiction: 'it wasn't actually a very good job, now I come to think of it more seriously.' But it's not the assessment of the merits of the job that leads to the conclusion; rather, it's the urgent psychological need to protect one's self-esteem.

7. Intellectualisation

Intellectualisation is similar. It involves ignoring something very painful and important by starting a highly plausible conversation inside one's head about something entirely different. The scarring sense of loss, guilt, betrayal and anger on breaking up with a partner might be neutralised by thinking about the history of the late Roman Empire or the government's plan to raise interest rates. Many intellectuals are not merely thinking a lot. They are also guilty of 'intellectualisation'; making sure their researches keep a range of more pertinent issues at bay.

8. Reaction formation

Reaction formation involves doing the opposite of our initial, unacceptable feelings. We might call it 'overcompensating'.

Someone who has a strong interest in sex with teenagers may, for instance, join a religion with a particular emphasis on abstinence among the young. We are often guilty of reaction formation in childhood. When we are embarrassed about being attracted to a classmate, we might be mean or aggressive towards them, instead of admitting our attraction.

9. Displacement

Displacement is the redirection of a (usually aggressive) desire to a substitute recipient. It is generally engendered by a frustrating person appearing to us as a threat and us reacting to it by directing our feelings towards someone/something else who is easier to blame.

So a classic case is someone who may feel threatened by their boss and comes home and shouts at their partner.

10. Fantasy

Fantasy is another escapist mechanism. It avoids problems by imagining them away or disassociating oneself from reality.

Fantasy manifests in a range of everyday scenarios – from daydreaming to reading literature to looking at porn. We use these moments to transport ourselves from the threatening world to find comfort elsewhere. After a bad day at work, for instance, you might sink into an action film, listen to psychedelic music or log on to youporn.com. Such activities enable us to escape our real problems or concerns. The travel industry relies on our need to fantasise.

***

In March 1938, two years after writing the book on defence mechanisms, Anna moved to London with her family to escape the Nazi occupation of Vienna. After the war, with a friend, Kate Friedlaender, who specialised in juvenile delinquency, she set up child therapy courses at a nursery and clinic in Hampstead.

She died in 1982. Her ashes were placed next to her parents in the Golders Green Crematorium in North London, in an ancient Greek funeral urn, together with those of her lifelong partner and colleague, Dorothy Tiffany-Burlingham.

Conclusions

Anna Freud started from a position of deep generosity towards defence mechanisms. We turn to them because we feel immensely threatened. They are our instinctive ways of warding off danger and limiting psychological pain.

Anna Freud keeps reminding us that defences are not voluntary. They are not conscious deliberate choices. We don't realise what we're doing. We don't think of ourselves as being defensive. We don't see that we're in denial, or that we're rationalising. The role of a defence mechanism isn't to get at a truth, but to ward off distress.

Anna Freud is teaching us a lesson in modesty. For she reveals the extreme probability that defence mechanisms are playing a marked and powerful role in one's own life – though without it being obvious to oneself that this is so. It's a humbling thought – and one that should induce a little more gratitude to those who consent to live their lives in close proximity to us.

Melanie Klein

1882–1960

Melanie Klein was a highly creative and original Viennese Jewish psychoanalyst who discovered the work of Freud at the age of 26 and devoted her life to enriching and nuancing it in intriguing and valuable ways. She is perhaps best remembered today for an unlikely-sounding but inherently sensible theory, advanced in her book *The Psychoanalysis of Children* (1932), about a 'good breast' and a 'bad breast' – of which more in a minute.

Freud had achieved renown by evoking for us just how deeply unacceptable many of our desires are in their raw, undisguised forms. Beneath the civilised surface, in our unconscious minds, we are motivated by what the inventor of psychoanalysis called 'the pleasure principle', which incites us to want a shifting array of surprising, anarchic and (from an everyday point of view) simply shocking things. We want to kill, castrate and maim our enemies, be the most powerful people on earth, have sex with unusual body parts of men, women and children, pair off with members of our own families and become immortal.

So explosive, peculiar and dangerous are these wishes, they must be overruled by the rational mind, or ego, if we are to get on in the world. But this process can go more or less well, depending on how our conscious minds emerge from the vagaries of childhood. At worst, in our attempts to quash these impossible unconscious demands, we fall prey to rigid neuroses and inhibitions, which defend us from what we want, but only at a high cost: we become uncreative and severely hampered in daily life. For example, we might become unable to leave the house (so afraid is a part of us that we could try to murder someone); we might become impotent (for we're somewhere deep down terrified of the aggression of a father figure in relation to our potency); or we might fail at everything we do (to make sure we don't rival a sibling we secretly envy and yet dread). It is these sort of neuroses that psychoanalysis was designed to help us understand and patiently unpick, so that we might eventually make more flexible, less inhibited adjustments to reality.

Melanie Klein discovered psychoanalysis in 1914 and was at once captivated by its ambition and wisdom. A highly intelligent woman, she had been held back by her father from her desire to become a doctor and had been pushed by her family into a loveless marriage with a coarse, unpleasant man with whom she had nothing in common. She was bored, sexually frustrated and mentally unwell. Psychoanalysis saved her. She left her husband, read everything she could, attended lectures, and started publishing papers of her own. She soon departed from Freud in an area that most other analysts had overlooked: the analysis of children. Freud had been sceptical that children could ever be analysed properly, their minds being in his view too unformed to allow for a perspective on the unconscious. But Klein now argued that an analyst could get a useable view into a child's inner world through studying how they played with toys in his or her presence. She therefore equipped her consulting room with small horses, figurines and locomotives and made the observation of how children played with them a centrepiece of her clinical work. She was to establish herself as a child psychoanalyst, first in Berlin and then in London, where she settled in 1926 and remained for the rest of her life (becoming a star among the Bloomsbury group and particular friends with Virginia and Leonard Woolf).

In her work with children, Klein wanted to understand how human beings evolve from the primitive pleasure-seeking impulses of early infancy to the more mature adaptations of later life – and in particular, she wanted to know what might go wrong on this journey, giving rise to the neurotic adaptations of adults.

She was first and foremost struck by the difficulty of the young infant's situation (in the words of the psychoanalyst Julia Kristeva, Klein described the newborn's days and

nights 'with the horror of a Hieronymus Bosch painting').
Weak, utterly at the mercy of adults, unable to grasp what is
happening, the infant cannot – in Klein's description – grasp
that people around it are in fact *people*, with their own alternative reality and independent points of view. In the early
weeks, the mother is not even 'a mother' to her child, she
is – to come to the crux of the issue – just a pair of breasts
that appear and disappear with unpredictable and painful
randomness. In relation to this mother, all the infant experiences are moments of intense pain and then, for reasons
it can't understand, moments of equally intense pleasure.
When the breast is there and the milk flows, a primordial
calm and satisfaction descends upon the infant: it is suffused with feelings of well-being, gratitude and tenderness
(feelings that will, in adulthood, be strongly associated with
being in love, a moment where breasts continue to play a
notable role for many). But when the breast is desired and yet
for whatever reason it is missing, then the infant is thrown
into unfathomable panic: it feels starving, enraged, terrified
and vengeful.

   This, thought Klein, leads the infant to adopt a primitive defence mechanism against what would otherwise be
intolerable anxiety. It 'splits' the mother into two very different breasts: a 'good breast' and a 'bad breast'. The bad
breast is hated with a passion; the infant wants to bite,
wound and destroy this object of unholy frustration. But
the good breast is revered with an equally thorough, though
more benign, intensity.

   With time, in healthy development, this 'split' heals. The
child will gradually perceive that there is in truth no entirely
good and no entirely bad breast; both belong to a mother
who is a perplexing mixture of the positive and the negative:
a source of pleasure *and* frustration, joy *and* suffering. The
child (for, by now, we are talking of someone aged around
4 years old) discovers a key idea in Kleinian psychoanalysis:
the concept of *ambivalence*. To be able to feel ambivalent

CLETOFONTE PRETI, *The Suckling*, 1843–1880

about someone is, for Kleinians, an enormous psychological achievement and the first marker on the path to genuine maturity.

But it isn't inevitable or assured. The grey area is hard to reach. Only slowly can a healthy child grasp the crucial distinction between intention and effect, between what a mother may have wanted for it and what the child might have felt at her hands nevertheless. While no sane mother would ever want to frustrate and scare her own child, this child might nevertheless have been badly hurt and confused by her. These complicated psychological realisations belong to what Klein called 'the depressive position', a moment of soberness and melancholy when the growing child takes on board (unconsciously) the idea that reality is more complicated and less morally neat than it had ever previously imagined: the mother (or other people generally) cannot be neatly blamed for every setback; almost nothing is totally pure or totally evil, things are a perplexing, thought-provoking mixture of the good and bad ... This is hard to take and – for Klein – explains the serious faraway look that may sometimes enter the eyes of children during daydreams. These small beings look oddly wise and grave at such moments; they are, somewhere deep inside, cottoning on to the moral ambiguity of the real world.

Unfortunately, in Klein's analysis, not everyone makes it to the depressive position, for some get stuck in a mode of primitive splitting she termed (somewhat dauntingly) the 'paranoid-schizoid position'. For many years, even into adulthood, these cursed people will find themselves unable to tolerate the slightest ambivalence: keen to preserve their sense of their own innocence, they must either hate or love. They must seek scapegoats or idealise. In relationships, they tend to fall violently in love and then – at the inevitable moment when a lover in some way disappoints them – switch abruptly and become incapable of feeling anything anymore. These unfortunates are likely to move from candidate to candidate, always seeking a vision of complete satisfaction, which is repeatedly violated by an unwitting error on the lover's part.

We don't have to believe in the literal truth of Klein's theory to see that it has value for us as an unusual but useful representation of maturity. The impulse to reduce people into what they can do for us (give us milk, make us money, keep us happy), rather than what they are in and of themselves (a multifaceted being with their own often elusive centre of gravity), can be painfully observed in emotional life generally. With Klein's help, we learn that coming to terms with the ambivalent nature of all relationships belongs to the business of growing up (a task we're never quite done with) – and is likely to leave us a little sad, if not for a time quite simply depressed.

Donald Winnicott

1896–1971

How do you build a better world? There are so many well-known, urgent places you might start: malaria, carbon emissions, tax evasion, the drug trade, soil erosion, water pollution …

Donald Winnicott deserves his place in history because of the dramatic simplicity of his approach. He proposed that the happiness and future satisfaction of the human race depended ultimately not so much on external political issues, but on something far closer to home: the way parents bring up their children. All the sicknesses of humanity were, in his view, in essence consequences of a failure of parental provision. Fascism, delinquency, rage, misogyny, alcoholism, these were only the symptoms of poor childhoods that the collective would have to pay for. The road to a better society begins in the nursery.

Donald Winnicott was an English paediatrician, who early on in his career became passionate about the then new field of psychoanalysis. He was analysed by James Strachey, who had translated Freud into English, and became Britain's first medically trained child psychoanalyst. He worked as a consultant in children's medicine at the Paddington Green Children's Hospital in London, and also played a crucial role in public education around child-rearing, delivering some fifty talks on the BBC, tirelessly lecturing around the country and authoring fifteen books, among which is the bestselling *Home is Where We Start From*.

It must have felt very odd, in 1954, to tune into BBC Radio at prime time and hear someone with a gentle, intelligent voice arguing incisively against the idea that babies cry 'to get attention' or that sending 7-year-olds to boarding school might be a good idea so as to 'toughen them up.'

It was rather strange, too, that Winnicott should even have been English, given that his country was notorious, then as now, for its lack of tenderness and its resistance to introspection (and its commitment to irony, detachment and sarcasm instead). As he pointed out: 'The Englishman does not want to be upset, to be reminded that there are personal tragedies all over the place, that he is really not happy in himself; in short, he refuses to be put off his golf.'

And yet Winnicott's brand of psychoanalysis was, on closer inspection, peculiarly English. He wrote pragmatic, homespun prose, expressing the deepest ideas in plain, unadorned language. There was no German incomprehensibility or abstraction here. There was also a characteristic English modesty about what he saw as the point of child psychoanalysis. He wanted to help people to be, in his famous formulation, 'good enough' parents; not brilliant or perfect ones (as other nations might have wished), but just OK. And that was because he displayed, to a high degree, the downbeat, modest, realistic, temperament that is the particular glory of the English mind.

In an early paper, he announced his project as such:

> I find it useful to divide the world of people into two classes. There are those who were never 'let down' as babies and who are to that extent candidates for the enjoyment of life and of living. There are also those who did suffer traumatic experiences of the kind that result from environmental letdown, and who must carry with them all their lives the memories of the state they were in at moments of disaster. These are candidates for lives of storm and stress and perhaps illness.

It was this second category that he wanted to save and spare in the next generation. So what would it take, in his eyes, to encourage the 'good enough' parent? Winnicott put forward a number of suggestions:

1. Remember that your child is very vulnerable
Winnicott begins by impressing on his audience how psychologically fragile an infant is. It doesn't understand itself, it

doesn't know where it is, it is struggling to stay alive, it has no way of grasping when the next feed will come, it can't communicate with itself or others. It is an undifferentiated, unindividuated mass of competing drives. It isn't a person. The early months are hence an immense struggle. Winnicott's work never loses sight of this, and he therefore repeatedly insists that it is those around the infant who have to 'adapt', so as to do everything to interpret the child's needs and not impose demands for which the child is not ready.

A child who has adapted to the world too early, or who has had inappropriate demands made upon it, will be a prime candidate for mental problems, just as health is the result of an environment that can respond appropriately to the child, which can keep elements of reality at bay until the small creature is ready.

At worse, a depressed mother might prematurely force an infant to be 'cheerful', to be together because she was not; a child of very angry, unstable parents might be terrified from expressing any of its darker emotions; or a child of intrusive parents might be prevented from developing a capacity to be alone.

2. Let a child be angry
Winnicott knew what violence, what hate there could be in a healthy infant. Referring to what happens if a parent forgets a feed, he cautioned: 'If you fail him, it must feel to him as if the wild beasts will gobble him up.'

But though the infant might sometimes want to kill and destroy, it is vital for the parents to allow rage to expend itself, and for them not in any way to be threatened or moralistic about 'bad' behaviour:

> If a baby cries in a state of rage and feels as if he has destroyed everyone and everything, and yet the people round him remain calm and unhurt, this experience greatly strengthens his ability to see that what

he feels to be true is not necessarily real, that fantasy and fact, both important, are nevertheless different from each other.

Winnicott interpreted violent feelings against parents as a natural aspect of the maturational process: 'For a child to be brought up so that he can discover the deepest part of his nature, someone has to be defied, and even at times hated ... without there being a danger of a complete break in the relationship.'

This is why he appreciated and spoke out for difficult adolescents, the sort that scream at their parents and try the odd bit of stealing from their purses. They were proof of children who had been properly loved and could hence dare to defy and test the adult world:

> A normal child, if he has confidence in mother and father, pulls out all the stops. In the course of time, he tries out his power to disrupt, to destroy, to frighten, to wear down, to waste, to wangle, and to appropriate. Everything that takes people to the courts (or to the asylums for that matter) has its normal equivalent in infancy and early childhood ... If the home can stand up to all the child can do to disrupt it, [things will settle down]. (Winnicott is almost always deeply encouraging in his tone).

3. Make sure your child isn't too compliant

Parents are delighted when infants and children follow their rules. Such children are called good. Winnicott was very scared of 'good' children. He had a messier view of childhood. The point of the early years was to be able to express freely a lot of 'bad' feelings without consequences, and without fear of retribution.

However, there might be parents who could not tolerate too much bad behaviour and would demand compliance too early and too strictly. This would lead, in Winnicott's formulation, to the emergence of a 'False Self' – a persona that would be outwardly compliant, outwardly good, but was suppressing its vital instincts; who was not able to properly balance up its social with its destructive sides and that couldn't be capable of real generosity or love, because it hadn't been allowed fully to explore selfishness and hate. Only through proper, attentive nurture would a child be able to generate a 'True Self'.

In Winnicott's scheme, adults who can't be creative, who are somehow a little dead inside, are almost always the children of parents who have not been able to tolerate defiance, parents who have made their offspring 'good' way before their time, thereby killing their capacity to be properly good, properly generous and kind (for the compliant personality is in truth only a fake version of a responsible, giving self).

4. Let your child be

Every failure of the environment forces a child to adapt prematurely. For example, if the parents are too chaotic, the child quickly tries to overthink the situation. Its rational faculties are overstimulated (it may, in later life, try to be an intellectual).

A parent who is depressed might unwittingly force the child to be too cheerful – giving it no time to process its own melancholy feelings. Winnicott saw the dangers in a child who, in his words, has to 'look after mother's mood'.

Winnicott had a special hatred for 'people [who] are always jogging babies up and down on their knees trying to produce a giggle.' This was merely their way of warding off their own sadness, by demanding laughter from a baby who might have very different things on its mind.

The primordial act of parental health for Winnicott is simply to be able to tune out of oneself for a time in the name of empathising with the ways and needs of a small, mysterious, beautiful fragile person whose unique otherness must be acknowledged and respected in full measure.

5. Realise the gravity of the job you've taken on

Many of the parents Winnicott saw were worn down by their labours. Winnicott tried to bolster them by reminding them of the utmost importance of what they were doing. They were, in their own way, as significant to the nation as the prime minister and the cabinet:

> The foundation of the health of the human being is laid by you in the baby's first weeks and months. Perhaps this thought can help a little when you feel strange at the temporary loss of your interest in world affairs. ... It is not surprising. You are engaged in founding the mental health of the next generation.

Winnicott called parenting: 'the only real basis for society, and the only factory for the democratic tendency in a country's social system.'

Of course, there will be errors. Things go wrong in childhood. And that's what psychoanalysis is for. In Winnicott's eyes, the analyst in later years acts as a substitute parent, a proxy 'good enough' figure who 'is in a position of the mother of an infant'. Good analysis has things in common with those early years. Here, too, the analyst should listen without forcing the patient to get 'better' ahead of time. She shouldn't force a cure down his or her throat, she should provide a safe place where bits of childhood that weren't completed or went awry can be recreated and rehearsed. Analysis is a chance to fill in the missing steps.

In his descriptions of what parents should do for their children, Winnicott was in effect referring to a term that he rarely mentioned directly: love. We often imagine love to be about a magical intuitive 'connection' with someone. But, in Winnicott's writings, we get a different picture. It's about a surrender of the ego, a putting aside of one's own needs and assumptions, for the sake of close, attentive listening to another, whose mystery one respects, along with a commitment not to get offended, not to retaliate, when something 'bad' emerges, as it often does when one is close to someone, child or adult.

Since Winnicott's death, we've collectively grown a little better at parenting. But only a little. We may spend more time with our children, we know in theory that they matter a lot, but we're arguably still failing at the part Winnicott focused on: adaptation. We still routinely fail to suppress our own needs or stifle our own demands when we're with a child. We're still learning how to love our children – and that, Winnicott would argue, is why the world is still full of the walking-wounded, people of outward 'success' and respectability who are nevertheless not quite 'real' inside and inflict their wounds on others. We've a way to go until we get to be 'good enough'. It's a task – Winnicott would have insisted – that's in its own way as important as curing malaria or slowing global warming.

John Bowlby

1907–1990

A mong our deepest and seemingly most natural aspirations is the longing to form stable, satisfying relationships: to thrive in partnerships that are good for both people. It doesn't seem much to ask. A lot of people are looking for roughly the same thing. But the painful fact is that very large numbers of relationships have one difficult episode after another, or seemingly intractable miserable conflicts running through them; relationships feel like a struggle, rather than a support. It's one of the biggest questions: why is it so hard for us to have the happy, constructive relationships we all want?

The huge – and not yet fully digested – insight of psychoanalysis is that the challenges of relationships do not start over dinner in an interesting restaurant or a college bar. They start, in fact, when we are children. There is no more important period of our lives than childhood; a good childhood is the bedrock of a happy life and a bad one just about dooms us to enduring misery. It was the contribution of the great psychoanalyst John Bowlby to trace the tensions and conflicts we have with our partners back to our early experience of maternal care.

His ideas are sound in part because he drew so deeply and honestly on his own experiences in order to formulate them. Born in 1907, Edward John Mostyn Bowlby had a quintessentially upper-class British childhood. His father was a famous and highly successful doctor, with a knighthood and royal connections. Young Bowlby hardly saw his parents and was looked after by a lovely nanny, Minnie. But Minnie was an employee, and when John was 4, she was sent away. His parents weren't being deliberately callous. They (like pretty much everyone else at the time) didn't realise how wounding her departure could be. At 7, Bowlby went off – in line with the conventions of his class – to boarding school, to a realm from which maternal warmth was rigorously excluded.

Bowlby was a brilliant medical student and an imaginative researcher. In 1952 he made a film, *A Two-Year-Old Goes to Hospital*, which showed the suffering a child went

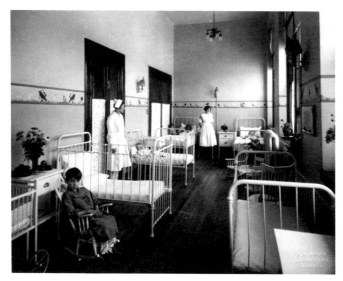

Hospital wards used to deprive children of connection with their mothers.

through when they were institutionally separated from their parents. In the wards, mothers were not allowed to hold their sick children, for instance, for fear of spreading germs. Visiting times were punitively restricted.

When he was a consultant to the World Health Organization in the early 1950s, Bowlby wrote a report, *Maternal Care and Mental Health*. He attacked prevalent assumptions (including those vigorously maintained by his own mother), arguing that kindness does not smother and spoil children. And he asserted the importance to both child and mother of developing an intimate and enjoyable relationship. This initiated a wave of reform: the visitation rules of many health institutions were reformed – a dry, bureaucratic move that ended countless afternoons of quiet sorrow and evenings of solitary anguish.

Bowlby poignantly invokes the loving care that a little boy needs: 'all the cuddling and playing, the intimacies of suckling by which a child learns the comfort of his mother's body, the rituals of washing and dressing by which through her pride and tenderness towards his little limbs he learns the values of his own ...' Such experiences teach a basic trust: that difficulties can be managed; that slip-ups are only that and can be put right, that we are naturally entitled to be treated warmly and considerately, without having to do anything to earn this and without having to make special pleas or demands. 'It is as if maternal care were as necessary for the proper development of personality as vitamin D for the proper development of bones.'

The ideal parent is there when the child needs it. They are good at actually listening to what the child is saying. They help the child work out for itself what it is feeling. The ideal parent is not anxiously hanging around trying to micro-manage everything. The ideal parent makes it feel that problems, difficulties and dangers don't always have to be avoided: they can be coped with, solved or skilfully overcome. Such a parent makes the child secure. Not just that the child feels secure at particular moments, but that they take this security with them into the tasks of life: they become secure people, so that they are less urgently in need of external validation, less devastated by failure, less in need of markers of status to reassure themselves of their own worth – because they carry within them a stable, reasonable, secure sense of who they are.

But the fact is that we often don't quite get the maternal care we need. Parents – without meaning to let anyone down – go wrong in endless ways. They are inconsistent: at one point they are hugely available, happy to play and do things; then suddenly they are sternly busy and remote. Or they might be sweet and tender – but equally they might be angry or grumpy. They are around, then they disappear. They might be busy almost all the time, or very much preoccupied by work or social life. Their own fears, anxieties or troubles may keep them from providing the wise, generous attention the child needs.

In a book published in 1959 called *Separation Anxiety*, Bowlby looks at what happens when there isn't enough maternal care. He described the behaviour of children he had observed who had been separated from their parents. They went through three stages: protest, despair and detachment. The first phase began as soon as the parent left, and it would last between a few hours and a week. Protesting children would cry, roll around and react to any movement as the possibility of their mother returning.

If something like this is frequently experienced, then the child craves the attention, love and interest of the parents but feels that anything good may disappear at any moment. They look for a lot of reassurance – and get upset if it is not forthcoming. They are volatile: they take heart, then they despair, then they are filled with hope again. This is the pattern of what Bowlby called 'anxious attachment'.

But the degree of separation from the parents may be greater. The child could feel so helpless they become detached: they enter their own world. To protect themselves, they become remote and cold. They are, Bowlby says, 'attachment avoidant': that is, they see tenderness, closeness, emotional investment as dangerous and to be shunned. They may, in truth, be desperate for a cuddle or for reassurance, but such things look far too treacherous.

The focus of Bowlby's thinking was about what happens to a child if there are too many difficulties in forming secure attachments. But the consequences don't magically get restricted only to the age of 8 or 12 or 17. They are lifelong. The pattern of relating that we develop in childhood gets deployed in our adult lives.

Our attachment style is fed by early experiences: it defines our individual way of being with others. It's how we sense what other people are up to, how we frame our own needs, how we expect things to go. It's a pre-existing script that gets written into our adult relationships – usually without us even realising that this happens. It all feels obvious and familiar (even when it is uncomfortable). We take this with us, from partner to partner.

In line with Bowlby's views about how children relate to their parents, there are three basic kinds of attachment we have to other adults.

1. Secure attachment is the (rare) ideal. If there is a problem, you work it out. You are not appalled by the weakness of your partner. You can take it in your stride, because you can look after yourself when you have to. So if your partner is a bit down, confused, or just plain annoying, you don't have to react too wildly. Because even if they can't be nice to you, you can take care of yourself and have, hopefully, a little left over to meet some of the needs of your partner. You give the other the benefit of the doubt when interpreting behaviour. You realise that maybe they were just busy when they didn't show any interest in your new haircut or insights into the news. Maybe they had a tricky time at work, and that's why they are not interested in your day. The explanations are accommodating, generous – and usually more accurate. You are slow to anger, quick to forgive and forget.

2. Anxious attachment is marked by clinginess: calling just to check where the other is and keeping tabs on what they are up to. You need to make sure that they haven't left you – or the country. Anxious attachment involves a lot of anger because the stakes feel very high. A minor slight, a hasty word, a tiny oversight can look – to the very anxious person – like huge threats. They seem to announce the imminent breakup of the whole relationship. Anxiously attached people quickly become coercive and demanding and focus on their own needs – not their partner's.

3. Avoidant attachment means that you would rather withdraw, and go away, than get angry with or admit you need the other person. If there is a problem, you don't talk. Your instinct is to say you don't really like the other person who has hurt you. Avoidant spouses often team up with anxious ones. It's a risky combination. The avoidant one doesn't give the anxious one much support. And the anxious one is always invading the delicate privacy of the avoidant one.

Bowlby helps us towards more generous – and more constructive – ways of seeing what our partners are doing when they upset or disappoint us. Almost no one, in truth, is purely anxious or avoidant. They are just a bit like that, some of the time. So, alerted by Bowlby, we can see that a partner's apparent coldness and indifference is not caused by their loathing of us, but by the fact that a long time ago they were too badly hurt by intimacy. They are protecting themselves out of fear. They deserve compassion, not a character assassination.

And it opens possibilities of self-knowledge that can help one reform (if only a little) one's own behaviour. Perhaps I work so hard because I can't trust anyone and because, a long time ago, I felt that work might help me to secure the fleeting unreliable love of my parents.

***

Bowlby died in September 1990 in his early eighties, at his summer home on the Island of Skye.

There's a powerful, modest but very real principle of hope at work in his theories. It took a long time for Bowlby's ideas about the importance of the early bond between the mother and child to get broader recognition and support. But it did happen, eventually. There was no single dramatic revolutionary moment. Many thousands of people changed their minds in small ways: an idea that sounded stupid came to seem mildly interesting. The slow revolution took place at dinner tables and at school gates, at conferences in out of the way places and in careful cost-benefit analyses worked out by civil servants. It is a process of social evolution in which there are few obvious heroes and many necessary participants who can never know exactly what contribution they made: so that today a child facing a frightening operation is surrounded by love and kindness and her parents get to sleep in a bed beside her.

How long it took in history for this need to be taken seriously – and so touching it should have been by this particular man, whose family background, childhood, and education could have been expected to close off any such sympathetic insights.

Research shows that in the UK population:

· 56 per cent are securely attached
· 24 per cent are avoidantly attached
· 20 per cent are anxiously attached

Art &
Architecture

Andrea Palladio

1508–1580

n Europe and the US, the average person spends 84 per cent of their life indoors: that is, inside architecture. Much of the rest of the time we are around buildings, even if we're not paying them a great deal of attention. Despite this massive exposure, on the whole we're not – as a culture – very ambitious about what buildings look like. We tend to assume that, mostly, the buildings we live around won't be anything special and that there's nothing to be done about this. We've come to imagine that great buildings are the unique and very expensive creations of genius-architects. You might travel to see great architecture on holiday perhaps, but it's hardly to be expected as standard at home. Vicenza, 25 miles inland from Venice, is one of the leading sites of global architectural tourism, and for one reason: many of the works of Andrea Palladio are located in and around that town.

Andrea Palladio was born at the end of November in 1508 in Padua. He was an apprentice stonemason and later a stone carver. His real name was Andrea di Pietro della Gondola (i.e. Andrew, son of Peter the Gondolier). And it was only when he was around 30 years of age that he got involved in designing buildings himself – and his first important patron suggested a stylish name change, to *Palladio*.

Over the next forty years of his working life, Palladio designed forty or so villas, a couple of town houses and a handful of churches. Not a huge list, given the amount of building that was going on at the time. For most of his career he had a mix of professional successes and setbacks; though during his sixties he finally emerged as the top architect in Venice – about the richest and most powerful city in the world at that time. He was a devoted father, but his two elder sons – who worked alongside him – died young. Palladio himself died in the summer of 1580. He was 71.

Palladio held views on architecture almost entirely opposite to those that are current today. His attitude can be summarised by two central ideas. First, architecture has a clear purpose, which is to help us be better people. And, second, there are rules for good building. Great architecture (he was convinced) is more of a craft than an art: it isn't necessarily expensive and it is for everyday life, for farms, barns and offices, not only for the occasional glamorous project.

1. The purpose of architecture

We tend not to ask this question; it can easily sound naive or pretentious. Either you are supposed to know already or someone is about to launch into a complicated disquisition.

Palladio held that architecture has an important purpose – above and beyond the provision of floors, walls and ceilings. He thought that we should build in order to encourage good states of mind in ourselves and others. In particular, he thought architecture could help us with three psychological virtues: calm, harmony and dignity.

a. Calm

Palladio reduces what's going on; all the elements in a room are centred, balanced, symmetrical. He only uses simple geometrical shapes. Generally, the walls are plain and neutral. There's not meant to be much furniture. The serenity of the space is designed to calm us down; it is not trying to surprise or excite us. It invites us to focus and concentrate, to be less distracted.

b. Harmony

Palladio was obsessed with making sure that every element of a building fitted perfectly with every other.

A fine building ought to appear as an entire and perfect body, wherein every member agrees with its fellow, and each so well with the whole, that it may seem absolutely necessary.

Villa Cornaro, Veneto, Italy, 1552

The design of a window is related to that of a door; every opening is aligned with every other; every room is a clear, simple shape; the doors always line up.

Powerfully coherent buildings are moving because they counter the natural tendency of life for things to get muddled, confused and compromised. They work against our anxiety that many of our concerns won't line up neatly: that work and home life, sex and love, desire and duty will all be continually fighting one another. The building creates an environment in which we are provided with a limited – but real – sense of everything important coming elegantly together.

c. Dignity

One of the ambitions of Palladio's architecture was to give greater dignity to parts of life that had been, unfairly, regarded as unworthy. And that, in his eyes, lacked the prestige they properly deserved.

Villa Barbaro, Veneto, Italy, 1560

At the Villa Barbaro – a farmhouse in the countryside about 40 miles north of Venice – the barns and stables and grain stores are just as grand as the owner's not especially large house. Rather than being hidden away or set at a distance, these working buildings are presented as honourable and important.

He wasn't disguising the utilitarian reality of the farm, rather he was demonstrating its genuine (though generally underappreciated) dignity.

In directing architecture towards these psychological states, Palladio wasn't flattering us. He wasn't pretending that his buildings were reflecting what we're normally like. He knew perfectly well that people tend to be (then as now) irate and agitated; that dignity is a mask that slips; that we get despondent. He wasn't trying to give expression to ordinary human nature. In keeping with the long Classical tradition, he believed that buildings should try to compensate for our weaknesses: encouraging us to be more collected, poised and measured than we manage to be day-to-day. We need serene, harmonious and confident buildings precisely because we're not reliably like that. Ideally, architecture embodies our better selves. The ideal building is like the ideal person.

Palladio is classically pessimistic about our ability to hold onto ideas; the mind is leaky: we very easily lose contact with our own better nature; we're very likely to forget, under pressure, what is important to us. The task of architecture is to provide us with the environment that continuously reminds us about – and encourages us to become – who we really want to be.

2. Rules

Of course, we accept that there are lots of useful rules – for airline safety, accounting practices or card games. But we're generally suspicious of the idea that rules might be important around anything deemed cultural, intimate or creative: the idea that there might be beneficial rules of conversation, art, relationships or indeed of architecture. We tend to see rules as secondary, lacking originality. Like Aristotle, Palladio took the view that many creative undertakings (like writing tragedies, having conversations or cultivating friendships) should be understood as skills or crafts. They are learnable. According to a Classical outlook, good outcomes in such areas are not simply to do with luck or chance. And rules ideally capture what it is we need to do in order to do them well.

In 1570, Palladio published *The Four Books on Architecture*.

It's an early, and very distinguished, example of the 'how to' genre. It gives instruction on how to build. There's a practical guide to digging foundations and how to judge the quality of cement and the various reliable ways of constructing walls and laying floors.

He also develops rules of proportion, based on simple mathematical ratios. The ancient Greek philosopher Pythagoras had famously discovered that two taut strings, one half the length of the other, sound harmonious when vibrated at the same time. The pleasing quality of the sound, he discovered, was governed by a simple mathematical principle. Palladio and others developed a visual equivalent of this.

The fancy surrounds are not the crucial thing. Without them, the window opening will still look lovely, because it is the proportions and not the decoration that make it harmonious. This meant that an equally beautiful building could be produced more cheaply (always one of Palladio's chief concerns) because the same proportions are beautiful irrespective of whether the building is made of marble, brick, concrete or wood.

And he went on to provide a wide range of simple rules for making buildings attractive: they should be symmetrical; there should be three, five or seven openings on a side – not an even number; rooms should have a simple geometrical shape; the length should be three-fifths of the width and the height three-fifths of the width.

Palladio saw himself as a craftsman. He was simply following a set of rules, which others could follow too. He was working against the idea that architecture requires special genius. The ideal of a pattern book is that visually elegant buildings can be put up as standard, as happened (to a significant extent under the influence of Palladio) in London and in many cities in the 18th century.

A central concern of the *Four Books* is to educate the potential client or the consumer of architecture. Often, we're not very sure why we like or dislike buildings. We might have quite positive or negative reactions and say something is great or rather horrible. But if pressed for an explanation, we often find ourselves struggling. We find it difficult to say what it is about one building that makes it attractive and what makes another unappealing. We're tempted to say that it's a purely personal matter, that taste in architecture is purely subjective. It's a well-intended sentiment. But it's also unfortunate. It plays into the hands of developers who have no concerns whatever for beauty – who are safe in the knowledge that they will never be taken to task for what they do.

Conclusion

Palladio's ideas have resonated down the ages. But it isn't when buildings have columns or make nods to ancient temples that they are necessarily at their most authentically 'Palladian'. Buildings are Palladian when they are devoted to calm, harmony and dignity on the basis of rules that can (and should be) widely reused. It's then they display the same underlying ambition of which Palladio is a central exponent and advocate: that it should be normal for buildings to present us with a seductive portrait of our calmest and most dignified selves.

Johannes Vermeer

1632–1675

We live in a world saturated with false glamour. In truth, the problem does not lie with glamour itself, but with the things we have collectively agreed to regard as glamorous. Progress wouldn't be found in eradicating the whole idea of glamour from our lives. Instead, what we need to do is direct our admiration and excitement more wisely: to turn it upon the things that genuinely do deserve prestige.

One of the fundamental things artists can do for us is turn the spotlight of glamour in the best – and most helpful – directions. They can identify things that we tend to overlook but that, ideally, we should care about a great deal. And by the tenderness, beauty, skill and wisdom with which they portray these things, we too can come to see their true worth.

Serving women – and bread and milk – were not regarded as especially exciting in the late 1650s, when Johannes Vermeer painted his famous milkmaid. He didn't seek out a model who was already highly admired. Instead he spent his time looking very carefully at a scene that he happened to love, but that most people at the time would have considered boring and not worth a moment's consideration.

Vermeer saw in the serving woman pouring milk something that he felt deserved prolonged contemplation and admiration. He thought something really important was going on. By worldly standards, it's a pretty humble situation. The room is far from elegant. But the care with which she works is lovely. Vermeer is impressed by the idea that our true needs might be quite simple. Bread and milk are really rather satisfying. The light coming through the window is beautiful. A plain white wall can be delightful.

Vermeer is redistributing glamour by raising the prestige of the things he depicts. And he's trying to get us to feel the same way. The milkmaid is a kind of propaganda (or an advert) for homely pleasures.

Vermeer was born in 1632 in the small and beautiful city of Delft, where his father was a modestly successful art dealer-cum-innkeeper. Vermeer stayed there most of his life.

JOHANNES VERMEER, *The Milkmaid*, 1657

He never travelled away from Delft after his marriage (aged 21). He hardly even left his pleasant house. He and his wife, Catharina, had ten children (and many more pregnancies) and he did a great deal of painting in the front rooms on the upper floor. Vermeer was a slow painter and – in fact – not only a painter. He continued the family businesses of inn-keeping and art dealing and he became the head of the local guild of painters. In contemporary terms, his career was not a huge success. He wasn't especially famous during his lifetime. He didn't make a lot of money.

JOHANNES VERMEER, *The Girl with the Pearl Earring*, 1665

He was in fact an exemplary member of (in those days) a newly important kind of person: the middle-class individual. Vermeer was in his teens when Holland (or technically the Seven Provinces) became an independent state – the first 'bourgeois republic' in the world. In contrast to the semi-feudal aristocratic nations that surrounded it, Holland gave honour and political power to people who were not at the pinnacle of society: to merchants, administrators, prosperous artisans and entrepreneurs. It was the first country in the world to be recognisably modern.

A great insight of Christianity – which is ultimately detachable from the surrounding theology – is that everyone's inner life is important, even if on the outside they do not seem particularly distinguished. The thoughts and feelings of an apprentice tailor count for as much (from a spiritual point of view) as those of a general or an emperor.

Vermeer paints *The Girl with the Pearl Earring* with the same kind of consideration. She isn't anybody famous or important in the eyes of the wider world. She isn't rich. The earring that she wears is nice, but it is a minor trinket by the standards of the fashionable world. It is the one rather pricey thing she owns. But she's not in need of justice – she's not downtrodden or badly treated by the world. She is (for want of a better term) ordinary. Yet, of course, in herself she is (like everyone) not in the least ordinary: she is uniquely, mysteriously and profoundly herself.

The picture that best sums up Vermeer's philosophy, *The Little Street*, has become one of the most famous works of art in the world. It has pride of place in Amsterdam's great Rijksmuseum; it is insured for £100 million and is the subject of a mountain of learned articles.

Yet the painting is curiously – and pointedly – out of synch with its status. Because, above all else, it wants to show us that the ordinary can be very special. The picture says that looking after a simple but beautiful home, cleaning the yard, watching the children, darning cloth – and doing these things faithfully and without despair – is life's real duty.

It is an anti-heroic picture: a weapon against false images of glamour. It refuses to accept that true glamour depends on amazing feats of courage or on the attainment of status. It argues that doing the modest things, things that are expected of all of us, is enough. The picture asks you to be a little like it is: to take the attitudes it loves and to apply them to your life.

JOHANNES VERMEER, *The Little Street*, 1658

If a good, decent society had a founding document, it could be this small picture. It is a central contribution to the world's understanding of happiness.

Vermeer did not live long. He died in 1675, still only in his early forties.

But he had communicated a crucial – and hugely sane – idea: much of what matters to us is not exciting, urgent,

JOHANNES VERMEER, *View of Delft*, 1660–1661

dramatic or special. Most of life is taken up dealing with things that are routine, ordinary, humble, modest and (to be honest) a touch dull. Our culture should focus on getting us to appreciate the average, the everyday and the ordinary.

When Vermeer painted the town where he lived, he didn't choose a special day; the sky is neither very overcast nor especially sunny. Nothing is happening. No celebrities are around. Yet it is, as he has taught us to recognise, all very special indeed.

Caspar David Friedrich

1774–1840

One of the unexpectedly important things that art can do for us is teach us how to suffer. It can do so by evoking scenes that are dark, melancholy or painful, and that normalise and lend dignity to the suffering we may ourselves be experiencing in isolation and confusion. They reveal – with grandeur and technical skill – that grief belongs to the human condition.

Caspar David Friedrich, a painter of sublime sadness, was born in 1774 in Greifswald, an ancient trading town in the far north of Germany, on the Baltic coast. It was a beautiful place in a severe, northern sort of way. As a child he loved the way the pinnacles, spires and towers of the town loomed up above the trees in the haze of very early summer mornings.

His father was a modest artisan of few words and little warmth. His beloved mother died when he was only a young child. At the age of 13, he saw his younger brother, Johann Christoffer, fall through the ice of a frozen lake and drown.

He grew up taciturn, intense and shy. He was trained as a painter from an early age, but it took many years of poverty and hardship before his own distinctive style began to emerge. The taste of the era favoured sunny, classical landscapes. Italy in summer was the ideal. But Friedrich was drawn to aspects of nature that – up to that point – people had thought of as disagreeable and uninteresting: cold damp mornings; glacial nights by the sea; the pale hour before the sun rises; the flooded fields of late spring.

Friedrich's first mature work – the first big picture in which he started to present his own view of life – was a shock to his contemporaries. Instead of the conventional angels, weeping saints and soldiers, he depicted the crucifixion of Jesus as happening on top of a mountainous crag amidst Teutonic fir trees, with the sun's rays striking the clouds behind.

Friedrich realised then that nature could express many of the solemn moods previously associated with a literal rendition of the Christian story. With time, he dispensed with direct references to Jesus altogether, but he kept the atmosphere of tragedy and grief associated with his life and death. He found that tall trees, mountains, mists, jagged reefs, the rising of the moon, the stillness of water at night, open heathland and fog could carry many of the same messages about pain, love, suffering and redemption as Christian theologians had once found in the Gospels. He remains a painter uniquely suited for those who no longer believe, but are attracted to the serious emotions that accompany belief.

In 1818, when he was 44, Caspar David married 25-year-old Christiane Caroline Bommer. They had three children: two daughters, Emma and Agnes Adelheid, and a son, Gustav Adolf. It seems to have been, on the whole, a good relationship. Caroline appears in many of his pictures, but always alone. He was drawn to painting men and women on their own, as if what is most important about us only comes to the surface when we are away from the chatter of civilisation. He himself had only a handful of friends and almost never left his simply furnished studio.

CASPAR DAVID FRIEDRICH, *Woman before the Rising Sun*, 1818–20

CASPAR DAVID FRIEDRICH, *The Sea of Ice*, 1824

Instead of solitude being something to evade (with business, drink or sexual fantasies), Friedrich suggests it as a state that brings us into contact with our deepest possibilities.

He also believed that the harshness of nature could put the sorrows of the human condition into a consoling, redeeming perspective.

Humans can be cruel, fate can be remorseless, but contemplating the ineluctable collision of ice packs takes us out of ourselves, beyond the particular envy, wound or disappointment that is tormenting us, reducing our sense of personal persecution.

Works like *Moonrise Over the Sea* make us aware of our insignificance, exciting a sense of how petty man's disasters are in comparison with the ways of eternity, leaving us a little readier to bow to the incomprehensible tragedies that every life entails. From here, ordinary irritations and worries are neutralised. Rather than try to redress our humiliations by insisting on our wronged importance, we can – through

CASPAR DAVID FRIEDRICH, Moonrise *Over the Sea*, 1822

the help of a great artwork – endeavour to apprehend and appreciate our essential nothingness.

Here, Friedrich uses a striking, jagged rock formation, a spare stretch of coast, the bright horizon, faraway clouds and a pale sky to induce us into a mood of redemptive sadness. We might imagine walking in the predawn, after a sleepless night, on the bleak headland, away from human company, alone with the basic forces of nature. The smaller islands of rock were once as dramatic and thrusting as the major formation just beyond. The long, slow passage of time will, one day, wear them down as well. The first portion of the sky is formless and empty, a pure silvery nothingness, but above them are clouds that catch the light on their undersides and pass on in their pointless, transient way, indifferent to all of our concerns.

The picture does not refer directly to our relationships or to the stresses and tribulations of our day-to-day lives. Its function is to give us access to a state of mind in which we are acutely conscious of the largeness of time and space and of the insignificance of our situation within the greater scheme. The work is sombre, rather than sad; calm, but not despairing. And in that condition of mind – that state of soul, to put it more romantically – we are left, as so often with Friedrich's work, better equipped to deal with the intense, intractable and particular griefs that lie before us in the days ahead.

Like many artists, Friedrich was not terribly successful. He was admired and his work purchased by a small number of serious people (and two of the most delightful painters of the era, Kersting and Dahl, were his friends). He died in his mid-sixties, in 1840, almost forgotten.

He did not know that, in the distant future, his work would be deeply admired – not because it cheers us, but precisely because it knows how to reframe and express the saddest parts of all of us.

Henri Matisse

1869–1954

T he cultural elite gets nervous about cheerful or sweet art. They worry that pretty, happy works of art are in denial about how bad the state of the world is and how much suffering there is in almost every life.

Look at the picture opposite of sailing boats shooting about in the Med, beyond the palm trees, while a chintzy-looking woman sits on a sofa. Has the artist forgotten that the world is filled with inequality, corruption and war? The fear is that we might be so absorbed in having a nice time that we forget about the bad things – and therefore won't trouble ourselves to do anything about them.

However, these worries are generally misplaced. Far from taking too rosy and sentimental a view, most of the time we suffer from excessive gloom. We are only too aware of the problems and injustices of the world. Our problem is actually that we feel debilitatingly small and weak in the face of them. It's because we feel overwhelmed and hopeless that we recoil into ourselves.

Cheerfulness is an achievement and hope is something to celebrate. If optimism is important, it is because many outcomes are determined by how much of it we bring to the task. It is an important ingredient of success. This flies in the face of an elite view that skill is the primary requirement of a good life. Yet in many cases, the difference between success and failure can be determined by nothing more than one's sense of what is possible and the energy one can muster to convince others of one's due. One can be doomed not by a lack of talent, but by an absence of hope.

Rarely are today's problems created by people taking too sunny a view of things; it is because the troubles of the world are so continually brought to our attention that we stand in need of tools that can preserve our more hopeful dispositions.

Matisse himself knew a huge amount about suffering and tragedy (which builds our confidence in his pleasing, hopeful, charming work), but his acquaintance with it made

HENRI MATISSE, *Seated Woman, Back Turned to the Open Window*, 1922

him all the more alive to its opposites. As he saw it, the real problem was that darkness and misery are so likely to overpower us that we actually need to make a deliberate effort to remind ourselves of cheerful and hopeful things.

Matisse was born in 1869 into a relatively prosperous family. His father was a hardware and grain merchant. He wasn't supposed to be an artist. His father was very keen that he should have a safe, respectable – and lucrative – career as a lawyer. In his twenties he became desperate to give up his day job in the law office but his father was strongly opposed. Eventually he relented and agreed that Matisse could study – but only so long as he kept to the most traditional and conservative style.

In order to develop as a painter of joyful, bright and sensuous pictures, Matisse had to face down his father, embrace poverty (when all family support was cut off) and be reviled by his teachers and mentors.

HENRI MATISSE, *The Window*, 1916

In the years before the outbreak of the First World War, Matisse started to build up a successful career. He was selling a few pictures. He was getting well known in adventurous artistic circles. Just as he seemed to be making it, the whole world started to fall apart.

In the year of the Battle of the Somme, he painted *The Window*.

It's not that Matisse didn't care about the trenches a day's journey from Paris. It intensified his sense of the loveliness of the trunk of a tree just glimpsed through the gap in the curtains, or his delight in the pattern of the floorboards – and the overall freshness and charm of a bowl of flowers in an elegant but unpretentious room in the city. It's as if he is reminding himself (and us) that these things are still here. They haven't been destroyed. It's not the work of someone who is indifferent. It is created in recognition of how easily one could be paralysed with despair. And the hint of light green leaves through the window might speak kindly to us, even today, when we're overburdened with our own sense of the weight of life.

Later, there were more private traumas. Matisse was diagnosed with duodenal cancer. He was involved in a protracted and very painful legal dispute with his estranged wife.

In 1942, when Paris had fallen and the German 6th Army was pushing through Russia towards the southern oilfields, Matisse painted a number of pictures of dancers, with fabulous legs, reclining in big, soft armchairs.

HENRI MATISSE, *Dancer and Rocaille*, 1942

HENRI MATISSE, *Tree of Life* at the Chapel of the Rosary, Vence

The most poignant of his cheerful, hopeful works were produced at the very end of his life, around about 1950, when he was in his eighties. He had been an invalid for years; mostly bedridden, occasionally able to get around in a wheelchair. He knew he was facing death.

The deep blue and yellow – and the simple pattern – of the stained glass seems to glow with delight in existence. But Matisse wasn't expressing a cheerfulness he had recently experienced. The vulnerable, suffering great painter was attempting to ward off his own fears of gloom and despondency; he was reminding us through his genius that there is nothing quite as serious as knowing how to hope.

Edward Hopper

1882–1967

E dward Hopper is a painter of gloomy-looking paintings that don't make us feel gloomy. Instead, they help
us to recognise and accept the loneliness that so often
lies at the heart of sadness.

In his *Automat*, a woman sits alone drinking a cup
of coffee. It is late and, to judge by her hat and coat, cold
outside. The room seems large, brightly lit and empty. The
decor is functional, and the woman looks self-conscious
and slightly afraid. Perhaps she's unused to sitting alone in
a public place. Something appears to have gone wrong. She
invites the viewer to imagine stories about her – of betrayal
or loss. She may be trying not to let her hand shake as she
moves the coffee cup to her lips. It may be eleven at night in
February in a large dark North American city.

Automat is a picture of sadness – and yet it is not a sad
picture. There can be something enticing, even charming,
about anonymous diners. The lack of domesticity, the bright
lights and anonymous furniture offer a relief from what can

EDWARD HOPPER, *Automat*, 1927

be the false comforts of home. It may be easier to give way to sadness here than in a cosy living room with wallpaper and framed photos. Home often appears to have betrayed Hopper's characters; something has happened there that forces them out into the night and onto the road. The twenty-four-hour diner, the train station waiting room or motel are sanctuaries for those who have, for sound reasons, failed to find a place in the ordinary world of relationships and community.

Hopper's ability to portray solitude grew from his own familiarity with it. He was born in 1882 in a shipbuilding town, Upper Nyack, New York, and had a comfortable, middle-class childhood as the son of merchant, yet inside, Hopper often felt awkward, a bit like an outsider.

He longed to be an artist, but his parents insisted he train in commercial art to stay afloat financially. He hated it, and to escape, he took several trips to Paris under the pretence of studying French art. But, in truth, he didn't feel a connection to the art salons. He absorbed some of the Impressionists but forgot Picasso's name. He preferred to be outdoors, watching the children playing in Luxembourg Gardens, listening to concerts in the Tuileries, and travelling up and down the Seine by boat.

In 1913, when he was 31, Hopper settled in Greenwich Village in New York City, where he remained for the rest of his life. There he discovered how crowded and yet isolated city life could be. The populations of American cities were skyrocketing, yet they were inhabited by passing strangers alienated from one another. Hopper would ride the L-train and look down at the 'dark glimpses of office interiors that were so fleeting as to leave fresh and vivid impressions on my mind.' In each room, a separate drama was unfolding, an unnoticed, oblivious island in a sea of people.

Although Hopper painted in New York for over a decade, his works didn't sell very well. He regularly struggled to find inspiration. Then, in his early forties, he met a beautiful, social painter named Josephine. Edward and Josephine took excursions to paint by the sea; they went to the movies and the theatre. Eventually, they married. Hopper was no longer so alone.

But of course – as most of us discover in our relationships – Hopper's marriage didn't permanently end his feelings of isolation and woe. He was still lonely at times. He and his wife couldn't quite figure out their sex life. She often seemed to prefer the company of her cat.

Hopper discovered that – even when others love us very much – some essential part of us is always alone. It is this recognition that makes his paintings so compelling. And indeed, it is by addressing loneliness that art can be most therapeutic: consoling us and reassuring us that estrangement and sorrow are normal, that we are neither very strange nor very shameful for experiencing them. Sad and lonely art allows us as viewers to witness an echo of our own griefs and disappointments, and thereby to feel less personally persecuted and beset by them.

Hopper's art helps us notice the landscape of loneliness in our own lives. A side effect of coming into contact with any great artist is that we start to notice things in the world that the painter would have been receptive to. Nowadays, we've become sensitised to what one might call the Hopperesque, a quality found not only in the North American places Hopper himself visited, but anywhere in the developed world where there are motels and service stations, roadside diners and airports, bus stations and all-night supermarkets.

Service stations readily evoke Hopper's famous *Gas*, painted thirteen years after *Automat*. In this painting, we see a petrol station on its own in the impending darkness. The isolation is made poignant and enticing. The darkness that spreads like a fog from the right of the canvas contrasts with the security of the station. Against the backdrop of night and the wild woods, in this last outpost of humanity, a sense of kinship seems easier to develop than in city daylight.

Top: EDWARD HOPPER, *Gas*, 1940
Below: EDWARD HOPPER, *Compartment C, Car 293*, 1938

Hopper loved the introspective mood that often comes with travelling. He liked painting the atmosphere inside half-empty train carriages making their way across a landscape, when we can stand outside our normal selves and look at our lives in a way we don't in more settled circumstances. We have all known the atmosphere in Hopper's *Compartment C, Car 293* – though we perhaps never recognise it as well as when Hopper holds a mirror up to it.

After Hopper's marriage, his professional life suddenly began to improve as well. It was the era of the Great Depression, and yet his paintings began to sell. Critics raved, museums bought his paintings and he won awards. But despite his success, he remained deeply introverted. Instead of escaping solitude, he embraced it. For decades he turned down awards, rejected speaking opportunities, and lived simply out of the public eye. He died in 1967, yet his art continues to help us see the loneliness in our own lives from a wiser and more mature perspective.

Oscar Wilde once remarked that there had been no fog in London before Whistler had painted it. There was, of course, lots of fog, it was just that little bit harder to notice its qualities without the example of Whistler to direct our gaze. What Wilde said of Whistler, we may well say of Hopper: that there were far fewer interesting, strangely haunting and consolingly beautiful service stations, train carriages, motels and diners visible in the world before Edward Hopper began to paint.

Oscar Niemeyer

1907–2012

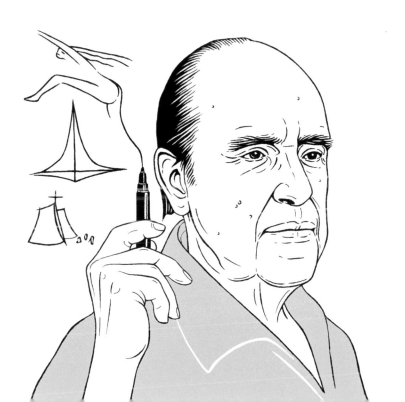

One of the most depressing aspects of travel is finding that the world often looks the same in many different places. The towers of downtown Tokyo are indistinguishable from those of Frankfurt or Seattle. That's no coincidence. Modern architecture was founded on the idea that buildings should logically look the same everywhere. The early figures of modernism were united in their bitter opposition to any kind of 'regionalism', which they saw as reactionary, folkloric and plain mediocre. If bicycles, telephones and planes (all harbingers of the new age) weren't going to be done up in a local style, why should buildings? Down with chalets, wigwams and gargoyles.

The Brazilian architect Oscar Niemeyer began his career as an orthodox modern architect, subscribing thoroughly to this universalist credo. He was born in Rio de Janeiro in 1907 – and developed a passion for architecture in his early teens. When he went to study at the National School of Fine Arts, he fell in with a group that venerated the great European modernist architects, especially Le Corbusier – who had insisted with particular vehemence on making sure buildings made no concession whatever to the culture in which they were located.

Niemeyer's professional ambitions were realised when, in 1936, Le Corbusier was commissioned to come to Rio to design the new Ministry of Education and Health. Niemeyer was invited to join the team of Brazilian architects charged with helping the European to realise his scheme on this large and prestigious building.

While working with him, Niemeyer retained the utmost respect for Le Corbusier, but at the same time, he couldn't help but observe how blind his guest was to the particularities of Brazilian culture and climate. With what would become his legendary charm, Niemeyer managed to persuade Le Corbusier to abandon some of his more hard-edged 'universalist' intentions for the building and to make some concessions to local conditions. Under his influence, the building's windows acquired 'louvres' against the sun and, most spectacularly of all, Niemeyer persuaded Le Corbusier to commission an enormous traditional Portuguese piece of tile work, done up with abstract motifs, for the public areas on the ground floor.

Emboldened by his success with the building, Niemeyer felt ready to break free from European modernism. He is to be celebrated for being perhaps the first architect anywhere in the world to practise a regional kind of modernism: in his case, a Brazilian-infused modernism.

His first wholly original work was completed in 1943 (when he was 36), and was commissioned by the local mayor of Belo Horizonte, the future president of Brazil, Juscelino Kubitschek. It was a building complex that included a casino, a restaurant, a dance hall, a yacht club and, most famously, a place of worship, now known as the Church of Saint Francis of Assisi, in Belo Horizonte.

Though the local clergy hated it (Archbishop Antonio dos Santos Cabral called it a 'devil's bomb shelter unfit for religious purposes'), it was quickly recognised as a masterpiece.

The complex had no straight lines on any plane, for Niemeyer now judged these to be European and (it was the heyday of fascism) appallingly authoritarian. Architecture had in theory been liberated from oppressive structural conventions by the invention of reinforced concrete – and Niemeyer proposed that one should use the new freedom in more creative ways.

Niemeyer was henceforth to include curves in all his buildings, and saw them in a nationalistic light as being particularly Brazilian in nature. 'It is not the right angle that attracts me, nor the straight line, hard and inflexible, created by man,' he said. 'What attracts me is the free and sensual curve – the curve that I find in the mountains of my country, in the sinuous course of its rivers and in the bodies of the beloved woman.' The latter point is telling. Niemeyer was

Pampulha Church, Belo Horizonte, 1944

deeply responsive to female beauty throughout his life. He was famous around Rio for his affairs, many with people dramatically younger than he was. At 92, he acquired a girlfriend who had just turned 25.

As in the Ministry of Health, the Pampulha church had tiles across it. They reminded viewers that Brazil could be both modern and recall its heritage – that a church might nod towards the forms of a futuristic airplane hangar, and yet could at the same time accommodate a depiction of Saint Francis and some (distinctly charming) chickens.

The sensuality that Niemeyer enjoyed in his life also came to infuse many of his buildings. His Casa das Canoas (1951) repositions sensuality as part of a sophisticated, mature life. Instead of suggesting that it might be the special province of the young, the carefree, the louche or the pretty, he creates a home where one imagines you can be an accountant or work in the Ministry of Infrastructure (be a responsible, hard-working person much concerned with technical and administrative problems) and relish your body. You can

Brazilian National Congress, Brasília, 1964

have a conversation that stretches your mind and also be gently exploring the back of your lover's knee; or you might kiss in the warm shadows before taking a conference call about worrying regional sales projections.

The house is a bit like a confident and encouraging friend who makes reassuring murmurs at the right time. One could imagine a couple feeling safe enough in this house to be sexually adventurous in a way that felt impossible for years in their normal home.

Niemeyer's most audacious attempt to use architecture to define Brazilian identity came with his designs for the new capital, Brasília. In 1956, Kubitschek asked Niemeyer to help create a wholly planned city in the centre of the country, free from the corruption of the old capital in Rio. Niemeyer drew up the National Congress, a cathedral, a cultural complex, many ministries and commercial and residential buildings. The atmosphere was dignified, hopeful, and in touch with the native environment. Apartment buildings were lifted on stilts to allow vegetation to grow beneath them, maintaining a connection with the local ecology and tropical climate.

Of course, Niemeyer's works depicted Brazil not as it was, but as he believed and hoped it might one day be. He knew that architecture can point hopefully and encouragingly in a good direction. Brazil is a country of frenetic economic activity, of rainforest and Amazonian villages, favelas, soccer, beaches and intense disagreement about political priorities ... none of which is apparent from contemplation of the National Congress in Brasília. Instead, the building imagines the Brazil of the future; it is a glass and reinforced concrete ideal for the country to develop towards. In the future, so the building argues, Brazil will be a place where rationality is powerful; where order and harmony reign; where elegance and serenity are normal. Calm, thoughtful people will labour carefully and think accurately about legislation; in offices in the towers, efficient secretaries will type up judicious briefing notes; the filing systems will be perfect – nothing will get lost, overlooked, neglected or mislaid; negotiations will take place in an atmosphere of impersonal wisdom. The country will be perfectly managed. The building, therefore, could be seen as an essay in flattery. It hints that these desirable qualities are already to some extent possessed by the country and by its governing class. Ideals flatter us – because we experience them not merely as intimations of a far distant future but also as descriptions of what we are like. We are used to thinking of flattery as bad – but in fact it is rather helpful, for flattery encourages us to live up to the appealing image it presents. The child who is praised for his or her first modest attempts at humour, and called witty as a result, is being guided and helped to develop beyond what he or she actually happens to be right now. They grow into the person they have flatteringly been described as already being. This is important because the obstacle to our good development is not usually arrogance, but a lack of confidence.

Niemeyer was prolific until his very last years, teaching around the world, writing and designing sculptures and furniture. He died in 2012, when he was 104 years old. He was given a hero's funeral, and thousands joined the cortege. What his nation was honouring was an architect who had given it a workable yet ideal portrait of itself. He had enabled Brazil to break free from a sterile European modernism – and to create buildings that better reflected the nation's uniqueness. Niemeyer remains an example to all architects who aspire to put up buildings that remember the distinctiveness of their locales – architects who may like their phones to be universal in design, but are as keen for their buildings to be culturally specific.

Louis Kahn

1901–1974

Modern architecture produces truly innovative work: glittering, staggeringly tall buildings, opera houses that look like folded origami, museums that look like spaceships. However, in turning towards everything new, architectural modernism also dogmatically left behind much of what makes buildings lovely. The best architects of the modern age have managed to avoid this pitfall, discarding older, dull conventions while retaining the meaningful and beautiful aspects of tradition. Perhaps one of the most successful architects at finding this balance was a whimsical, absent-minded American named Louis Kahn.

Kahn was born in 1901. As a young man he studied architecture at the University of Pennsylvania, but his career truly blossomed in the 1950s after a trip to Rome led him to a new appreciation of ancient designs. Kahn's important contribution to modern architecture was to include these older and even ancient elements in his work without losing the innovation and clarity of modernism.

One example of this successful rehabilitation of old ideas was Kahn's affection for symmetry, which modern

Salk Institute at the Vernal Equinox

architects usually saw as unimaginative and conformist. Kahn designed the Salk Institute in La Jolla, California, as a complex of buildings, identical on either side of a central fountain. Such symmetry was characteristic of the Beaux-Arts style, but Kahn was unperturbed by this apparent regression. 'If people want to see Beaux-Arts, it's fine with me,' he said. 'I'm [as] interested in good architecture as anybody else.'

Kahn used the identical rows of buildings to draw the viewer's eye to the centre of his design, and to the sea beyond it. The fountain that runs through the centre of the institute aligns with the path of the sun on both the autumnal and vernal equinox. Thus Kahn used symmetry not as an aesthetic default but instead with great intentionality, to provide one with a sense of balance, focus and momentum.

Kahn also managed to create a sense of grandeur in his designs rarely seen in modern architecture. We might gape at the height of a skyscraper, but it rarely instils the sense of awe that a great cathedral generates.

Yet Kahn managed to reintroduce this sense of wonder and magnificence to modern works. In the Yale Centre for British Art, he draws the viewer's eyes upward to the high windowed ceiling, much as though it were the dome of a church. The building's width is imposing; even the staircases create a sense of lofty space and height. The viewer feels reverence and appreciation not only for the art on display, but for buildings, museums and the idea of culture itself.

Most modern architects have relied mainly on steel, concrete and glass, but Kahn sought a wide variety of sensory materials. He regularly brought consultants into his office to find new uses for ceramic, copper and other unusual substances, and once he had his class at Yale think of as many possible uses for clay as they could imagine. Most of all, he rejected the idea that architects should always use modern building materials. Instead, he instructed his students to ask the materials for advice: 'You say to a brick, "What do you

Atrium, Yale Center for British Art, New Haven, Connecticut

want, brick?" And brick says to you, "I like an arch." And you say to brick, "Look, I want one, too, but arches are expensive and I can use a concrete lintel." And then you say: "What do you think of that, brick?" Brick says: "I like an arch."' In short, the brick should have its way.

Kahn especially liked to cleverly juxtapose unexpected materials like concrete and oak, as he did in his Esherick House, built in 1959. Usually, we associate oak wood with Victorian smoking rooms and dusty, ancient libraries, while concrete reminds us of impersonal factories and remote, futuristic buildings. But together, the two mediums

Kimbell Art Museum, Fort Worth, Texas

demonstrate strikingly different, yet remarkably complementary virtues. The wood gives the space a warmth and domesticity that makes the house a good place for a bookworm, while the concrete provides a sense of strength and stability that lends it a reassuring feeling of refuge from the outside world. This combination of materials subtly suggests that we can find comfort and strength together.

Finally, Kahn is remembered as a monumental architect – in both senses – during a time when most modern architects firmly rejected monuments as useless and sentimental. In 1938 the architectural critic Lewis Mumford firmly declared, 'If it is a monument it is not modern and if it is modern it cannot be a monument.' But Kahn liked monuments. After his important trip to Rome, he wrote: 'I finally realise that the architecture of Italy will remain as the inspirational source of the works of the future … those who don't see it that way ought to look again. Our stuff looks tinny compared to it.' The marble Kahn used in his Kimbell Arts Museum, in Fort Worth, Texas is, for example, a clear reference to the ancient buildings that Kahn so admired.

When Kahn died in 1974, he was perhaps the most famous architect in the United States, and he remained deeply influential. Kahn's importance lay in his ability to transcend dogmatic modernism and return beautiful traditional elements of architecture to their rightful place in the canon of design, where they could continue to bring gravitas, elegance, and splendour for future generations.

Coco Chanel

1883–1971

The world of fashion can seem very silly. It can come across as intensifying vanity and encouraging snobbery; it distributes prestige in unhelpful ways.

This skittish, narcissistic side of fashion is unfortunate, for at its best, fashion circles round important territory. Clothes convey ideas about what is admirable or exciting, they influence mood and help define identity. Fashion is potentially a very serious part of life – but it has largely been abandoned to pretension, eccentricity and foolishness.

The person who did the most to realise the positive potential of fashion – and direct it to its true task – was the French designer Coco Chanel. She was born on 19 August 1883 in Saumur in the Loire valley. Her mother died when she was a child; she grew up poor and isolated. She was educated by charitable nuns. She was called Gabriel until her early twenties, when she was trying to make it as a cabaret performer and changed her name to the more distinctive 'Coco'.

She started out as a designer of hats, made a lot of influential friends and had several liaisons with British and Russian dukes – perhaps in compensation for her early very fragile social status.

Although we don't often give the fact a great deal of attention, clothes are instruments of communication. We are very much open to being influenced by what a person wears. Before Chanel, stylish clothes were complicated and very expensive. They were designed to stress the delicate, passive characteristics of their wearers.

These garments put forward an image of delicacy and refinement. The wearer was presented as poetic, perhaps a little dreamy and sensitive. They looked like they wouldn't have much of an appetite for dinner. This wasn't meant to be an actual accurate portrait of any particular person. The clothes signalled an aspiration. The Victorian woman might be insecure, have a raucous laugh and be keen on eating meringues; yet the clothes provided an idealised portrait of

Ladies fashion magazine
Les Grandes Modes de Paris (1901–1933)

the desired direction of travel: a picture of what this person would ideally like to be like.

What Coco Chanel did was invent a new and better destination. In 1926 she introduced a very simple garment: the little black dress.

It spoke of a different vision of existence: a different ideal. The dress spoke of being energetic and focused; the wearer would be sharp-witted, engaged in how the world works; they might have spent the day running a business or working at the finance ministry – or writing an experimental novel.

She was also making this ideal much more widely accessible. The dress was a fraction of the price of its more splendid rivals. It was designed to be long-lasting. Not just in sheer physical durability but in the psychological sense of

Coco Chanel, Paris, 1936

not feeling dated. So the dress you bought in 1926 would do just as well in 1927 or 1937. In fact, it was intended to last for years and years – which radically changed the economics of being chic.

Another side of Coco's proposal was to limit options. The dress only came in black – so you didn't have to put your mind to considering and deciding. She was making the idea of being stylish simpler and easier. The little black dress was designed to make it easy and inexpensive to look elegant.

The little black dress was conceived as the clothing equivalent of the Model T Ford (which – not by chance – also came only in black). The Model T had revolutionised the automobile industry by bringing cars, for the first time, within the budget of many more people. Instead of being a luxury for the few, personal transport became more widespread – and, eventually, normal. Coco shared a similar noble ambition: to make her vision of elegance simple, timeless and – most importantly – widespread. Chanel was searching – as *Vogue* put it in a perceptive article from 1926 – for a 'uniform for the woman of taste'.

The uniform of the Chanel dress – or something less costly inspired by it – stresses a range of admirable virtues: the idea that you can be efficient, organised, serious, and in control – without becoming puritanical or dour. Such clothes stress the long term, they hint that we should care about things that last, and not chop and change our enthusiasms at every turn. They argue that elegance is a key concern in a crowded and busy world: it means efficiency without loss of grace.

Over her long and very successful career, many of Coco Chanel's efforts were devoted to developing a distinctive brand. She didn't just stick with clothes. She also designed jewellery and handbags. And – most importantly from a commercial point of view – her Chanel No.5 scent.

Chanel No. 5, created in 1921

The Catholic Church had long used scents to promote religious devotion. They recognised that scents influence mood. The smell of burning incense could encourage the congregation to concentrate, to feel that something special was occurring.

Coco wanted her scent to summon up associations of a particular kind of person – confident, strong, attractive and independent.

The aim wasn't simply to expand her business empire. It was to take a good experience from one part of life, where it might already be familiar, and apply it more widely. Coco loved beaches and bathing costumes, she liked the clothes people wore when playing sports. She wasn't at all unusual in that. The kind of move she made always seems obvious in retrospect – but never was at the time. She took the pleasure of the beach very seriously and sought to extract the general, reusable essence from a local, particular kind of happiness.

***

Chanel was far from admirable in all respects.

During the Second World War, when Paris was occupied by the Third Reich, she lived in the Ritz and spent a lot of time around senior Nazis. She was more than friendly and eventually worked as an agent, though exposure of her conduct did not occur until much later. Like many artists, her work was better than she was herself. She died in Paris, aged 87, in 1971.

In the utopia, there would still be fashion, but it would differ from what we are currently most familiar with. It would take up Chanel's attitude to classic style.

A classic isn't just something that is famous or distinctive from a past era. It's something that continues to be relevant and useful outside of the specific time it was first made. The true task of fashion isn't to chop and change every year. Clothes are not emblems of vanity or clutter (as our fears sometimes suggest); they have a potential to be aids and prompts, friends, in our quest to become more mature, focused, sane and balanced versions of ourselves.

In the end, Chanel didn't do all that could be done with her brand. But she's inspiring in how she teased out some of what can be most serious about clothes. In the ideal world, a clothing company would – with the help of in-house philosophers – define what really matters most in life and then set out to make clothes that constantly support and amplify these ethical and moral commitments. Nice clothes would be honoured for what they really are: embodiments of good ideas.

Jane Jacobs

1916–2006

There is something compelling and exciting about cities that makes many of us love (and some of us dread) them. They are full of bright attractions, intriguing strangers and endless, unimaginable possibilities. Yet despite a great migration towards city living in the modern era, we haven't quite got cities figured out. Some parts of them are full of delightful surprises, and others are dreadfully boring – or worse, dangerous. One of the most instrumental people in understanding how urban areas work was a woman who spent her life explaining just how complex and vital cities really are.

Jane Jacobs was born in 1916 in Scranton, Pennsylvania, to a doctor and a nurse. As a young girl, she disliked school, which bored her, but liked telling her imaginary friend, Benjamin Franklin, about the world around her and why it was built the way it was. As she explained it, Franklin 'was interested in lofty things, but also in nitty-gritty, down-to-earth details, such as why the alley we were walking through wasn't paved, and who would pave it if it were paved.' This kind of thinking would later make her a great writer about practical ideas for a less imaginary audience.

After graduating from high school and briefly working as an unpaid assistant at a newspaper, she moved with her sister to New York City during the height of the Great Depression. Looking for jobs, Jacobs liked to choose a different subway stop to get off at each day, and thus she discovered a new neighbourhood each time. One day she got off at the Christopher Street stop in Greenwich Village and fell in love with the tree-lined, winding streets. She decided to move there.

In New York, Jacobs worked first as a secretary for a candy factory and later as a freelance writer and journalist for several magazines. She also took classes in various topics at the School of General Education at Columbia University, refusing to conform to any undergraduate curriculum. (Fortunately, she would always explain, her grades were too low for the undergraduate colleges to accept her, and so she was left alone to get an education.)

Edmund N. Bacon, left, then executive director of the Philadelphia City
Planning Commission, describing the Market East Project.

During the Second World War, Jacobs worked for the
Office of War Information and then the Department of
Defence's magazine, *Amerika*. There she met her husband,
Robert, an architect, and married him a month later. They
would have three children.

After the war, Jacobs switched to working for another
magazine, *Architectural Forum*. She was assigned to write
about a new housing development in Philadelphia designed
by Edmund Bacon. Bacon, like many architects at the time,
wanted to make American cities hubs of modernity, encircled
with freeways that would bring thousands of automobiles
and trucks through the city, and crowned with impressive,
towering skyscrapers. Such projects were very well funded

The NYCHA Jacob Riis Houses complex of apartments in the
East Village neighbourhood of New York.

by the government and considered enormously important
(Bacon himself would grace the cover of *Time* magazine for
his contributions).

Yet when Jacobs went to see the developments in Philadelphia and interview Bacon, she decided she didn't like his
vision much at all. She found, for example, that the projects looked sleek and modern, but the streets around them
were empty compared to older streets. People didn't actually
want to be around the housing projects, much less live in
them. Jacobs decided that the problem with much of modern architecture, and particularly designs like Bacon's, was
that they bore no relation to what people actually needed.
Instead, too many projects were simply the result of government funding and overzealous 'reformers' who sought
to line their pockets. Cities were being ruined by top-down
planning.

Jacobs surprised her editors with a negative story about
the Philadelphia housing project. Nevertheless, her criticism
was well received, and in 1956 she was invited to lecture at

Street intersection in Boston's historical North End.

Harvard University. There she spoke about the foolish plans for urban renewal underway in American cities, urging famous architects to 'respect – in the deepest sense – strips of chaos that have a weird wisdom of their own not yet encompassed in our concept of urban order.' Later, she wrote a related piece, 'Downtown is for People', for *Fortune* magazine, emphasising the flaws of many redevelopment plans. 'They will have all the attributes of a well-kept, dignified cemetery,' she warned.

Impressed by her work, The New School, a research institute in New York City, gave Jacobs a position, while the Rockefeller Foundation gave her a grant to write a critical study of urban planning in America, which would result in *The Death and Life of Great American Cities* (1961). The book was an extended criticism of modernist, rationalist planners and of one architect in particular, Robert Moses (1888–1981). Moses had worked his way up through elite connections to become one of the biggest urban planners of the New York City area, cleverly using money from toll roads to fund parks, pools, bridges and highways. His designs can still be seen throughout the city.

Jacobs wrote that Moses and his fellow designers were like children playing with blocks. They made large towers and then cried: 'look what I made!', not realising that what they had made was a social mess. In Jacob's view, their urban planning theories were simply pseudoscience.

Why then were such terrible projects conceived? Because they were the result of bad thinking about the needs of others. Not least, they lacked charm and originality, which Jacobs believed was good for the soul. Of one building in San Francisco, she wrote, 'A look at this Buddhist Temple is better than a trip to the psychoanalyst.'

Finally, all this was a self-perpetuating social problem in Jacob's view because the idea that certain areas with old buildings or crowded streets were slums had been absorbed by bankers, who then didn't invest money in these areas for the minor restorations that might actually improve city life.

Union Square, San Francisco

In her book, Jacobs offered an alternative to the gigantic and unfriendly designs of architects like Moses. She wrote that the best way to see what a city needs is to look at the way people actually use it. 'If you get out and walk,' she wrote, 'you see all sorts of other clues. Why is the hub of downtown such a mixture of things? Why do office workers on New York's handsome Park Avenue turn off to Lexington or Madison Avenue at the first corner they reach? Why is a good steak house usually in an old building? Why are short blocks apt to be busier than long ones?'

Jacobs suggested that what ultimately makes cities successful is their 'diversity', their varied resources, and the closeness with which these very different people, businesses, and communities are knitted together. Ultimately, Jacobs argued for a city that was meant for people, one that protected their social and economic needs, one that made them happy and comfortable, and one that brought out what people really like about cities. 'In short,' she insisted on asking, 'will the city be any fun?' A 'fun' city, in Jacob's view, needs all of the four 'generators of diversity'. These can be rephrased as guidelines for city planning:

1. Cities should be like ecosystems

Jacobs described the ideal city as having 'mixed primary uses', meaning that it should be both residential and commercial in any given area, and ideally that each block should have activity throughout the day. This is because movement and involvement is what makes cities dynamic, desirable places to live. Cities are almost like the lunch hour of life on earth: they are where all the busy, frenzied, social exchanges take place and new relationships are formed. (And indeed, one of Jacob's main arguments for why areas need multiple kinds of uses is that an area with, say, both office buildings and theatres supplies restaurants with both lunch and dinner business.) In order for cities to appropriately capitalise on their potential, different kinds of businesses and people need to be living in close proximity, so that exchanges can happen at all hours of the day.

2. City blocks should be small

Shorter blocks give people more opportunities to turn corners. This is good because it allows them more paths between one point and another, and more opportunities to discover new places and meet people. Shorter blocks also mean more ground-floor spaces for businesses.

3. There should be a mix of old and new buildings

Because old buildings have already paid off the costs of construction, their rent is lower. This allows poorer people and companies to have places to live and work, rather than forcing them out, which happens when there is a neighbourhood-wide renovation. A few newer buildings can then be permitted in order to draw in wealthier people and businesses. Jacobs believed that each neighbourhood should have both old and new, preventing areas from simply being 'rich' or 'poor', and encouraging people of very different backgrounds to live together.

4. Cities should be dense

Architects like Moses and Le Corbusier (1887–1965) argued for the benefits of wide open parks and boulevards. Jacobs disagreed profoundly. In her view, streets should be places for people to encounter one another, to literally and metaphorically run into new things. Enormous plazas or business districts ruin this possibility. Jacobs insisted that in redesigning cities 'the whole point is to make the streets more surprising, more compact, more variegated, and busier than before – not less so.'

Moreover, Jacobs believed that density was part of how cities remained safe spaces. In dense neighbourhoods with relatively short buildings, she argued, everyone knows everyone and they know what is and isn't normal (this knowledge

Jacobs at a Greenwich Village press conference.

is a form of what she called 'social capital'). As a result, the neighbourhood has what Jacobs termed 'eyes on the street', an innate communal awareness and safety mechanism. In a city with giant skyscrapers, Jacobs wrote, 'nobody … was going to have to be his brother's keeper anymore.' Such urban designs destroy the very nature of cities, their lifeblood of sociability and interdependence.

Jacobs was not the first person to have such ideas, but she was one of the people who expressed them most clearly and succinctly. She was an especially fierce opponent of urban development in her own area of New York City, Greenwich Village, during the 1950s and 1960s. Robert Moses had made his way there, hoping to tear down much of the neighbourhood and convert it to a new highway, the Lower Manhattan Expressway. The project included 'slum clearance', which meant the removal of hundreds of small businesses and family homes, all to be replaced with high rises. Jacobs's own home, which she had carefully renovated with her husband (even adding a small garden) was slated for destruction. Consequently, Jacobs recruited a number of high-profile figures like Margaret Mead and Eleanor Roosevelt to resist this change. With the support of the community and the media, Moses's plans were eventually scrapped.

Jacobs, who had become a local hero, was arrested in April 1968 after being charged with inciting a riot at a public hearing about the project. Though she was largely exonerated of her charges, she moved shortly thereafter to Canada. Her decision to leave the US was based partly on her growing frustration with the City of New York, and partly to avoid her teenage sons being conscripted during the Vietnam War. Jacobs quickly assumed a similar role in Toronto, becoming a vociferous figure in blocking projects for an expressway (one of her common themes was to ask whether cities were built for people or cars), and campaigning for the regeneration of the St Lawrence neighbourhood, which has been widely acclaimed as a great success in city planning.

Jacobs was a woman of strong political convictions. During her lifetime she not only advocated for better urban planning, but also for equal pay for women and the right to unionise. She turned down honorary degrees from almost thirty institutions, always giving credit to the people working the protest lines instead. *Dark Age Ahead*, her final book, published shortly before she died in 2006, is a pessimistic treatise on the decline of North American civilisation, which she saw as endangered by excessive capitalism and too little emphasis on education and community. She was, in short, always working to defend modern life from 'reforms' that actually make life worse.

Cy Twombly

1928–2011

Abstract art continues to provoke annoyance and confusion in equal measure. You know the kind of thing: a large empty white canvas, with a solitary deep black line down the middle. A splodge of purple paint against a yellow background. Ten steel beams arranged in a random pile. What does it mean? Is someone making fun of us? A child could have …

To adopt a more sympathetic approach (which can be useful and fair), we need to go back to first principles and ask: what's so good about not showing what things look like? The central intention in abstract art is to get directly to emotion and to bypass representation. Like music, abstract art is best interpreted as echoing, or giving a form to, certain of our inner states or moods. Some might be relatively straightforward, like 'calm' or 'anger', and others will defy easy definition in language. It is therefore not very helpful to say: this painting doesn't look like anything. It is true that it doesn't look like anything in the outer world, but that's because the intention is to represent the inner one. We should be asking: what does this work feel like? Does it evoke any of my emotional states? What piece of mankind's inner landscape is being summoned?

The great abstract artist, Cy Twombly, was born in 1928 in the pretty, ultraconservative town of Lexington, Virginia. His father had been a pitcher for the Chicago White Sox – in UK terms today, the equivalent of being a Premier League footballer. The artist was actually christened Edwin Parker Twombly but became known as 'Cy' in honour of one of the most prominent figures in the history of baseball, Cy Young. He went to Darlington School – a smart, expensive private school. Eventually he made his way to study art in New York in the early 1950s and then spent a year touring round the Mediterranean. The journey changed his life. He found himself an aristocratic girlfriend, moved to Rome, and inaugurated his trademark abstract style.

Top: CY TWOMBLY, *Academy*, 1955
Bottom: CY TWOMBLY, *Hero and Leandro*, 1985

He hadn't left reason behind. He was deeply alive to the lessons of Roman and Renaissance art. What he wanted to do was give form to the inner states of humankind, just as the ancient masters had represented our outer ones.

Take his *Academy* of 1955, now in the Museum of Modern Art in New York. We can't see the marks precisely, but they fill the canvas, like mysterious script on a blackboard. We are held at the moment of being on the cusp of something. We are about to understand, but have not yet understood.

Twombly's work is like a specially designed mirror of a part of our inner lives, deliberately constructed to draw attention to it and to make it clearer and easier to identify. This work homes in on what it is like when you almost know what you think about something but not quite. It pictorialises a moment in reflective life, suggestive of ambition and confusion.

It shouldn't surprise us in any way that Twombly loved figurative, representational art. His favourite artist was the 17th-century painter Poussin (who also lived in Rome). But he wanted to do something else in his own work:

The title of the painting *Hero and Leandro* makes reference to a tragic couple in Classical Greece. Leander used to swim three kilometres each night across the Hellespont to meet his lover (Lord Byron tried it too and now there's a club). But Twombly hasn't tried to show us the dripping torso or the treacherous moonlit waves, as Poussin would have done. Instead he has made a picture of what a certain feeling of love is like – the feeling, perhaps, of knowing that the person you love is making great efforts to get to you, or the sense that someone you love is desperately longing to make contact with you. It is a work of drama and passion, showing without representing. Gazing at the intricate, soft, swirling surface, one is drawn into a precious sense of the price of love.

Twombly's career was devoted to making portraits of inner life so that we might learn to communicate its fruits to other people. Getting others to share our experiences is notoriously difficult. Words can feel clumsy.

One might simply say to a close friend: 'Inside, it feels a little like this.' And they would understand. Apart from abstraction, Twombly had a tendency to go in for some very simple-looking bits of writing.

It's a bit like a note to oneself – half-doodled on the back of a company report – a phrase, an idea, that's come into one's head but doesn't yet have a definite meaning.

It looks like graffiti – something scrawled on a neighbour's wall to give offence, to express antisocial aggression. But in Twombly's hands, that urgency, the excitement and daring, the risk-taking, the readiness to cause offence and upset people's comfortable expectations – are being deployed in the name of wise cultivation, of true self-development of the enlargement and refinement of the spirit (all things for which 'Goethe in Italy' is shorthand). It's a reminder of what we should think about, and pay attention to, far more than the slogans and brand names we are otherwise continually exposed to.

Cy Twombly died in 2011 in his beloved Rome. He was 83 – and he had lived to see his works gain immense prestige and appreciation among those whose opinions he respected.

His paintings are simultaneously about nothing – and about everything that is most powerful, private and hitherto incommunicable but important within us. He will last – as long as some of those great Romans he so deeply admired.

Andy Warhol

1928–1987

A ndy Warhol was the most glamorous figure of 20th-century American art. He is famous for making prints of tins of Campbell's soup and brightly coloured portraits of celebrities like Marilyn Monroe and Michael Jackson. Much about his life was eccentric – he wore a silver wig; he liked to peel potatoes while lying in bed; he liked to go to the dry cleaners and stand in the corner, to enjoy the smells and sounds of the chemicals and cleaning machines. He loved airports, and used to go through airport security multiple times because he said he found it fascinating and inspiring.

Andy Warhol's great achievement was to develop a generous and helpful view of two major forces in modern society: commerce and celebrity. He spent most of his life as an international celebrity, but he was also keen on business. Warhol was born in Pennsylvania in 1928 to Czechoslovakian parents and lived most of his life in New York. Today his name is one of the most commercially successful artistic brands on the planet (his pictures of Elvis sell for 50 to 100 million dollars).

There are four big ideas behind Andy Warhol's work, which can teach us a more inspired way of looking at the world, and prompt us to build a better society.

1. Appreciating everyday life

We spend much of our life working to reach some kind of better place: to have a nicer house, to buy better things, perhaps to move to a different country. We are often down on average things and positive about the exotic: a meal from Panama with Japanese infusions, a holiday in Tbilisi. It is normal to feel that the exciting things are not where we are.

Andy Warhol aims to remedy this by getting us to look again at things in everyday life. The soup can is an intriguing object.

Putting them on the wall and looking at them helps us to see their beauty, to notice their appealing labels, their strong but elegant form, perfectly fitted to their job. When they are in a picture, we look at them with the same interest we might bestow on a candlestick holder or a spoon dug up from Roman times. Art can put us in the mindset of appreciation, which is hard to hold onto when we are busy using or consuming the objects around us.

In the same spirit of redirecting our attention, Andy Warhol made a video of himself eating a hamburger.

He is trying to get us to practise a mental habit: feeling that the things we do in our daily life are interesting and worthy of note. Warhol wants us to realise that we are already living an appealing life – to stop being down on ourselves, and ignoring ordinary experiences – filling up a car with petrol, dropping something off at the dry cleaners, microwaving a premade meal … We don't need to fantasise about other places. We just need to see that the things we do all the time and the objects around us have their own merits and are enchanting in their own ways.

2. Creating celebrities
During the 1960s, Warhol groomed a retinue of bohemian and countercultural eccentrics to whom he gave the title 'Superstars', including Nico, Joe Dallesandro, Edie Sedgwick, Viva, Ultra Violet, Holly Woodlawn, Jackie Curtis and Candy Darling.

Warhol understood that celebrities have an important power: they can distribute glamour and prestige. He thought that glamour needed to be distributed in the right way for society to work well.

For example, Warhol believed that the job of being a maid had too little status. He wrote:

> They should have a college course now for maids and call it something glamorous, I think. People don't want to work at something unless there's a glamorous name tagged to it. The idea of America

is theoretically so great because we've gotten rid of maids and janitors, but then, somebody still has to do it. I always think that even very intelligent people could get a lot out of being maids because they'd see so many interesting people and be working in the most beautiful houses. I mean, everybody does something for everybody else – your shoemaker does your shoes for you, and you do entertainment for him – it's always an exchange, and if it weren't for the stigma we give certain jobs, the exchange would always be equal. A mother is always doing things for her child, so what's wrong with a person off the street doing things for you?

Warhol suggested that the president could use his status to shift perceptions.

If the President would go into a public bathroom in the Capitol, and have the TV cameras film him cleaning the toilets and saying 'Why not? Somebody's got to do it!' then that would do so much for the morale of the people who do the wonderful job of keeping the toilets clean.

Warhol saw that celebrity culture has great potential. But he wants us to get the right celebrities. If we were to anoint some 'Superstars' today, we might choose, for example, a nurse, a janitor, an airport security manager, an engineer in a logistics warehouse, a philosophy student, an economist, or an 11-year-old who has just started drawing classes.

3. Combining art and business
He didn't call his place in New York a *studio* – the prestigious term used by artists since the Renaissance to describe their place of work. Instead he called it 'The Factory'.

We tend to feel that the idea of art and the idea of a factory don't mix. But Warhol's point was that business and art actually do very much belong together: 'Being good in business is the most fascinating kind of art. During the hippie era people put down the idea of business – they'd say, "Money is bad", and "Working is bad", but making money is art and working is art and good business is the best art.'

He began to like business when he made an agreement with a local theatre to make them one film per week. This moved his filmmaking from being something done on the side, to an organised production. He learned more skills and moved from short movies into longer movies and feature films (he also tried to learn the logistics of distributing movies, but decided he needed a partnership after all).

The lesson of The Factory is that we can organise ourselves to produce good things more reliably and cheaply. One example of this for Warhol was Coke. He pointed out that wherever you go, Coke is always the same. Whether you're the president or a cleaner, you still drink the same Coke – and it's a good drink. Art has generally not been able to live up to this ideal of being good *and* widely distributed. Artists make a few things, and only a few people get to own them. Andy Warhol tried to counteract this. One day, after reading that Picasso had made 4,000 masterpieces in his lifetime, Warhol set out to make 4,000 prints in one day. As it turned out, it took him a month to make 500. But he believed that art should be mass-produced and widely distributed. 'If the one "master painting" is good, they're all good.'

The lesson we can draw from Warhol is that mass production needs to apply beyond making prints and other kinds of 'high art'. We need the organising, commoditising and branding powers of business to reliably produce and distribute good clothing, high-quality childcare, psychotherapy, careers advice, and good architecture – to start the list.

Warhol at work in The Factory, 1966.

4. Brand extension

Most art does not have an impact on the world. But Warhol was keen to do so. He mastered many genres – from
drawing, painting and printing, to photography, audio recording, sculpture and theatre; he started a magazine, designed clothes, managed a band, made over 100 films and
had plans to start his own TV chat show. What held all this
together was his approach to life, which came through in
everything he did. He was sensitive: he noticed details, he
was aware of how he felt, and he was moved by the sur-
faces of the world. He was also kind: he was unbullying. He
was not vindictive against the world. He was untroubled by
people's strangeness. This openness and lack of vindictive-
ness gave him freedom to play and enjoy the world.

All these values together make up his 'brand'. 'Brand
extension' means taking the values that have been realised
in one thing, and making them real in another thing. For
example, if we looked at the values embodied in the VW
Golf car, we might say that it is a car that is unaware of class

distinctions, practical, elegant, affordable. These qualities are needed in many places elsewhere in the world. Brand extension might take VW from making cars, to designing clothes, or setting up a school.

Warhol was able to extend his work into different channels partly because of his populism. Being populist means he was unafraid to reach people where they started. The chat show is populist because it plays to what masses of people find funny or interesting. Warhol was populist out of generosity. He wanted to translate the things he cared about (sensitivity, love of glamour and spectacle, playfulness) into objects and experiences that touched many people.

The only pity is that he finished where he did. He could have founded his planned TV chat show, then gone on – in ever broader and broader partnerships – to start a fashion label, design a hotel, a chain of schools, a financial advisory service, a medical centre, a supermarket chain and an airport …

This is the task still open to people who are drawn to art but also want to change the world.

He died in 1987 when he was only 58, after complications following routine gallbladder surgery in New York Hospital. He is buried at a small cemetery near where he was born, in Bethel Park, Pennsylvania.

Dieter Rams

1932–present

D ieter Rams is one of the world's greatest designers of everyday objects. His mind, which might in other eras have been employed making sculptures for altarpieces or precision scales for diamond traders, is devoted to producing carefully and beautifully made calculators, shelving, office chairs, TVs, radios, watches, shavers, record players, egg-beaters, fruit juicers, video cameras, and electric shavers.

His career has been extraordinarily successful. The company he made famous, Braun, was – when he joined – a medium-sized manufacturer of radios in Germany and grew to become a global titan of consumer goods production. As head of design, Rams's work ended up in hundreds of millions of homes. Apple took up his work with enthusiasm, finding inspiration in his T3 pocket radio for the first iPod.

Why is design important? Partly because poorly designed things slow us down and sadden us – the stapler that doesn't work, the bag of walnuts that doesn't open, the TV remote control that is impossible to figure out. All are symbols of miscommunication and lack of empathy. Bad design is also depressing given the price it exacts on the planet. Modern capitalism can seem to be stuck filling the world with junk, much of which ends up floating around the Pacific Ocean choking sea turtles and albatrosses.

Rams shows us that capitalism need not produce poor-quality products. His life and work are a guide to the values that we might make more central to our lives and our businesses. There are five underlying lessons to be taken from his work:

1. The value of simplicity

Rams wanted to reduce everything back to just a few things that matter most. You can see this in the design of one of his early products, the RT 20 tabletop radio. Rams had been inspired by the design of the SK Phonosuper, which he previously worked on with Hans Gugelot. You can see the similarities of the two pieces when reviewed side by side.

Top: The iPod takes inspiration from the T3 pocket radio.
Bottom: RT 20 Radio, designed by Dieter Rams, made by Braun, Germany, 1963.

There are many more things that could be done with a radio: one could add in more dials and controls, an alarm clock, an output cord for larger speakers, and so on. Rams pushed in the opposite direction. He sacrificed things that were valuable, but not top-priority, in order to achieve simplicity.

Simplicity is so satisfying because our lives are cluttered, and the experience of having too many options is a constant drag on us. When we see simplicity, we know that we value it. But in many other contexts in our lives we find it difficult, even embarrassing, to be simple. If we get promoted to manager, we might find ourselves feeling a bit awkward around still using a biro. Or we might feel the need to beef up a report a little, even though all we really wanted to say could be said in one paragraph.

Our true selves might secretly yearn for something basic, but we might have lost touch with ourselves so much that it feels weird to seek it out. For example, in an expensive restaurant, there is a pressure to order something elaborate, even though deep down we might actually just feel like ordering cheese on toast.

Being simple can make you feel vulnerable. But simplicity is really an achievement – it follows from hard-won clarity about what matters.

2. The value of modesty

When designing a toothbrush, Rams spent weeks thinking about and experimenting with the ratio of the handle to the bristles, the width of the handle, the number of ridges for the thumb to grip onto. But this large amount of work is not obvious in the final product. This follows from a principle of modesty that Rams lives by, and that goes back to the Roman poet Horace: 'the art lies in concealing the art.'

Rams had modesty as a person. Although he originally trained as an architect (and a carpenter), he wanted to make products that improved people's lives, rather than design

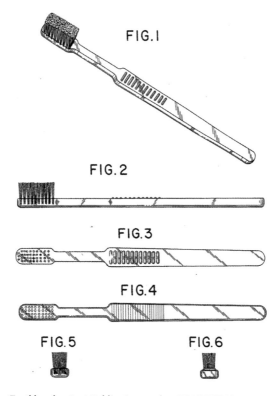

FIG.I

FIG.2

FIG.3

FIG.4

FIG.5   FIG.6

Toothbrush patent. Publication number: US D305386 S.

spectacular one-off buildings to promote his own glory. And the products he designed are also imbued with modesty: they don't try to attract your attention for no reason. They are happy to sit in the background and do the work.

Modesty is the opposite of being showy. It is part of a broader ideal of service – which is a central ideal of good capitalism. One is not there to attract attention; one is there to help the customer to live a better life – like a discreet waiter. There can be few more quietly helpful tools out there

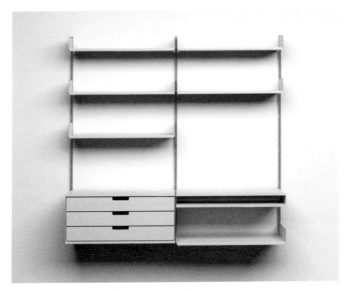

606 Universal Shelving System by Dieter Rams for Vitsoe

than the 606 Universal Shelving System, which Rams designed for the company Vitsoe, and that has been in continuous production since 1960.

True modesty comes from confidence. Modesty is a lack of anxiety about being ignored.

3. Empathy with the customer
One of Rams's principles is that an object should be easy to live with, and easy to encounter for the first time. His objects communicate how to use them, not via an instruction manual, but by the way they look.

The ability to create a welcoming experience for another person is a great skill. Not many people can do it well, however, because it derives from an unusual source. That is, Rams's user experience is guided by remembering what it is like to be distressed. He is in touch with what it is like to be lost – to feel abandoned, frustrated. Although his work looks serene, it comes from knowing how easily we get angry and muddled and ashamedly confused by instructions that any normal adult should be able to understand.

We are more like simpletons than we pretend to be. We actually want things to be easy and user-friendly. But we don't readily tell other people that we are a bit stupid – although everyone is in many ways. Which is why it is the job of the designer (or the hotelier, or the customer feedback agent) to remember with tenderness the fact that we are all childlike and a little bit lost. Rams is like a parent: he is making the world friendlier for us.

Rams is not making things for actual 6-year-olds. Rather, he mixes insights about our childlike nature with a context of elegance and dignity.

Remembering that everyone is more easily confused than they pretend to be should be a basis for the reform of architecture, hotels, street design, websites, car manufacturing, phone companies, and writing books.

4. Being classic

Rams was classic, which means he tapped into things that don't change. This means we don't have to buy new things all the time. A classic book, for instance, is La Rochefoucauld's *Maxims*. It is a classic because the essential lessons in it are still useful for us to hear, many hundreds of years after it was written.

Overall, the global economy needs to be more classic. The fashion industry, to take what is currently the least classic business, could play more to our need to have items of clothing that are versatile and dignified in many contexts and less to our drive to set ourselves apart.

We have a Romantic ideology, which tends to emphasise what is new. Rams, in contrast, is interested in what is permanent. His goal was to create a product that wouldn't go out of date, so we would never have to throw it away.

5. Art and product design

If you cared about bringing more attention and care to the little things of everyday life in 1650, you might have gone into painting. The Dutch painter Johannes Vermeer was an advocate for paying more attention to the humble objects in daily life. In *The Little Street* (valued at £100 million) he portrays a life governed by simplicity and modesty.

Vermeer notices the details: the lived-in neatness and order, the sturdy seats outside, the basic broom. Rams values the same things that Vermeer does, but he has turned these values into products we can use in our own lives.

There is no dividing line between art and product design. Paintings were originally meant to be part of daily life, to hang in your kitchen or the hallway, so they would seep into your life. Nowadays, we might only see Vermeer's work once or twice every few years, whereas Rams's work we can buy and live with every day.

Rams raises product design to new heights. The true artist of our age designs phones and alarm clocks, rather than pieces of canvas. All the intensity, focus, high standards, and the pursuit of integrity that is found in art can be brought into the realm of everyday design. And this is where it stands more chance of affecting people, as they check the time, or press the snooze button on their alarm.

Conclusion

Rams shows us what good business could be: elegant, long-lasting, dignified. All capitalism should be like this. Ideally, entrepreneurs would study his work and devote themselves to the values of simplicity and modesty at the heart of his worldview. Rams's mindset is currently unique, but it should become mainstream and widespread.

Christo and Jeanne-Claude

Christo, 1935–present
Jeanne-Claude, 1935–2009

Traditionally, artists made small, lovely things. They laboured to render a few square inches of canvas utterly perfect or to chisel a single bit of stone into its most expressive form.

For several centuries, the most common size for art was between three and six feet across. And while artists were articulating their visions across such expanses, the large-scale projects were given over wholesale to governments and private developers – who generally operated with much lower ambitions. Governments and the free market made big ugly things rather often.

We're so familiar with this divergence that we tend not to think about it at all. We regard this polarisation as if it was an inevitable fact of nature, rather than what it really is – a cultural failing.

It is because of this failing that the artists Christo and Jeanne-Claude stand out as quite so important. Christo and Jeanne-Claude point the way to a new kind of art and a new kind of public life. Christo and Jeanne-Claude have been the artists most ambitious about challenging the idea that artists should work on a tiny easel – and keenest to produce work on a vast industrial scale.

Other artists have experimented more widely and addressed us more intimately. What's distinctive and important about Christo and Jeanne-Claude is that they want to make art that can fill the sort of expanses previously associated with airports, motorways, supermarkets, light industry zones, marshalling yards, factories and technology parks.

Christo and Jeanne-Claude started exploring the effect of having an impact on quite big things around 1961, in Cologne, where they produced the works *Dockside Packages* and *Stacked Oil Barrels*. They wrapped their first public building, the Kunsthalle Bern in Switzerland, 1967–68.

The idea was pushed much further when they wrapped a whole bit of coastline in Australia. Next they slung an enormous orange curtain across a valley in Colorado, and

Surrounded Islands, Biscayne Bay, Greater Miami, Florida, 1983

then they got around to surrounding several islands in Biscayne Bay, in the heart of Miami, with 6.5 million square feet (603,870 square metres) of floating pink woven polypropylene fabric.

They then wrapped the Pont-Neuf in Paris, and in 1991, in a simultaneous project, they installed 3,100 umbrellas along two valleys, one for 18 miles in the USA and another for 12 miles in Japan. In 1995, they carried out a monumental project in Berlin. They veiled the German Reichstag, which was the traditional seat of national authority and also the focus of intensely painful memories because of its association with the rise of the Nazi party. The whole event was seen as a symbolic act of national renewal.

Christo and Jeanne-Claude has gone far beyond even traditional architecture, the standard next step up from art: they occupy a space normally occupied by city planners or civil engineers constructing a container port or landscape architects laying out parkland around a town.

Christo and Jeanne-Claude can look very innovative, but in a way their conception of art is deeply traditional. What they mean by art is making beautiful things. They

Wrapped Reichstag, Berlin, 1995

might be wrapping things or surrounding them, but what guides them is the search to make the world more beautiful. Only not just a little bit at a time. The scale of their efforts to make the world beautiful has been stupendous – and inspiring.

Valley Curtain, catching the sunlight, was visible for miles. Millions of people wandered through the enchantingly remade Central Park.

Perhaps the biggest thing Christo and Jeanne-Claude has done, however, is to indicate a direction of travel, which doesn't stop with the great things they themselves happen to have done.

One key move is not to stop with imagining something wonderful but to work out how to make the imagined thing become real. Rather than picture a revitalised Central Park, they revitalised it. Rather than imagine Germany renewing its feelings about its historic centre of government, they made it happen. The ideal task of the artist isn't just to dream of a better world, or complain about current failures (though both are honourable); rather it is to actually make the world finer and more elegant.

The Gates, Central Park, New York City, 2005

The primary identity of Christo and Jeanne-Claude is as an artist. But to operate realistically on a large scale, they needed to deploy many of the skills traditionally associated with business and that we think of as the domain of the entrepreneur.

Christo and Jeanne-Claude had to negotiate with city councils and governments; they had to draw up business plans, arrange large-scale finance, employ the talents and time of hundreds and even thousands of people, coordinate vast efforts and deal with millions of users or visitors. And all the while, they held on to the high ambitions associated with being an artist.

Furthermore, crucially, Christo and Jeanne-Claude worked out how make a profit while doing all this. Profit wasn't the primary goal. But profitability meant it was possible to go onto the next project (they have never received private or public subsidy). Christo and Jeanne-Claude have made a fortune out of what they have been doing.

The way they made money was fascinating: they financed a project by selling the plans and drawings for it. It was like Plato financing a new state by selling copies of the Republic (except, unlike Plato, Christo and Jeanne-Claude made their utopia happen).

Christo and Jeanne-Claude are a key exemplar of the crucial proposition that the creation of beauty isn't a commercial luxury but potentially a central plank of good commerce. They hint at a tremendous ideal: if making something beautiful could become a major way of increasing shareholder value, then the immense forces of investment could start to line up in the right direction.

Christo and Jeanne-Claude are showing us that ideally artists should absorb the best qualities of business. Rather than seeing such qualities as opposed to what they stand for, artists, following Christo and Jeanne-Claude's lead, should see these as great enabling capacities, which help them fulfil their beautifying mission to the world. In the future, an artist might spend as much time being trained by the Wharton School of Business or INSEAD as by the Royal College of Art.

Christo and Jeanne-Claude have never got to build an airport or a supermarket or lay out a new city – but the ideal next version of them will.

Literature

Jane Austen

1775–1817

Jane Austen is loved mainly as a charming guide to fashionable life in the Regency period. She is admired for portraying a world of elegant houses, dances, servants and fashionable young men driving barouches. But her own vision of her task was radically different. She was an ambitious – and stern – moralist. She was acutely conscious of human failings and she had a deep desire to make people nicer: less selfish, more reasonable, more dignified and more sensitive to the needs of others.

Born in 1775, Jane Austen grew up in a small village in Hampshire where her father was the Anglican rector. They had quite a high social status but were not at all well-off. She started writing young: at only 21 she had a novel turned down by a major publisher. During most of her adult life, Britain was at war with Napoleon. Two of her brothers became admirals. She did much of her writing at a tiny octagonal table. She was a very good dancer and very interested in being well dressed. She was neat, elegant and lively. She never married, though on a couple of occasions she was tempted. Mostly she lived in pleasant small houses in the country with her sister Cassandra.

The novel was her chosen weapon in the struggle to reform humanity. She completed six: *Northanger Abbey, Pride and Prejudice, Sense and Sensibility, Mansfield Park, Emma* and *Persuasion*.

Some of the main things she wants to teach you are:

1. Let your lover educate you

In *Pride and Prejudice*, Mr Darcy and Elizabeth Bennet start off heartily disliking each other and then gradually realise they are in love. They make one of the great romantic couples. He is handsome, rich and well connected; she is pretty, smart and lively. But why actually are they right for one another?

Jane Austen is very clear. It's for a reason we tend not to think of very much today: it is because each can educate and improve the other. When Mr Darcy arrives in the

Elizabeth Bennet and Mr Darcy in *Pride and Prejudice.*

neighbourhood, he feels 'superior' to everyone else because he has more money and higher status. At a key moment, Elizabeth condemns his arrogance and pride to his face. It sounds offensive in the extreme, but later he admits that this was just what he needed:

> What did you say of me that I did not deserve? ... The recollection of what I then said, of my conduct, my manners, my expression ... is inexpressibly painful to me. Your reproof, so well applied, I never shall forget. ... You taught me a lesson, hard indeed at first, but most advantageous. By you I was properly humbled.

Elizabeth shares this view of love as education. They suit each other because:

> It was a union that must have been to the advantage of both; by her ease and liveliness, his mind might have been softened, his manners improved; and from his judgement, information, and knowledge of the world, she must have received benefit of greater importance.

It's a lesson that sounds strange because we still tend to think of love as liking someone for who they already are, and of total acceptance. The person who is right for us, Austen is saying, is not simply someone who makes us feel relaxed or comfortable; they have got to be able to help us overcome our failings and become more mature, more honest and kinder – and we need to do something similar for them.

In *Pride and Prejudice*, Darcy and Elizabeth improve one another and then the novelist lets them get engaged. The story rewards them because they have developed well. That's why the novel feels so beautifully constructed. It's not merely ingenious. It illustrates a basic truth: marriage depends on maturity and education.

2. We shouldn't stop judging people; but we have to judge more carefully

Mansfield Park starts when quiet, shy Fanny Price goes to live with her much richer cousins, the Bertrams, at Mansfield Park, their big house in the country. The Bertrams are smart, fashionable, confident and well-off. In social terms they are stars and Fanny is a very minor character indeed (her cousin Julia looks down on her because she doesn't know where the different European countries are). But Jane Austen judges people by a completely different standard.

Austen exchanges the normal lens through which people are viewed in society, a lens that magnifies wealth and power, for a moral lens, which magnifies qualities of character. Rather than focus on who has the nicest dress, the best carriage, or the most servants, she examines who is vain, selfish or cruel, who has integrity, humility and true dignity.

Through this lens, the high and mighty may become small, the forgotten and retiring figures may grow large. Within the world of the novel, virtue is spread without regard to material wealth: the rich and well mannered are not (as in the dominant status schema) immediately good nor the poor and unschooled bad. Virtue may lie with the lame ugly child, the destitute porter, the hunchback in the attic or the girl who doesn't know the first facts of geography. Certainly Fanny has no elegant dresses, has no money and can't speak French – but by the end of *Mansfield Park,* she has been revealed as the noble one, while the other members of her family, despite their titles and accomplishments, have fallen into moral confusion.

Jane Austen is not the enemy of status. She just wants to see it properly distributed, and at the end of her novels it always is. Fanny is raised up, and will become the mistress of Mansfield Park. Her selfish, empty-headed cousin Julia is disgraced.

3. Take money seriously

Jane Austen is quite frank about money. She tells us the details of people's financial status: In *Pride and Prejudice* she explains that Mr Bingley has an income of £4,000 a year (which is clearly rather a lot); while Darcy has more than twice that. Rather than feeling that it is not quite polite to go on about people's money or lack of it, she thinks that money is an eminently suitable topic for highbrow literature. Because how we deal with our finances has a huge effect on our lives.

She takes aim at two big mistakes people make around money. One is to get over-impressed by what money can do. In *Mansfield Park,* Julia Bertram gets married to Mr Rushworth (the richest character in all Jane Austen's novels), but they are miserable together and their marriage rapidly falls apart. But, equally, she is convinced that it is a serious error to get married without enough money. At one point in *Sense and Sensibility*, it looks like Elinor Dashwood and Edward Ferrars, who are otherwise well suited, won't be able to get married: 'they were neither of them quite enough in love to think that three hundred and fifty pounds a year [a little below the middle-class average] would supply them with the comforts of life.'

Elinor takes the view that 'wealth has much to do with happiness' – though by wealth she doesn't mean great luxury, just enough to live carefully in moderate comfort. Marriage, without a reasonable economic basis, is folly.

Jane Austen is steering her way towards an elusive – but crucial – attitude. Money is in some ways extremely important and in other ways unimportant. We can't just be for it or against it. It sounds simple, of course, to assert this; and yet we are continually going wrong in practice.

4. Don't be snobbish

In *Emma*, the heroine – Emma herself – takes Harriet Smith, a pretty girl from the village, under her wing. Harriet is a very pleasant, modest and unassuming young woman. But Emma decides she should be much more than this. She wants Harriet to make an impressive match with the smart vicar. Harriet is swept off her feet by Emma's excessive praise. She turns down a very suitable offer of marriage from a farmer because she thinks him not good enough, though in fact he is thoroughly good-hearted and quietly prosperous. The vicar turns out to be horrified at Emma's idea and Harriet has her heart broken.

It's droll in the novel, but the underlying point is serious: Emma is unwittingly, but cruelly, snobbish. She is devoted to the wrong kind of hierarchy. Jane Austen does not think that the cure for snobbery is to think that everyone is equal. In her eyes, that would be immensely unjust. Rather, the real cure is to pay attention to true merit. The farmer is essentially a better person than the vicar; but social conventions and manners make it easy to ignore this.

Few people are deliberately snobbish. And Jane Austen is careful to give this fault to Emma, who is in many ways an enchanting character. But eventually Emma is corrected. We see her recognise her error, feel very sorry and learn a lifelong lesson. In other words, Jane Austen does not mock snobbery as the behaviour of ghastly and contemptible people. Instead, she regards the snob with pity – as someone who lives a blighted life (however materially comfortable); they are in need of instruction, guidance and reform. But mostly, of course, they don't get this help.

But Austen does not simply assert her concept of true hierarchy with the bluntness of a preacher, she enlists our sympathies for it and marshals our abhorrence for its opposite with the skill and humour of a great novelist. She does not tell us why her sense of priorities is important; she shows us why within the context of a story that also happens to make us laugh and grips us enough that we want to finish supper early to read on (as an early critic of Austen, Richard Whately, later the Archbishop of Dublin, put it in the *Quarterly Review* of 1822: 'Miss Austen has the merit of being evidently a Christian writer: a merit which is much enhanced, both on the score of good taste, and of practical utility, by her religion being not at all obtrusive. She might defy the most fastidious critic to call any of her novels a "dramatic sermon".') Upon finishing one of the novels, we are invited to go back into the sphere from which Austen has drawn us aside and respond to others as she has taught us, to pick up on and recoil from greed, arrogance and pride and to be drawn to goodness within ourselves and others.

***

During her late thirties, Jane Austen had several productive years, living in a congenial and well-ordered house in the little village of Chawton in Hampshire. Her novels were increasingly well received, and she started making some money from them (though she never became famous because they were always published anonymously during her lifetime). In 1816, when she was 40, her health declined rapidly. She died the following year and was buried in Winchester Cathedral.

Austen modestly and famously described her art as 'the little bit (two inches wide) of ivory on which I work with so fine a brush, as produces little effect after much labour,' but her novels are suffused with greater ambitions. Her art is an attempt, through what she called a study of 'three or four families in a country village' to criticise and so alter life. She has the usual assumption that the exciting, important things are going on somewhere else and that we, unfortunately, are missing out.

Austen might have written sermons. She wrote novels instead. Sadly, we refuse to read her novels as Austen would have wanted. The moral ambition of the novel has largely disappeared in the modern world, yet it is really the best thing that a novel can do. The satisfaction we feel when reading Austen is really because she wants the world to be a certain way that we find immensely appealing; it's the secret, largely unrecognised, reason why she is so much loved as a writer.

Johann Wolfgang von Goethe

1749–1832

People have always had trouble pronouncing his name. The 19th-century British prime minister Benjamin Disraeli was once mocked in Parliament for getting it wrong. If you don't speak German, it's not at all obvious how you are supposed to say it. A safe bet is to start with a hard 'g' on 'Ger...' and end with a 'ter': Ger-ter.

Johann Wolfgang von Goethe has often been seen as one of Europe's big cultural heroes – comparable to the likes of Shakespeare, Dante and Homer. He excelled in a wide range of areas: he wrote many poems, was a huge hit as a novelist and made scientific contributions in physiology, geology, botany and optics. He was also a diplomat, fashion guru, a senior civil servant, a pornographer, the head of a university, a fine artist, an adventurous traveller, the director of a theatre company and the head of a mining company.

During his life, Goethe's admirers were impressed by his literary works. But more than any of his books, what impressed people at the time was how he lived his life, the kind of person he was. The life was more significant than the books (which helps explain why, unlike Jane Austen or Marcel Proust, his literary works are relatively unknown).

Goethe was born in the city of Frankfurt in 1749. His family was comfortably off – it was new money, made from innkeeping.

Goethe's parents took great care with his schooling: he was mainly educated at home; he wrote poetry for his friends, took art classes, learned Italian. He went to the theatre a lot and became friends with actresses. As a member of the upper class, he wore a sword in public from the age of 12.

He studied at the University of Leipzig and later did a master's degree in law at the University of Strasbourg. He often skipped lectures and went to a viewing platform high up on a nearby cathedral tower. He was afraid of heights. But he made himself do it because he liked to overcome obstacles – and loved the view.

We can pick up some vital lessons from Goethe:

1. From Romanticism to Classicism in love

Goethe's first proper job, after law school, was as an assistant at a national tribunal judging cases between the many
minor German states that, at that time, made up the Holy
Roman Empire. While he was working, he fell in love with
the fiancée of one of his colleagues. He then committed a
huge indiscretion and wrote up the love affair as a novel. He
called it *The Sorrows of Young Werther*. The central character, Werther, is a lightly disguised self-portrait.

It tells the story of how Werther/Goethe falls in love with
a young woman, Charlotte. It's a very detailed description of
all the tiny steps one takes on the road to infatuation: they
dance together, and at one point their feet accidentally touch
under the table; they smile, they write each other flirtatious
little notes. It makes being in love seem like the most important experience in life. Werther asks himself: 'What is a life
without romantic love? A magic lantern without a lamp.'

This deeply charming novel was a bestseller across Europe
for the next twenty-five years. Napoleon boasted he had read
it seven times. The story has a miserable ending. Charlotte
doesn't really love Werther and finally rejects him. In despair
he kills himself. The tragic dénouement shows Goethe beginning to see the limitations of the romantic view of life. Romantic love is deeply attractive but it causes immense problems too.

The core problem – as Goethe sees it – is this: Romantic
love hopes to 'freeze' a beautiful moment. It's a summer's
evening, after dinner. Werther is walking in the woods with
his beloved. He wants it to be always like this, so he feels
they should get married, have a house together, have children. Though, in reality, marriage will be nothing at all like
the lovely June night. There'll be exhaustion, bills to pay,
squabbles and a sense of confinement. By comparison with
the extreme hopes of Romanticism, real love is always necessarily a terrible disappointment.

That's why Goethe gradually moved away from Romanticism towards an ideology of love that he termed Classicism – marked by a degree of pessimism, an acceptance of the troubles that afflict all couples over time, and of the need to abandon some of the heady hopes of the early days for the sake of tranquillity and administrative competence. Goethe was a critic of Romantic ideology not because he was cold-hearted or lacking in imagination but because he so deeply and intimately understood its attractions – and therefore its dangers.

Goethe's career shows us a journey away from the initial Romanticism of Werther towards a mature, Classical view of life. His later play, *Iphigenia,* fully develops the Classical alternative to Romanticism.

Iphigenia is a Greek princess at the time of the Trojan War, the daughter of the chief king of the Greeks, Agamemnon. She and her family are caught up in a horrific sequence of murders and feuds: a dramatic exaggeration of the traumas of ordinary family life.

Typically, the cycle of intense passion continues itself from one generation to the next. Goethe imagines Iphigenia as the person who finally brings forgiveness and peace.

Iphigenia sees her role in life as that of 'making men mild.' She is always encouraging people to calm down and be merciful. She is committed to love, but a love marked not by wild passion, but by understanding, sympathy and a desire for harmony:

> Remembering that we all must die
> Should move the hardest heart to tenderness;
> Are we not required to show others
> The best kindness we ourselves have known?

Goethe's first audiences, brought up on Romanticism, were slow to get the message. Was Goethe turning his back on Romantic love? Where was all the passion? They described the story of Iphigenia as like 'watching grey mist.' Goethe, now in middle age, was undaunted. He'd had enough of Werther and expressed his own view emphatically – 'Romanticism is sickness, Classicism is health.' But he encountered an elemental cultural problem: Romanticism feels more exciting. Goethe pinpointed one of the central problems of culture: how to make things that are good for us compete successfully for attention with the thrilling passionate stuff?

2. The dignity of administration

In April, 1775, not long after his big success with Werther, Goethe took a job as a civil servant.

Carl August, the Duke of Weimar, appointed him as his chief advisor and senior administrator to help run his country.

Goethe continued in this employment for most of the rest of his life; his main jobs were as minister for roads – which was vital to trying to improve trade. He was the overseer of the state-owned silver-mining operation. He undertook diplomatic missions and made major decisions around education and urban planning. He spent a lot of time in the twice-weekly cabinet meetings (which involved a lot of writing and reading of briefing papers).

It can sound like a strange move for a very successful creative figure: as if the winner of the Booker Prize became a civil servant at the Department of Environment, Food and Rural Affairs. We just assume that art and literature are at odds with an enthusiasm for government administration.

But Goethe didn't see it that way. Over the years, he spent a lot of his time drawing up reports and sitting in meetings about the pros and cons of purchasing specialist drainage equipment, the best material for resurfacing a highway and how to deal with the overbearing neighbour, Prussia.

He felt that he needed responsibility, power and experience to become a more mature and wiser person – and a better poet and philosopher. But it did something else as well: it enabled him to put ideas into practice.

Later, he held the position of arts minister. He was able to establish the best theatre in Germany – and put on the first performances of many of the plays of the era. In modern terms, it was like setting up as a major film producer. The encounter with power, responsibility, budgets and money – with the mechanisms by which the world is run – enabled Goethe to pursue a crucial developmental path. He moved from being a solitary creative thinker working essentially on his own to someone able to put his ideas into action. Instead of writing about how good it would be to have a national theatre, he was able to establish one; instead of just saying that cities should have green spaces, he was able to rev the governmental machinery into action and actually create a model urban park.

3. Travel as therapy

In September 1786, after ten years in the Weimar civil service, when his fortieth birthday was coming into view, Goethe was gripped by the fear that he was wasting his life. He was weary of the cold winters, the endless meetings, the workload that made it hard to find time for writing. He headed for Italy – first to Vicenza and Venice, where he was especially impressed by the buildings of Andrea Palladio.

Then he went to Rome, which was his main base. He spent nearly two years in Italy. He had a very Classical idea of the point of travel. The outer journey was intended to support an inner journey towards maturity. He felt that there was a part of himself that could only be discovered in Italy – 'I am longing for grapes and figs.'

But like many visitors to Rome, when he got there he felt disappointed.

In a collection of poems he wrote about his experience – *The Roman Elegies* – he describes how the great city seemed to be filled with lifeless ruins that were famous but didn't actually mean anything to him: 'Speak to me, you stones!' he pleads. It's a feeling many later visitors have had.

He realised that what he needed was not a more elaborate guidebook, but the right person to have an affair with – someone who would share their love of Rome with him and show him the real meaning of the place. In a poem, he describes the woman he meets – he calls her Faustina. They spend lazy afternoons in bed; she's not a great intellectual; she tells him about her life, about the buildings she passes on her way to the market – the Pantheon, a baroque church designed by Bernini – which she hadn't realised were famous; they were just the buildings that happened to be around, that she happened to like. In his bedroom next to Faustina, Goethe realises that he's entering into the spirit of Classical culture: a simple, comfortable relationship to sex and beauty; and the idea that the Classical poets were people like him.

For Goethe, the point of travel isn't relaxation or just taking a break from routine. He's got a bigger goal in mind: the aim of travel is to go to a place where we can find the missing ingredient of our own maturity.

Goethe didn't stay in Italy. After nearly two years, he had developed enough to go back to Weimar and get on with his political and creative work.

4. Living life to the full: the Faustian hero

One of the most striking things about Goethe is how much he did, how broad his horizons were, and how wide his interests were. He explored this particularly through his most famous work, *Faust*. Goethe worked on *Faust* all his life. The earliest sketches go back to his teens. And he only decided he'd done with it when he was in his early eighties. *Faust* comes in two parts, and together the performance takes about thirteen hours. Goethe himself never saw the whole thing – and few people have since.

Faust is a medieval academic and scholar. He's very learned, but he doesn't do very much: he is unfulfilled in love, he hasn't made any money, and he has no power. His knowledge is sterile. His life feels pointless and he wishes he could die.

But then he is visited by a devil – called Mephistopheles – who offers him boundless energy, good looks and the ability to do whatever he wants. The question is: what will Faust want to do? The first danger for Faust is to stay an academic who resists worldly impact.

With the devil's help he could be the ultimate bookworm: he could get his hands on the oldest, rarest manuscripts. But he gets weary of words and longs for action.

The second danger is that he will use his new powers to gratify every sensual appetite. He will become a pure hedonist. Faust goes some way down this path: he goes to a bar and gets everyone very drunk, he goes to a huge orgy – but then he realises that what he really seeks is beauty and love, and this leads him on from sex and alcohol.

The third danger is that Faust will become a confident but shallow political leader. But in the second part of the play, Faust pursues a grand purpose: eventually he organises the development of a new country – along the lines of the Dutch Republic – which at that time was the most enlightened and successful society in the world.

Faust is a morality tale for all of us: he shows us both the pitfalls of life and how we might avoid them. Faust knows a great deal, but he resists being an academic; he loves sex, but he doesn't give way to debauchery. He likes power, but he doesn't use it for megalomania: he puts it to work in the service of noble ends.

Faust's career path is not unlike Goethe's. Faust is essentially tracing for us a theory of how to live a full life. He is very interested in ideas, but not a scholar. He visits Italy, but doesn't stay there. He goes back to work. He tries out administration and learns how to wield power, but once he has mastered this side of himself he moves on. The Faustian idea is that in order to develop fully, we have to flirt with things that are quite dangerous, but hold on to a sense of higher purpose.

5. Science for artsy people

Goethe was the last European to do a certain kind of remarkable thing – to write great novels and plays and also play a significant role in science. His interests ranged through geology, meteorology, physiology and chemistry. But his most important work was in botany – in 1790 he produced his study, *Metamorphosis of Plants* – and on optics and colour, where his research was summed up in the *Theory of Colours*, which was published in 1810.

Thereafter, this combination of very significant work in the arts and in the sciences disappears from European civilisation completely. Goethe gives us some guidance as to why this has happened. Goethe is a hero for people of a more literary and artistic sensibility who are attracted from a distance to the broad subject matter of science – but who find the details of science less appealing.

Goethe likes science that you can do yourself, by looking carefully at the world around you.

He did a lot of his research on optics with candles and coloured pieces of paper in his study. He liked the training this gave in asking oneself: what do I actually see? This could combat our tendency to see only what we expect. And also, it usefully turned our attention outwards, as a relief from a preoccupation with ourselves.

Goethe was very interested in the psychological aspect of our relationship to the sort of things that science investigates: plants, light, stones. Rather than exclude the issues of personal meaning, Goethe sees these as central to the proper and full investigation of nature.

He was struck that different kinds of rock have a different character. And he was very moved by the continuity between human life and the life of plants and animals. The point of studying an elephant's jaw was to understand the traces of our evolution. Goethe thought of human nature as being a gradual refinement of animal nature.

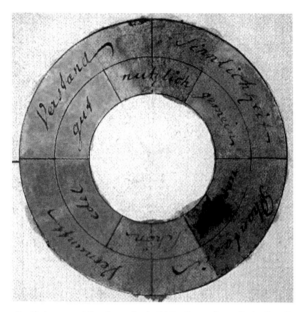

Goethe's symmetric colour wheel with 'reciprocally evoked colours'.

Goethe was very worried by the direction that science was taking – which he particularly associated with the work of Isaac Newton. As Goethe saw it, the academic, professional scientist wasn't interested in the personal meaning of the things they investigated.

Goethe's point isn't that Newton is technically wrong. It's that he dislikes the direction of his efforts.

Conclusion

As he aged, Goethe kept on working. And he kept on seeking love – and sex.

Goethe died at his house in Weimar in 1832. He was 83.

We have so much to learn from him. We don't often hear people declaring a wish to be a little more like Goethe. But if we did, the world would be a more vibrant and humane place.

Leo Tolstoy

1828–1910

L eo Tolstoy was a believer in the novel not as a source of entertainment, but as a tool for psychological education and reform.

It was, in his eyes, the supreme medium by which we can get to know others, especially those who might from the outside seem unappealing, and thereby expand our humanity and tolerance.

He was born in 1828 at Yasnaya Polyana, a huge family estate 100 miles south of Moscow. It was to be his home, on and off, for the rest of his life.

His parents died when he was young, and he was brought up by relatives. He flopped at university. One lecturer described him as being 'unable and unwilling to learn.'

He spent a few years gambling and drinking and chasing gypsy women, before signing on as an artillery officer in the Crimean War.

He got married in his early thirties. His wife Sophia, who came from a sophisticated, high-cultured background, was only 18. They had thirteen children, nine of whom survived infancy.

It was a difficult marriage; there were huge arguments about sex, and bitterness on both sides. Leo grew a very long beard, became a fitness fanatic, and spent most of his time in his study.

What he did there was to write several hugely successful books, among them *War and Peace, Anna Karenina* and *The Death of Ivan Ilych*.

Tolstoy did not believe in the idea of art for art's sake. He was deeply invested in the belief that good art should make us less moralistic and judgemental and should be a supplement to religion in terms of developing our reserves of kindness and morality. This crusading moralistic side of Tolstoy has often been ignored by modern critics – who don't wish to dirty art with a mission – but it is in fact the most important side of Tolstoy, and none of his efforts can properly be appreciated without keeping it in mind.

Tolstoy's first great novel was *War and Peace*, published in 1869, when he was 41. In it, we meet Natasha Rostov, a delightful, free-spirited young woman.

At the start, she is engaged to Andrey, a kind and sincere man who loves her deeply but is also rather emotionally remote and avoidant. While Andrey is away travelling in Italy, Natasha meets a handsome cynical waster called Anatole and falls under his spell. He almost manages to seduce her and persuades her to run away with him, though her family manage to stop her at the last minute. Everyone is appalled and furious with Natasha. This sort of madness wrecks her own prospects and deeply shames her family.

By the world's standards, Natasha has failed terribly. If we encountered a news clip about such a person we might rapidly come to the conclusion that she lies beyond the range of normal sympathy. She had so much, she thought only of herself, and she got what she deserved.

And yet Tolstoy's view is that if we grasp what things are like for Natasha inside her mind, we can't and won't withdraw our sympathy. She isn't, in truth, self-indulgent, frivolous or totally lacking in devotion. She's just a sexually inexperienced young woman who feels abandoned by her preoccupied boyfriend. She is someone who has a deeply impulsive and warm nature and is easily carried away by joy and happiness. She is also acutely worried about letting other people down, which is what leads her into trouble with the scheming and manipulative Anatole.

Tolstoy keeps us on Natasha's side, and by doing so, he is getting us to rehearse a move he believes is fundamental to an ethical life: if we more accurately saw the inner lives of others, they couldn't appear to us in the normal cold and one-dimensional way – and we would treat them with the kindness that they truly need and deserve. No one should be outside the circle of sympathy and forgiveness.

For Tolstoy, a particular task of the novel is to help us to understand the so-called 'dislikeable' characters. One of the most initially repellant characters in his fiction is the husband of Anna Karenina, the heroine of his great novel of the same name, the pompous and stiff Karenin. The novel, a tragedy, tells the story of the beautiful, clever, lively and very generous-hearted married Anna, whose life falls apart when she falls in love with Vronsky – a splendid young cavalry officer.

Anna's husband – Count Alexei Alexandrovich Karenin – is a fussy, status-conscious, mannered, high-ranking government official, who is often callous towards Anna and is unable to answer any of her emotional yearnings. As Anna's affair with Vronsky develops, her husband's main worry is that it might lead to social gossip that could undermine his public standing. He appears to have no feelings at all about the marriage itself. He comes across as simply cold and brutish.

But then Anna gives birth to her lover's child, she is ill, and – in a highly touching scene – Karenin is deeply moved, weeps for the infant, for the mother, and forgives Anna:

> 'No, you can't forgive me!' [says Anna]. And yet he suddenly felt … a blissful spiritual condition that gave him all at once a new happiness he had never known. … a glad feeling of love and forgiveness for his enemies filled his heart. He knelt down, and laying his head in the curve of Anna's arm … he sobbed like a little child.

The hitherto cold Karenin falls in love with Anna's baby:

> [F]or the little newborn baby he felt a quite peculiar sentiment, not of pity, only, but also of tenderness. At first, from a feeling of compassion alone, he had been interested in the delicate little creature … he would go into the nursery several times a day … Sometimes for half an hour at a stretch he would sit silently gazing at the downy, wrinkled

face of the sleeping baby, watching the movements
of the frowning brows, and the fat little hands, with
clenched fingers, that rubbed the little eyes and nose.

Thanks to the judicious Tolstoy, we see entirely unexpected aspects of the man. His inner life is not at all what we
would expect, judging from the outside. But Tolstoy's point
is that Karenin is not really an exceptional character in this
respect. He is just the normal mixture of bad and very good.
It is highly usual for rather off-putting people to have huge
reserves of buried tenderness: to have dimensions to their
characters very different from and often much nicer than
those that their forbidding appearance suggests.

We are invited on a comparable journey in relation to
another character in Tolstoy's fiction, the hero of *The Death
of Ivan Ilych* (published in 1886). At the start of the novel,
we meet Ivan, a high court judge at the pinnacle of society
who appears selfish, vain and cynical. But one day, while
helping hang some curtains, Ivan falls from a ladder and
becomes aware of an inner pain, which is the first sign of a
disease that is soon diagnosed as fatal. He will have just a
few months left to live. As his health declines, Ivan spends a
lot of time sitting on the sofa at home.

His family, aware of just how inconvenient his death will
be to their social and financial standing, begin to resent him
and his illness. He's short and ill-tempered back. And yet
inside, Ivan is going through a range of epiphanies. He looks
back over his life and atones for its shallowness. He becomes
newly sensitive to nature – and to the ordinary kindness of
his manservant, a humble uneducated man of peasant stock.
He grows furious at the stupid way in which everyone avoids
paying attention to the one really crucial fact about life: that
we all die. He realises that our mortality should be constantly before our minds and should inspire continual kindness
and sympathy. As he dies, Tolstoy imagines him finally feeling pity and forgiveness for all those around him.

As is typical in his writing, Tolstoy recounts in detail the vast philosophical and psychological dramas going on inside his hero's head. All that those around him – the doctors and his family – get to see is a sullen man who spends a lot of time with his face to the wall, who is always saying 'go away, leave me alone' and who at times howls with misery, yet we can see a visionary, a prophet and a man of outstanding moral courage and generosity. In writing about Ivan, Tolstoy wanted us to see his life as representative of all human potential, if only we could wake up to it before it is too late.

**

When he was about 70, Tolstoy pulled together his thinking about being a writer in a long essay, *What is Art?*

It is one of his most important books. In it, Tolstoy proposes that art has a great mission. Through great art, he tells us 'Lower feelings – less kind and less needed for the good of humanity – are forced out and replaced by kinder feelings which better serve us individually and collectively. This is the purpose of art.'

As a supremely skilled and seductive writer, Tolstoy knew that novels need to be entertaining or we simply won't bother to read them. But he was also convinced that they have to aspire to be something else as well: key supports for our own stumbling path to maturity and kindness. And they can do this because they are able to get into a place we need but rarely have access to: the inner lives of other people.

In *What is Art?* Tolstoy was mostly writing about the works of other authors, but it is really his own achievement that he is, indirectly and modestly, summing up. Great writers shouldn't ever be just helping their readers pass the time. Their writing must be a form of therapy, an attempt to educate us towards emotional health and ethical good sense.

As they aged, the tensions between Leo and his wife Sophia grew. He complained that they had 'totally opposite ideas of the meaning of existence'. Yet he insisted that even as Sophia 'grew more and more irritable, despotic and uncontrollable' he continued to love her, though he admitted that he had given up trying to express his feelings. 'There is no greater tragedy than the tragedy of the marital bed', he wrote. Finally, when he was past 80, Tolstoy couldn't take it anymore, and deserted his wife and family. He ran away in the middle of a freezing November night, caught pneumonia and died at the nearby railway station, where he was waiting for a train.

Tolstoy's funeral was a major public occasion. Thousands showed up from across Russia and the world.

This was fitting, for his central proposal has enormous social implications. He realised that our picture of what other people are like is a great driving force of relationships, economics and politics. He held up the tantalising idea that art could be the major vehicle for getting more accurate – and often much kinder – ideas about what is going on in the minds (and lives) of others.

His body was taken back to his house and buried in the garden, under some trees where he liked to play as a child.

Marcel Proust

1871–1922

M arcel Proust was an early 20th-century French writer responsible for what is officially the longest novel in the world: *À la recherche du temps perdu* – which has 1,267,069 words in it; double those in *War and Peace*.

The book was published in French in seven volumes over fourteen years:

Du côté de chez Swann, 1913
À l'ombre des jeunes filles en fleurs, 1919
Le Côté de Guermantes, 1920
Sodome et Gomorrhe, 1922
La Prisonnière, 1923
Albertine disparue, 1925
Le Temps retrouvé, 1927

It was immediately recognised to be a masterpiece, ranked by many as the greatest novel of the century, or simply of all time.

What makes it so special is that it isn't just a novel in the straight narrative sense. It is a work that intersperses genius-level descriptions of people and places with a whole philosophy of life.

The clue is in the title: *À la recherche du temps perdu* – *In Search of Lost Time*.

The book tells the story of one man – a thinly disguised version of Proust himself – in his developing search for the meaning and purpose of life. It recounts his quest to stop wasting time and start to appreciate existence.

Marcel Proust wanted his book to help us. His father, Adrien Proust, had been one of the great doctors of his age, responsible for wiping out cholera in France. Towards the end of his life, his frail, indolent son Marcel, who had lived on his inheritance and had disappointed his family by never taking up a regular job, told his housekeeper Celeste: 'If only I could do for humanity as much good with my books as my father did with his work.' The important news is that he amply succeeded.

Proust's novel charts the narrator's systematic exploration of three possible sources of the meaning of life.

The first is **social success.**

Proust was born into a comfortable bourgeois household; but from his teens, he began to think that the meaning of life might lie in joining high society, which in his day meant the world of aristocrats, of dukes, duchesses and princes. We shouldn't think ourselves superior for having no interest in these types. We're much more likely to be implicated if we convert this category to its present-day equivalent: celebrities and business tycoons.

For years, the narrator devotes his energies to working his way up the social hierarchy; and because he's charming and erudite, he eventually becomes friends with lynchpins of Parisian high society, the Duc and Duchesse de Guermantes.

But a troubling realisation soon dawns on him. These people are not the extraordinary paragons he imagined they would be. The Duc's conversation is boring and crass. The Duchesse, though well mannered, is cruel and vain.

Marcel tires of them and their circle. He realises that virtues and vices are scattered throughout the population without regard to income or renown. He grows free to devote himself to a wider range of people. Though Proust spends many pages lampooning social snobbery, it's in a spirit of understanding and underlying sympathy. The urge to social climb is a highly natural error, especially when one is young. It is normal to suspect that there might be a class of superior people somewhere out in the world and that our lives might be dull principally because we don't have the right contacts. But Proust's novel offers definitive reassurance: life is not going on elsewhere.

The second thing that Proust's narrator investigates in his quest for the meaning of life is **love.**

In the second volume of the novel, the narrator goes off to the seaside with his grandmother, to the voguish resort of Cabourg (the Barbados of the times).

There he develops an overwhelming crush on a beautiful teenage girl called Albertine. She has short hair, a boyish smile and a charming, casual way of speaking.

For about 300 pages, all the narrator can think about is Albertine. The meaning of life surely must lie in loving her. But with time, here too, there's disappointment. The moment comes when the narrator is finally allowed to kiss Albertine:

> Man, a creature clearly less rudimentary than the sea-urchin or even the whale, nevertheless lacks a certain number of essential organs, and particularly possesses none that will serve for kissing. For this absent organ he substitutes his lips, and perhaps he thereby achieves a result slightly more satisfying than caressing his beloved with a horny tusk ...

The ultimate promise of love, in Proust's eyes, is that we can stop being alone and properly fuse our life with that of another person who will understand every part of us. But the novel comes to dark conclusions: no one can fully understand anyone. Loneliness is endemic. We're awkward, lonely pilgrims trying to give each other tusk-kisses in the dark.

This brings us to the third and only successful candidate for the meaning of life: **art.**

For Proust, the great artists deserve acclaim because they show us the world in a way that is fresh, appreciative, and alive.

Now the opposite of art for Proust is something he calls 'habit'. For Proust, much of life is ruined for us by a blanket or shroud of familiarity that descends between us and everything that matters. It dulls our senses and stops us appreciating everything, from the beauty of a sunset to our work and our friends.

Children don't suffer from habit, which is why they get excited by some very key but simple things like puddles, jumping on the bed, sand and fresh bread.

But we adults get ineluctably spoilt; which is why we seek ever more powerful stimulants (like fame and love).

The trick – in Proust's eyes – is to recover the powers of appreciation of a child in adulthood, to strip the veil of habit and therefore to start to look upon daily life with a new and more grateful sensitivity.

This for Proust is what one group in the population does all the time: artists.

Artists are people who strip habit away and return life to its deserved glory, for example, when they lavish appropriate attention upon water lilies or service stations.

Proust's goal isn't that we should necessarily make art or be someone who hangs out in museums. It's to get us to look at the world, our world, with some of the same generosity as an artist, which would mean taking pleasure in simple things – like water, the sky or a shaft of light on a roughly plastered wall.

It's no coincidence that Proust's favourite painter was Vermeer: a painter who knew how to bring out the charm and the value of the everyday.

The spirit of Vermeer hangs over his novel: it too is committed to the project of reconciling us to the ordinary circumstances of life – and some of Proust's most compelling pieces of writing describe the charm of the everyday: like reading on a train, driving at night, smelling blossom in spring time and looking at the changing light of the sun on the sea.

Proust is famous for having written about the dainty little cakes the French call 'madeleines'.

The reason has to do with his thesis about art and habit. Early on in the novel, the narrator tells us that he had been feeling depressed and sad for a while when one day he had a cup of herbal tea and a madeleine – and suddenly the

JULIAN MERROW-SMITH, *Madeleine*, 2005

taste carried him powerfully back (in the way that flavours sometimes can) to years in his childhood when as a small boy he spent his summers at his aunt's house in the country. A stream of memories comes back to him and fills him with hope and gratitude.

Thanks to the madeleine, Proust's narrator has what has since become known as **a Proustian moment:** a moment of sudden involuntary and intense remembering, when the past promptly emerges unbidden from a smell, a taste or a texture.

Through its rich evocative power, what the Proustian moment teaches us is that life isn't necessarily dull and without excitement – it's just that one forgets to look at it in the right way: we forget what being alive, fully alive, feels like.

The moment with the tea is pivotal in the novel because it demonstrates everything Proust wants to teach us about appreciating life with greater intensity. It helps his narrator to realise that it isn't his life that has been mediocre, so much as the image of it he possessed in voluntary memory.

> The reason why life may be judged to be trivial although at certain moments it seems to us so beautiful is that we form our judgement, ordinarily, not on the evidence of life itself but of those quite different images which preserve nothing of life – and therefore we judge it disparagingly.

That's why artists are so important. Their works are like long Proustian moments. They remind us that life truly is beautiful, fascinating and complex, and thereby they dispel our boredom and ingratitude.

Proust's philosophy of art is delivered in a book that is itself exemplary of what he's saying: a work of art that brings the beauty and interest of the world back to life.

Reading it, your senses are reawakened; a thousand things you normally forget to notice are brought to your attention; he makes you, for a time, as clever and as sensitive as he was – and for this reason alone, we should be sure to read him and the 1.2 million life-giving words he so deftly assembled.

Virginia Woolf

1882–1941

Virginia Woolf was a writer concerned above all with capturing in words the excitement, pain, beauty and horror of what she termed the 'Modern Age'. Born in 1882, she was conscious of herself as a distinctively modernist writer, at odds with a raft of the staid and complacent assumptions of 19th-century literature.

She realised that a new era – marked by extraordinary developments in urbanism, technology, warfare, consumerism and family life – would need to be captured by a different sort of writer. Along with Joyce and Proust, she was relentlessly creative in her search for new literary forms that would do justice to the complexities of modern consciousness. Her books and essays retain a power to convey the thrill and drama of the 20th century.

Virginia Woolf was born in London: her father was a famous author and mountaineer, and her mother a well-known model. Her family hosted many of the most influential and important members of Victorian literary society. Woolf was largely cynical about these grand types, accusing them of pomposity and narrow-mindedness. Woolf and her sister weren't allowed to go to Cambridge like their brothers, but had to steal an education in their father's study.

After her mother died when she was 13, Woolf had the first of a series of mental breakdowns that were to plague her for the rest of her life – partly caused by the sexual abuse she suffered at the hands of her half-brother George Duckworth.

Despite her illness, she became a journalist and then a novelist – and a central figure in the Bloomsbury group, which included John Maynard Keynes, E.M. Forster and Lytton Strachey. She married one of the members, the writer and journalist Leonard Woolf.

She and Leonard bought a small hand-printing press, named it The Hogarth Press, and published books from their dining room. They printed Woolf's radical novels and political essays when no one else would; and they produced the first full English edition of Freud's works.

In just four short years between the First and Second World Wars, Woolf wrote four of her most famous works: *Mrs Dalloway* (1925), *To the Lighthouse* (1927), *Orlando* (1928), and the essay *A Room of One's Own* (1929).

In March 1941, feeling the onset of another bout of mental illness, she drowned herself in the river Ouse.

Her work has many vital things to teach us.

1. Notice everything

Woolf is one of the great observers of English literature. Perhaps the finest short piece of prose she ever wrote was the essay, 'The Death of the Moth', published in 1942. It contains her observations as she sits in her study watching a humble moth trapped by a pane of glass. Rarely have so many profound thoughts been eked out from such an apparently minor situation (though for Woolf, there were no such things as minor situations):

> One could not help watching him. One was, indeed, conscious of a queer feeling of pity for him. The possibilities of pleasure seemed that morning so enormous and so various that to have only a moth's part in life, and a day moth's at that, appeared a hard fate, and his zest in enjoying his meagre opportunities to the full, pathetic. He flew vigorously to one corner of his compartment, and, after waiting there a second, flew across to the other. What remained for him but to fly to a third corner and then to a fourth? That was all he could do, in spite of the width of the sky, the far-off smoke of houses, and the romantic voice, now and then, of a steamer out at sea.

Woolf noticed everything that you and I tend to walk past: the sky, the pain in others' eyes, the games of children, the stoicism of wives, the pleasures of department stores, the interest of harbours and docks ... Emerson (one of her

Virgina Woolf at Monk's House, 1932.

favourite writers) may have been speaking generally, but he captured everything that makes Woolf special when he remarked: 'In the work of a writer of genius, we rediscover our own neglected thoughts.'

In another great essay, 'On Being Ill', Woolf lamented how seldom writers stoop to describe illness, an oversight that seemed characteristic of a snobbery against the everyday in literature:

English, which can express the thoughts of Hamlet and the tragedy of Lear, has no words for the shiver and the headache. ... The merest schoolgirl, when she falls in love, has Shakespeare, Donne, Keats to speak her mind for her; but let a sufferer try to describe a pain in his head to a doctor and, language at once runs dry.

This would be her mission: Woolf tried throughout her life to make sure language would do a better job at defining who we really are, with all our vulnerabilities, confusions and bodily sensations.

Woolf raised her sensitivity to the highest art form. She had the confidence and seriousness to use what happened to her – the sensory details of her own life – as the basis for the largest ideas.

2. Accept the everyday

Woolf was always profound, but never afraid of what others called trivial. She was confident that the ambitions of her mind – to love beauty and engage with big ideas – were

Traffic on Oxford Street, London, 1930s

completely compatible with an interest in shopping, cakes and hats, subjects on which she wrote with almost unique eloquence and depth.

In another particularly good essay of hers, called 'Oxford Street Tide', she celebrates the gaudy vulgarity of this huge London shopping street.

> The moralists point the finger of scorn [at Oxford street] ... [it] reflect[s], they say, the levity, the ostentation, the haste and the irresponsibility of our age. Yet perhaps they are as much out in their scorn as we should be if we asked of the lily that it should be cast in bronze, or of the daisy that it should have petals of imperishable enamel. The charm of modern London is that it is not built to last; it is built to pass.

In an accompanying essay, equally open to the unprestigious side of modern life, Woolf goes to visit the giant docks of London:

> A thousand ships with a thousand cargoes are being unladen every week. And not only is each package of this vast and varied merchandise picked up and set down accurately, but each is weighed and opened, sampled and recorded, and again stitched up and laid in its place, without haste, or waste, or hurry, or confusion by a very few men in shirtsleeves, who, working with the utmost organisation in the common interest ... are yet able to pause in their work and say to the casual visitor, 'Would you like to see what sort of thing we sometimes find in sacks of cinnamon? Look at this snake!'

3. Be a feminist

Woolf was deeply aware that men and women fit themselves into rigid gender roles, and as they do so, overlook their

WILLIAM STRANG, *Lady with the Red Hat*, 1918

fuller personalities. In her eyes, in order to grow, we need to do some gender-bending; we need to seek experiences that blur what it means to be 'a real man' or 'a real woman'.

Woolf had a few lesbian affairs in her life, and she wrote a magnificently bold queer text, *Orlando*, a portrait of her lover Vita, described as a nobleman who becomes a woman.

'It is fatal to be a man or woman pure and simple; one must be woman-manly or man-womanly.' (*A Room of One's Own*.)

In her anti-war tract, *Three Guineas*, Woolf argued that we will only ever end war by rethinking the habit of:

> pitting of sex against sex ... all this claiming of superiority and imputing of inferiority, belong to the private-school stage of human existence where there

are 'sides', and it is necessary for one side to beat another side, and of the utmost importance to walk up to a platform and receive from the hands of the Headmaster himself a highly ornamental pot.

Woolf wished desperately to raise the status of women in her society. She recognised that the problem was largely down to money. Women didn't have freedom, especially freedom of the spirit, because they didn't control their own income: 'women have always been poor, not for two hundred years merely, but from the beginning of time. Women have had less intellectual freedom than the sons of Athenian slaves. Women, then, have not had a dog's chance of writing poetry.'

Her great feminist rallying cry, *A Room of One's Own*, culminated in a specific, political demand: in order to stand on the same intellectual footing as men, women needed not only dignity, but also equal rights to education, an income of 'five hundred pounds a year' and 'a room of one's own.'

***

Woolf was probably the best writer in the English language for describing our minds without the jargon of clinical psychology. The generation before her, the Victorians, wrote novels focused on external details: city scenes, marriages, wills ... Woolf envisioned a new form of expression that would focus instead on how it feels inside to know ourselves and other people.

Books like Woolf's – which aren't overly sarcastic, caught up in adventure plots, or cradled in convention – are a contract. She's expecting us to turn down the outside volume, to try on her perspective and to spend energy with subtle sentences. And in turn, she offers us the opportunity to notice the tremors we normally miss, and to better appreciate moths, our own headaches, and our fascinating and fluid sexualities.

Credits

Political theory
NICCOLÒ MACHIAVELLI p.119 Portrait of Girolamo Savonarola (Ferrara, 1452–Florence, 1498), Italian preacher, Dominican friar. Painting by Bartolomeo della Porta or Fra' Bartolomeo (1472–1517). Florence, Museo Di San Marco (Art Museum). Photo by DeAgostini / Getty Images). THOMAS HOBBS p.125 Title page of *Leviathan* by Thomas Hobbes (London, 1651). Hobbes (1588–1679). English political philosopher. © World History Archive / Alamy Stock. JEAN-JACQUES ROUSSEAU p.131 Kitchen gardens and town of Secota, Virginia, America, engraving by Theodore de Bry, 1528–98. © The Art Archive / Alamy Stock Photo. KARL MARX p.143 Close-up of an antique rosewood chair. De Agostini / Getty Images. p.146 *Production and Manufacture of Engine and Transmission* by Mexican artist Diego Rivera is part of his 1932 Ford Industry fresco mural project at the Detroit Institute of Arts on Woodward Avenue in Detroit, MI. © Art Directors & TRIP / Alamy Stock Photo. JOHN RUSKIN p.154 Exterior of Ducal Palace, Venice, 19th century (pen, ink and wash on paper). Ruskin, John (1819–1900) / Ashmolean Museum, University of Oxford, UK / Bridgeman Images. p.155 A view of suburban houses and rooftops in the West Midlands, England, UK. © Simon Hadley / Alamy Stock Photo. HENRY DAVID THOREAU p.163 Thoreau's Cabin, 1854. Courtesy of the Walden Woods Project's Thoreau Institute. WILLIAM MORRIS p180 Design for Trellis wallpaper by William Morris, 1862. William Morris Gallery, London Borough of Waltham Forest. JOHN RAWLS p.186 Chicago, Il – November 06: U.S. President Barack Obama waves to supporters after his victory speech at McCormick Place on election night November 6, 2012 in Chicago, Illinois. Obama won re-election against Republican candidate, former Massachusetts Governor Mitt Romney. Chip Somodevilla / Getty Images.

Eastern philosophy
THE BUDDHA p.195 Prince Siddhartha Gautama (563–483 BC) meditates (far left) while the king performs the ploughing ceremony; he shows his skill at archery (above right); Siddhartha Gautama. Or 14297 fol.8–9 The Future Buddha Grows Up, c.1800–20 (gouache on paper), Burmese School, (19th century) / British Library, London, UK / © British Library Board. All Rights Reserved / Bridgeman Images. p.196 A golden Dharma Wheel deer adorn the roof of the Jokhang Tibets holiest temple Lhasa Tibet © Craig Lovell / Eagle Visions Photography / Alamy Stock Photo. LAO TZU p.201 *The Vinegar Tasters* (three sours; vinegar tasting old men), is a traditional subject in Chinese religious painting. The allegorical composition depicts the three founders of China's major religious and philosophical traditions: Confucianism, Buddhism and Taoism. The theme in the painting

has been interpreted as favouring Taoism and critical of the others. China: Buddha, Confucius and Laozi as the *Three Vinegar Tasters*, c. late 19th century / Pictures from History / Bridgeman Images. **CONFUCIUS** p.208 Silk painting (probably Sung Dynasty) showing Chinese philosopher and teacher Confucius lecturing students in the *Classics of Filial Piety* around 500 BC. Howard Sochurek / The LIFE Picture Collection / Getty Images. **SEN NO RIKYŪ** p.215 Taian tea house in Oyamazaki city, Kyoto prefecture, Japan, 22 December 2013. The tea house is one of the oldest in Japan and the only extant tea house designed by Sen Rikyū , the founder of Japanese tea ceremony. The structure is designated as a Japanese National Treasure. © epa european pressphoto agency b.v. / Alamy Stock Photo.

Sociology
ST BENEDICT p.231 Guest bedroom in monastery of Novy Dvur, Czech Republic. Designed by John Pawson. Photography by Stepan Bartos. **ALEXIS DE TOCQUEVILLE** p.239 Painting of Stu-mick-o-súcks (Buffalo Bull's Back Fat) a Blood chief by George Catlin. © FineArt / Alamy Stock Photo. **ÉMILE DURKHEIM** p.260 *Le Suicide*, 1887 by Édouard Manet. DEA / E. LESSING / De Agostini / Getty Images. **MARGARET MEAD** p.267 Bus, Samoa, 2012. © Scott McLennan. **RACHEL CARSON** p.285 Cropduster over a cornfield. dlewis33 / istock.

Psychology
SIGMUND FREUD p.294 Photograph of Sigmund Freud, Carl Jung and Sándor Ferenczi along with other members of the growing world of psychoanalysis, in front of Clark University. Taken in 1909. Carl Jung was Swiss, and lived 26 July 1875–6 June 1961. Sigmund Freud was Austrian, and lived between 6 May 1856–23 September 1939. Sándor Ferenczi was Hungarian, and lived between 7 July 1873–22 May 1933. All were involved in the founding stages of psychoanalysis. The three other members of the group are American psychoanalyst G. Stanley Hall, Austrian/American Abraham Brill and British/Welsh psychoanalyst Ernest Jones. © World History Archive / Alamy Stock Photo. p.295 *Master Baby*, 1886, Orchardson, Sir William Quiller (1832–1910). © Scottish National Gallery, Edinburgh / Bridgeman Images. p.301 The famous couch in the Freud Museum in London. © Bjanka Kadic / Alamy Stock Photo. **ANNA FREUD** p.304 Sigmund Freud with daughter Anna Freud walking in Dolomite Alps. © Keystone Pictures USA / Alamy Stock Photo. **MELANIE KLEIN** p.316 *The Suckling* , painting by Cletofonte Preti (1843–1880). DeAgostini / Getty Images. **JOHN BOWLBY** p.329 Sunbeam Ward. © WS Collection / Alamy Stock Photo.

Art & Architecture

ANDREA PALLADIO p.341 Villa Cornaro. Luxproductions.com. p.342 Veneto – Maser (TV). Villa Barbaro, the sixteenth century. © Universal Images Group North America LLC / DeAgostini / Alamy Stock Photo. **JOHANNES VERMEER** p.348 Johannes Vermeer, *The Milkmaid*. Oil on canvas. Circa 1660. Rijksmuseum Amsterdam, Amsterdam. © PAINTING / Alamy Stock Photo. p.349 Johannes Vermeer – *The Girl With The Pearl Earring*, 1665. © FineArt / Alamy Stock Photo. p.350 View of Houses in Delft. Known as *The Little Street* – by Johannes Vermeer, 1658. © FineArt / Alamy Stock Photo. p.352 Mauritshuis Johannes Vermeer – *Gezicht op Delft* 1660–1661 *View of Delft* 1660–1661 by Johannes Vermeer. © Peter van Evert / Alamy Stock Photo. **CASPAR DAVID FRIEDRICH** p.355 Friedrich, Caspar David, (1774–1840), painting, *Frau in der Morgensonne*, *(Woman in Morning Sun)*, circa 1818, oil on canvas, 22 cm x 30 cm, Folkwang Museum, Essen. © INTERFOTO / Alamy Stock Photo. p.356 Caspar David Friedrich – *The Sea of Ice*. © classicpaintings / Alamy Stock Photo. p.357 Caspar David Friedrich – *Moonrise over the Sea* – 1822 – XIXth century – German school – Alte Nationalgalerie – Berlin. © Masterpics / Alamy Stock Photo. **HENRI MATISSE** p.361 1949.1015 Henri Matisse, Le Cateau-Cambrésis, France, 1869–Nice, 1954, *Seated Woman, Back Turned to the Open Window*. About 1922, Oil on canvas, 73.3 x 92.5 cm, The Montreal Museum of Fine Arts Purchase, John W. Tempest Fund Photo MMFA, Christine Guest. © 2016 Succession H. Matisse/DACS, London. p.362 *The Window*, 1916 (oil on canvas), Matisse, Henri (1869–1954). Detroit Institute of Arts, USA / City of Detroit Purchase / Artwork © 2016 Succession H. Matisse/DACS, London / Digital image © Bridgeman Images. p.363 *Danseuse, fond noir, fauteuil rocaille. Dancer and Rocaille Armchair on a Black Background*, 1942 (oil on canvas), Matisse, Henri (1869–1954). Private Collection / Artwork © 2016 Succession H. Matisse/DACS, London / Digital image © Bridgeman Images. p.364 *Tree of Life* stained glass behind the altar in the Chapel of the Rosary at Vence, 1948–51 (stained glass), Matisse, Henri (1869–1954) / Chapelle du Rosaire, Vence, France. © 2016 Succession H. Matisse/DACS, London / Digital image © Bridgeman Images. **EDWARD HOPPER** p.366 *Automat,* 1927, by Edward Hopper (1882–1967), oil on canvas, 71x91 cm. United States of America, 20th century. Des Moines, Des Moines Art Center, Iowa, USA. De Agostini Picture Library / Bridgeman Images. p.369 *Gas* by Edward Hopper. © Artepics / Alamy Stock Photo. p.369 Edward Hopper *Compartment C, Car.* © Artepics / Alamy Stock Photo. **OSCAR NIEMEYER** p.374 An exterior view of the church of Sao Francisco de Assis, on November 22, 2012, in Belo Horizonte, Brazil. Designed by Oscar Niemeyer, is known as the Pampulha Church. www.julianasanches.com.br. p.375 Brasilia, Brazil – July 4: National Congress, designed by Brazilian architect

Oscar Niemeyer, the city of Brasilia, Federal District government, which was chosen as one of the cities hosting the next World Cup to be held in Brazil in 2014. The left hemisphere is the seat of the Senate and the right is the seat of the House of Representatives. Rubens Chaves / CON / Getty Images. **LOUIS KAHN** p.379 Salk Institute Vernal Equinox. © Sameer Mundkur. p.381 Yale Center for British Art, New Haven, United States, Louis Khan, Yale Center for British Art central view of the atrium. © VIEW Pictures Ltd / Alamy Stock Photo. p.382 Kimbell Art Museum, Fort Worth, Texas. Carol M. Highsmith / Buyenlarge / Getty Images. **COCO CHANEL** p.386 *Modes de Paris / Journal des Demoiselles*. On loan from the M.A. Ghering-van Ierlant Collection. Courtesy of Rijksmuseum, Amsterdam. p.387 Circa 1936: Coco Chanel, French couturier. Paris, 1936. LIP-6958-101. Lipnitzki / Roger Viollet / Getty Images. p.389 Paris, France – October 10, 2008: Chanel No. 5 perfume on white. A brand of luxury perfume, Chanel No. 5, produced by Chanel SA, France. Created in 1921 by the French couturier Gabrielle 'Coco' Chanel. Plainview / istock. **JANE JACOBS** p.393 Edmund N. Bacon, left, executive director of the Philadelphia City Planning Commission describing the Market East Project, which Philadelphia now has underway between 8th and Market Streets. The men at right are visiting from Norfolk, Va. They are, from left: Donald R. Locks, Clifford L. Adams and Harvey Lindsay Jr. Bill Ingraham / AP / AP / Corbis. p.394 The NYCHA Jacob Riis Houses complex of apartments in the East Village neighbourhood of New York. © Richard Levine / Alamy Stock Photo. p.395 Street intersection in Boston's historical North End. Elena Elisseeva / Shutterstock.com. p.400 Union Square, San Francisco, California. Ken Lund / Flickr Creative Commons. p.399 Jane Jacobs (1916–2006). American born Canadian writer and activist. Jacobs at a press conference at the Lions Head Restaurant in Greenwich Village, New York City, 5 December 1961. The Granger Collection / TopFoto. **CY TWOMBLY** p.403 *Academy*, 1955, Cy Twombly. © Peter Horree / Alamy Stock Photo. p.403 *Hero and Leandro*, 1985. Cy Twombly. Photograph: Dulwich Picture Gallery, courtesy Thomas Ammann Fine Art and Cy Twombly Dulwich Picture Gallery, courtesy Thomas Ammann Fine Art AG, Zurich and Cy Twombly. **ANDY WARHOL** p.411 Circa 1966: Andy Warhol in his factory in New York, United States in 1966. © 2016 The Andy Warhol Foundation for the Visual Arts, Inc. / Artists Rights Society (ARS), New York and DACS, London. Herve GLOAGUEN / Gamma-Rapho via Getty Images. **DIETER RAMS** p.415 RT 20 Radio, beechwood, sheet steel, designed by Dieter Rams, made by Braun, Germany, 1963. © Victoria and Albert Museum, London. p.416 The old pocket radio 'T3' by Braun from 1958 (left) can be seen next to an iPod by the company, Apple in the Braun exhibition in Kronberg im Taunus. © Uwe Anspach / dpa / Corbis. p.417 606 Universal Shelving System by Dieter Rams for Vitsoe. www.vitsoe.com.

p.418 Toothbrush Patent. Publication number: US D305386 S. http://www.google.com/patents/USD305386. CHRISTO AND JEAN-CLAUDE p.423 Christo and Jeanne-Claude: *Surrounded Islands*, Biscayne Bay, Greater Miami, Florida 1980–1983. Credit for 2.18759246 Copyright: Wolfgang Volz / Laif, Camera Press. p.428 Christo and Jeanne-Claude: *Wrapped Reichstag*, Berlin 1971–1995. Credit for 2.00806418 Copyright: Wolfgang Volz / Laif, Camera Press. p.425 Christo and Jeanne-Claude: *The Gates*, Project for Central Park, New York City 1979–2005 Credit for 2.00824890 Copyright: Wolfgang Volz / Laif, Camera Press.

Literature

JANE AUSTEN p.432 Matthew Macfadyen and Kiera Knightly, *Pride and Prejudice* (2005). © AF archive / Alamy Stock Photo. JOHANN WOLFGANG VON GOETHE p.447 A colour wheel or colour circle is an abstract illustrative organisation of colour hues around a circle that shows relationships between primary colours, secondary colours, tertiary colours, etc. Germany: Goethe's symmetric colour wheel with 'reciprocally evoked colours'. Zur Farbenlehre ('Theory of Colours'), 1810 / Pictures from History / Bridgeman Images. MARCEL PROUST p.460 A daily painting titled *Madeleine*. Postcard from Provence: a daily painting blog, fresh daily since 2005. ©copyright 2005–2012 Julian Merrow-Smith. VIRGINIA WOOLF p.465 Virginia Woolf – portrait of the English novelist and essayist, 25 January 1882–28 March 1941. © Lebrecht Music and Arts Photo Library / Alamy Stock Photo. p.466 Traffic on Oxford Street, London, 1930s. © Chronicle / Alamy Stock Photo. p.468 Portrait of Vita Sackville-West (1892–1962) poet, novelist and gardener; created the gardens at Sissinghurst Castle, Kent, England; wife of Harold Nicolson (1886–1968) diplomat, author and politician. *Lady with a Red Hat* (oil on canvas). Strang, William (1859–1921) / Art Gallery and Museum, Kelvingrove, Glasgow, Scotland / © Culture and Sport Glasgow (Museums) / Bridgeman Images.

The School of Life is dedicated to developing emotional intelligence through the help of culture – believing that a range of our most persistent problems are created by a lack of self-understanding, compassion and communication. We operate from ten physical campuses around the world, including London, Amsterdam, Seoul and Melbourne. We produce films, run classes, offer therapy and make a range of psychological products. The School of Life Press publishes books on the most important issues of cultural and emotional life. Our titles are designed to entertain, educate, console and transform.